PEP GUARDIOLA

Coaching Fluid Positional Rotations from Build Up to Attack

**Written by
Massimo Lucchesi**

Published by

PEP GUARDIOLA

Coaching Fluid Positional Rotations from Build Up to Attack

Published in English February 2025 by SoccerTutor.com
First Published in Italian February 2023 by Allenatore.net S.A.S.

info@soccertutor.com | www.SoccerTutor.com

UK: 0208 1234 007 | **US:** (305) 767 4443 | **ROTW:** +44 208 1234 007
ISBN: 978-1-910491-77-5

Copyright: SoccerTutor.com Limited © 2025. All Rights Reserved.

All rights reserved. No part of this publication may be reproduced, stored in a retrieval system, or transmitted in any form or by any means, electronic, mechanical, photocopy, recording or otherwise, without prior written permission of the copyright owner. Nor can it be circulated in any form of binding or cover other than that in which it is published and without similar condition including this condition being imposed on a subsequent purchaser.

Written by Massimo Lucchesi

Edited by Alex Fitzgerald - SoccerTutor.com

Diagram designs by SoccerTutor.com - All diagrams have been created using SoccerTutor.com Tactics Manager Software available from www.SoccerTutor.com

Note: While every effort has been made to ensure the technical accuracy of the content of this book, neither the author nor publishers can accept any responsibility for any injury or loss sustained as a result of the use of this material.

Contents

Coach Profile: Massimo Lucchesi 7
Introduction 8
Pep Guardiola's Achievements 9

Manchester City Seasons (2016-2024) 10
Pep Guardiola's Manchester City 4-3-3 Formation 11
Manchester City Team During the 2016-17 Season 12
Manchester City Team During the 2017-18 Season 13
Manchester City Team During the 2018-19 Season 14
Manchester City Team During the 2019-20 Season 15
Manchester City Team During the 2020-21 Season 16
Manchester City Team During the 2021-22 Season 17
Manchester City Team During the 2022-23 Season 18
Manchester City Team During the 2023-24 Season 20

Foundations of Pep Guardiola's Game Model 21
Foundations of Pep Guardiola's Game Model at Manchester City 22
Pep Guardiola's Fluid Formations for Different Game Situations 23
Tactical Solution 1 to Change Formations with Inverted Full Back 28
Tactical Solution 2 to Change Formations with Both Full Backs Inverted 30
Tactical Solution 3 to Change Formations with Centre Back Pushing into Midfield 32
Tactical Solution 4 to Change Formations with Full Backs Pushing High and Wide 34
Tactical Solution 5 to Change Formations with a 3-Player Rotation 36

Session Based on the Tactics of Pep Guardiola
(Switching Play and Breaking Lines with Inverted Full Back) 38
Positional Patterns of Play Setup with 4-1-4-1 Shape 39
1. Ball Circulation After Winning Possession + Break the Lines Pass (4-1-4-1 Shape) .. 40
2. Switch Play + Break Lines while Changing Team Shape with Inverted Full Back 41
3. Build Up Play + Break Lines while Changing Team Shape with Inverted Full Back
   (4-1-4-1 to 3-2-4-1) 43
4. Switch Play while Changing Shape from 4-1-4-1 to 3-2-4-1 + Attack with 2-3-5
   Shape 45
5. Build Up Play + Finish while Changing Shape with Inverted Full Back Positional
   Possession Game 47

Contents

Pep Guardiola's Passing Structures with Rhombus Shapes 48
Rhombus Shapes in Different Areas and Phases of the Game........................ 49
Rhombus Shapes in the Final Third with the Right Centre Back in Possession 53

Session Based on the Tactics of Pep Guardiola 59
1. 4v2 Rhombus Shape Positional Passing Practice in Different Areas of the Pitch 60
2. 5 (+GK) v 3 Positional Build Up Play Against High Press with TWO Rhombus Shape Structure 63
3. 7 (+GK) v 4 Positional Build Up Play Against High Press with THREE Rhombus Shape Structure 64
4. Positional Build Up Play Against High Press with FOUR Rhombus Shape Structures .. 65
5. Positional Build Up Play Against High Press with THREE Rhombus Shape Structures Using a "False 9" 66
6. 10 v 6 Positional Play in the Middle Third with Rhombus Shapes 67
7. Integrated and Dynamic Possession Play in the Defensive and Middle Thirds 68
8. 10 v 6 Positional Play in the Final Third with Rhombus Shapes 69

Direct Attacking Play Against Ultra-Aggressive Pressing 70
Direct Attacking Play Against Ultra-Aggressive Pressing Tactics 71

Session Based on the Tactics of Pep Guardiola 74
1. Direct Attack from Goal Kicks 7 (+GK) v 8 Functional Multi-Zone Practice........... 75
2. Direct Attack with Breaking Lines Passes 7 (+GK) v 8 Functional Multi-Zone Practice 76

Build Up Play to Break Lines Against High Pressing 77
Tactical Solutions for Build Up Play Against High Pressing 78

Session Based on the Tactics of Pep Guardiola 86
1. Build Up Play to Break Lines Through the Defensive Midfielder Functional Passing Circuit 87
2. Build Up Play to Break Lines with Double Rhombus Structure Functional Target Player Game 89
3. Build Up Play to Break Lines Against High Pressing Teams Target Player Game....... 90

Patient Build Up and Possession Against High Pressing 91
Tactical Solutions for Patient Build Up and Possession Against High Pressing 92
Passing Options for the Full Back in Possession 103

Session Based on the Tactics of Pep Guardiola 106
1. Position Specific Patient Build Up and Possession Technical Passing Circuit 107

Contents

2. Patient Build Up and Possession Against High Press Positional Two Phase Game 108

Overloading the Central Zone with an Inverted Full Back 110
Tactical Solutions for Possession Play Against a Mid-Block 111
Overloading the Central Zone by Changing the Team Shape 112

Session Based on the Tactics of Pep Guardiola 115
1. Position Specific Technical Passing in the Central Zone with an Inverted Full Back 116
2. Positional Possession in the Central Zone Combined Two Phase Practice 117
3. Switching Play with Inverted Full Back 6 (+3) v 6 Positional Possession Game 119
4. Positional Rotations in Possession Phase Against a Back 5 in a 9v5 Conditioned Game 120

Through Passes in Behind from the Middle Third 121
Through Passes in Behind from the Middle Third 122
Through Passes for the Winger's Run in Behind 123
Through Passes for the Attacking Midfielder's Run in Behind 125
Through Passes for the Forward's Run in Behind 127

Session Based on the Tactics of Pep Guardiola 128
1. Through Passes for the Winger's Run in Behind Combination Play 129
2. Through Passes for the Winger's Run in Behind Combination Play and Finishing 130
3. Through Passes for the Attacking Midfielder's Run in Behind Combination + Conditioned Game 131
4. Through Passes for Winger's Run in Behind Combination + Conditioned Game 133
5. Possession in the Centre + Through Passes for the Forward's Run in Behind 135
6. Through Passes in Behind from the Middle Third 10v6 (+GK) Tactical Game 136

Attacking in the Final Third with Positional Rotations 137
Tactical Solutions for Attacking in the Final Third 138
Changing Shape from 3-2-4-1 to 2-3-5 in the Final (Attacking) Third 139
Providing Two Outside and Two Inside Options for Player in Possession 141
Coordinated Development of Play and Positional Rotations 144
Full Back's Options for Ball Circulation or Line Breaking Passes 145
Winger's Options for Ball Circulation or Line Breaking Passes 147
Defensive Midfielder's Options for Ball Circulation or Line Breaking Passes 149

Practice Based on the Tactics of Pep Guardiola 151
Ball Circulation in the Final Third with Fluid Positional Rotations + Conditioned Attack 151

Contents

Attacking Through Dynamic Half Spaces in the Centre 153
Attacking Through Dynamic Half Spaces in the Centre 154
Utilising the Dynamic Half Spaces to Receive in Between the Lines 155
The Role and Decision Making of Dynamic Half Space Players 156
Quick Passing Combinations Through the Dynamic Half Spaces 157
Key Insights for "Quick Passing Combinations Through the Dynamic Half Spaces" 158
Fluid Positional Rotations Through the Dynamic Half Spaces 159
Crossing for Runs into the Box Against a Very Deep Defensive Line 160
Receiving in Dynamic Half Space to Finish Attacks Against Compact Block 161

Session Based on the Tactics of Pep Guardiola 162
1. Attacking Combinations Through Dynamic Half Spaces in the Centre + Finishing 163
2. Functional 6v5 (+GK) Attacking Through Dynamic Half Spaces in the Centre 164
3. Functional 8v5 (+GK) Attacking Through Dynamic Half Spaces in the Centre + Winger's Runs in Behind 165

Attacking High Up on the Flank 166
Attacking High Up on the Flank when the Winger Receives Near the Sideline 167
Alternative Option 1: Deep Cross Towards the Far Post 172
Alternative Option 2: Switch Play to the Weak Side 173

Practices Based on the Tactics of Pep Guardiola 174
1. Attacking High Up on the Flank with Full Back's Overlap Run + 3v3 in Box for Cross 175
2. Attacking High Up on the Flank with Attacking Midfielder's Underlap Run + 3v3 in Box for Cross 176

Cutting Inside Off the Flank to Create Shooting Chances 177
Cutting Inside Off the Flank to Create Shooting Chances 178
Cutting Inside and Passing for a Shooting Chance on Edge of the Box 179
Switching Point of Attack for the Opposite Winger to Shoot 181

Session Based on the Tactics of Pep Guardiola 183
1. Cutting Inside to Create Shooting Chances in the Horizontal Channel 184
2. Cutting Inside to Create Shooting Chances 7v5 (+GK) Functional Attack 185
3. Attacking in the Final Third 10v10 (+GK) with Transitions Game 186

Bibliography 187

Coach Profile: Massimo Lucchesi

Coach Profile: Massimo Lucchesi

Massimo Lucchesi
UEFA B Coach and Football Tactics Expert

- **Director of Allenatore.net**
  Italy's #1 football coaching publisher and digital platform.

- **Author of 20+ Top Selling Football Coaching Books**
  Published in English, German, Greek and Russian language.

- **Italian FA (FIGC) "Best Coaching Book" Award 2018**
  For "Liquid Organisation," 2018 (Allenatore.net).

- **Football Tactics Expert:**

  Conducted 100+ coaching seminars in Italy, USA, Russia, Greece, Mexico, Romania, Jamaica, Cyprus and Slovakia.

  Observed training sessions led by top coaches including **Pep Guardiola, Carlo Ancelotti, Antonio Conte, Diego Simeone, Luis Enrique, Maurizio Sarri**, and many more.

  Visited elite academies of **FC Barcelona, Benfica, Anderlecht, Schalke**, and **Dinamo Zagreb**, Massimo to learn the best approaches for developing young players.

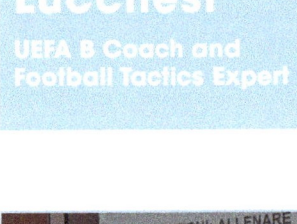

Introduction

Pep Guardiola is widely regarded as one of the greatest managers in football history, and arguably the best. Few coaches have impacted modern football as significantly. His journey has been defined not only by success but also by an unparalleled influence on the way football is played.

What sets Guardiola apart is his philosophy of a proactive, **possession based approach that combines creativity with precision**. His teams are recognised not only for their results but also for their **fluid, attacking style of football**. From his ground breaking success at Barcelona, creating one of the best teams in history, to his transformative spells at Bayern Munich and Manchester City, his teams have consistently displayed:

- A distinct identity to control football matches.
- Ability to dictate the tempo.
- Consistency in breaking down opponents with intelligence and flair.

This book examines the playing model Pep Guardiola has refined at Manchester City, exploring his **tactical innovations** and **strategic principles**. It highlights how his methods produce **organised, attacking football and provides valuable insights for coaches seeking to develop their teams**.

Pep Guardiola's philosophy is not just about tactics, as it reflects meticulous preparation, adaptability, and an unrelenting commitment to excellence.

Our aim is to inspire coaches to draw on Guardiola's ideas, encouraging them to create **high-quality training sessions that promote intelligent and ambitious football**. Achieving this requires more than ambition as it demands dedication, creativity, and a deep understanding of the game's demands.

Pep Guardiola's methods offer a road map for coaches looking to instil a clear philosophy in their teams.

This book invites readers to embrace the **principles that underpin Guardiola's legacy**, refining their approaches to coaching and developing a greater appreciation for football's possibilities. By studying his philosophy, we hope to **inspire the next generation of coaches and players** to reach new heights while upholding the beauty of the game.

Pep Guardiola's Achievements

COACHING ROLES

- **Manchester City** (2016 - Present)
- **Bayern Munich** (2013 - 2016)
- **Barcelona** (2008 - 2012)
- **Barcelona B** (2007 - 2008)

HONOURS (Europe / World)

- **UEFA Champions League x 3** (2009, 2011, 2023)
- **FIFA Club World Cup x 4** (2009, 2011, 2013, 2023)
- **UEFA Super Cup x 3** (2009, 2011, 2013)

HONOURS (Domestic Leagues)

- **English Premier League x 6** (2018, 2019, 2021, 2022, 2023, 2024)
- **German Bundesliga x 3** (2014, 2015, 2016)
- **Spanish La Liga x 3** (2009, 2010, 2011)
- **Spanish Tercera (2nd) División** (2008)

HONOURS (Domestic Cups)

- **English FA Cup x 2** (2019, 2023)
- **German DFB-Pokal x 2** (2014, 2016)
- **Spanish Copa del Rey x 2** (2009, 2012)
- **English EFL Cup x 4** (2018, 2019, 2020, 2021)
- **Spanish Super Cup x 3** (2009, 2010, 2011)

INDIVIDUAL AWARDS

- **Globe Soccer Awards Coach of Century** (2020)
- **FIFA World Coach of Year x 2** (2011, 2023)
- **UEFA Best Coach of Year x 3** (2009, 2011, 2023)
- **Premier League Manager of Season x 5** (2018, 2019, 2021, 2023, 2024)
- **La Liga Coach of Year x 4** (2009, 2010, 2011, 2012)

Manchester City Seasons (2016-2024)

Manchester City Seasons (2016-2024)

Pep Guardiola's Manchester City 4-3-3 Formation

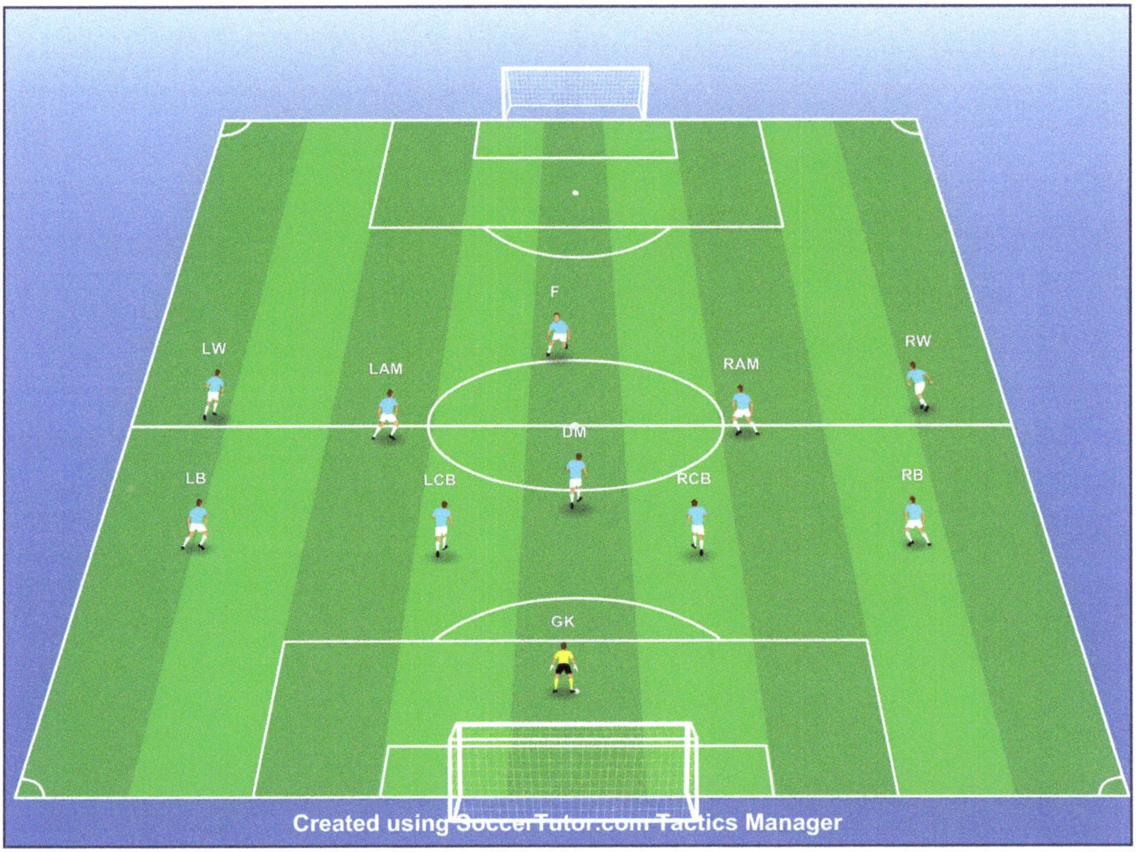

- **GK:** Goalkeeper
- **LCB:** Left Centre Back
- **RCB:** Right Centre Back
- **LB:** Left Back
- **RB:** Right Back
- **DM:** Defensive Midfielder
- **LAM:** Left Attacking Midfielder
- **RAM:** Right Attacking Midfielder
- **LW:** Left Winger
- **RW:** Right Winger
- **F:** Forward

Manchester City Seasons (2016-2024)

Manchester City Team During the 2016-17 Season

In his first season at Manchester City, Pep Guardiola's team finished third in the league, reached the Champions League quarter-finals, and the FA Cup semi-finals.

- **GK:** Bravo
- **LB:** Clichy (or Kolarov)
- **LCB:** Otamendi
- **RCB:** Stones
- **RB:** Sagna (or Zabaleta)
- **DM:** Fernandinho
- **LAM:** D. Silva
- **RAM:** De Bruyne
- **LW:** Sané
- **RW:** Sterling
- **F:** Agüero

Manchester City Seasons (2016-2024)

Manchester City Team During the 2017-18 Season

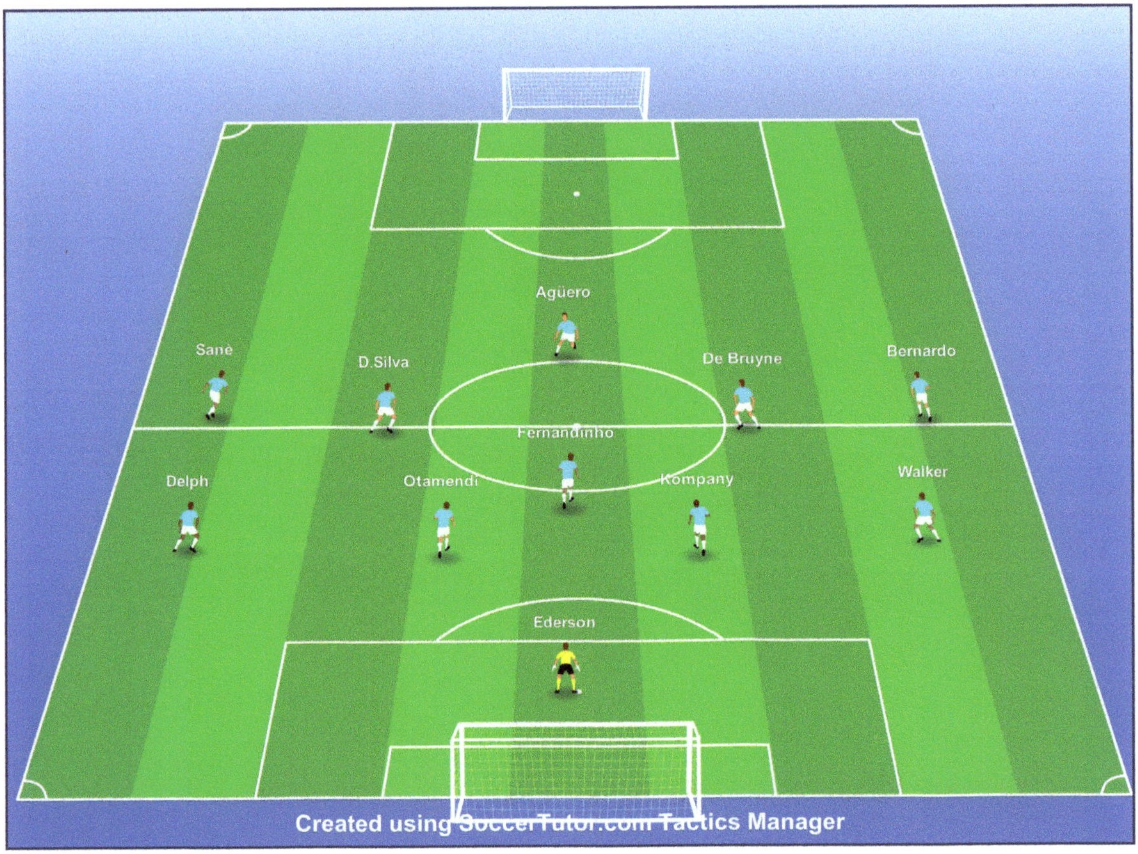

In his second season at Manchester City, Pep Guardiola's team won the Premier League with an incredible 100 points and won the EFL Cup (domestic double).

- **GK:** Ederson
- **LB:** Delph
- **LCB:** Otamendi
- **RCB:** Kompany or Stones
- **RB:** Walker
- **DM:** Fernandinho
- **LAM:** D. Silva (or Gündoğan)
- **RAM:** De Bruyne
- **LW:** Sané
- **RW:** Bernardo (or Sterling)
- **F:** Agüero

Manchester City Seasons (2016-2024)

Manchester City Team During the 2018-19 Season

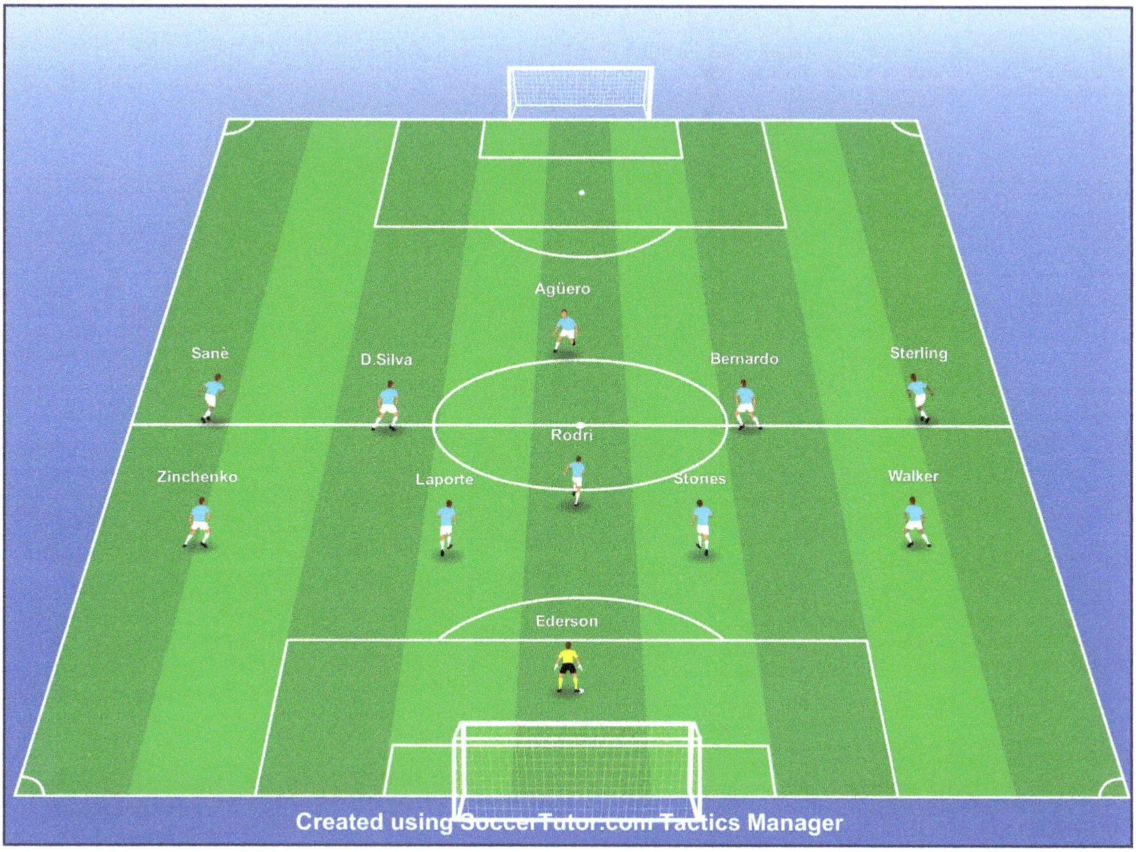

In his third season at Manchester City, Pep Guardiola's team won the Premier League, FA Cup, and EFL Cup to win a landmark domestic treble.

- **GK:** Ederson
- **LB:** Zinchenko
- **LCB:** Laporte (or Otamendi)
- **RCB:** Stones (or Kompany)
- **RB:** Walker
- **DM:** Rodri
- **LAM:** D. Silva (or Gündoğan)
- **RAM:** Bernardo
- **LW:** Sané
- **RW:** Sterling (or Mahrez)
- **F:** Agüero

Manchester City Seasons (2016-2024)

Manchester City Team During the 2019-20 Season

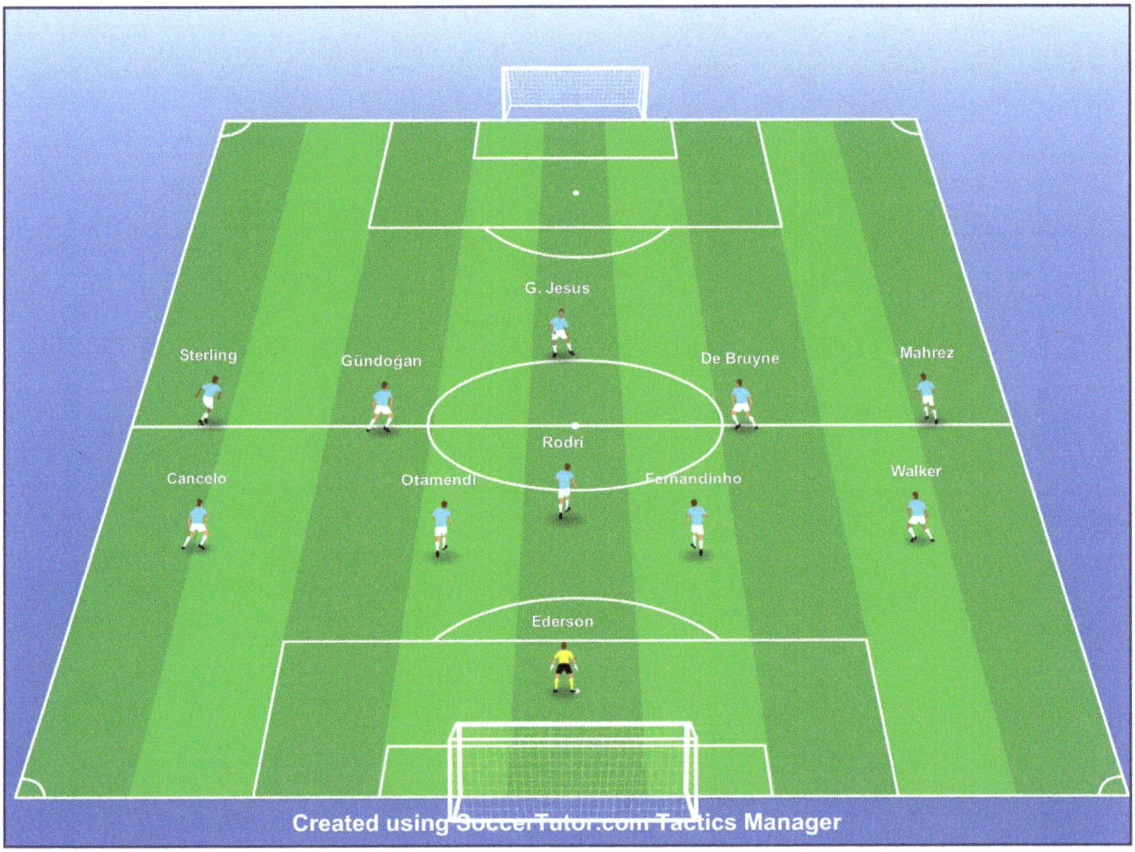

In his fourth season at Manchester City, Pep Guardiola's team won the EFL Cup, finished second in the Premier League, and reached the quarter-finals of the Champions League.

- **GK:** Ederson
- **LB:** Cancelo (or Mendy/Zinchenko)
- **LCB:** Otamendi (or Laporte)
- **RCB:** Fernandinho (or Stones)
- **RB:** Walker (or Cancelo)
- **DM:** Rodri
- **LAM:** Gündoğan (or Bernardo)
- **RAM:** De Bruyne (or Bernardo)
- **LW:** Sterling
- **RW:** Mahrez (or Bernardo)
- **F:** G. Jesus (or Agüero)

PEP GUARDIOLA - COACHING FLUID POSITIONAL ROTATIONS

Manchester City Seasons (2016-2024)

Manchester City Team During the 2020-21 Season

In his fifth season at Manchester City, Pep Guardiola's team won the Premier League and EFL Cup, reached the FA Cup semi-finals, and the Champions League final.

- **GK:** Ederson
- **LB:** Cancelo (or Zinchenko)
- **LCB:** Dias
- **RCB:** Stones
- **RB:** Walker
- **DM:** Rodri
- **LAM:** Gündoğan
- **RAM:** De Bruyne (or Bernardo)
- **LW:** Sterling
- **RW:** Mahrez (or Bernardo)
- **F:** G. Jesus

Manchester City Seasons (2016-2024)

Manchester City Team During the 2021-22 Season

![Formation diagram showing: Ederson (GK); Cancelo, Laporte, Dias, Walker (defense); Rodri (DM); Bernardo, De Bruyne (AM); Grealish, Foden (wingers); G. Jesus (forward)]

In his sixth season at Manchester City, Pep Guardiola's team won the Premier League and reached the FA Cup and Champions League semi-finals.

- **GK:** Ederson
- **LB:** Cancelo
- **LCB:** Laporte (or Stones)
- **RCB:** Dias
- **RB:** Walker
- **DM:** Rodri
- **LAM:** Bernardo
- **RAM:** De Bruyne
- **LW:** Grealish
- **RW:** Foden (or Mahrez)
- **F:** G. Jesus

Manchester City Seasons (2016-2024)

Manchester City Team During the 2022-23 Season

Option 1: 4-3-3

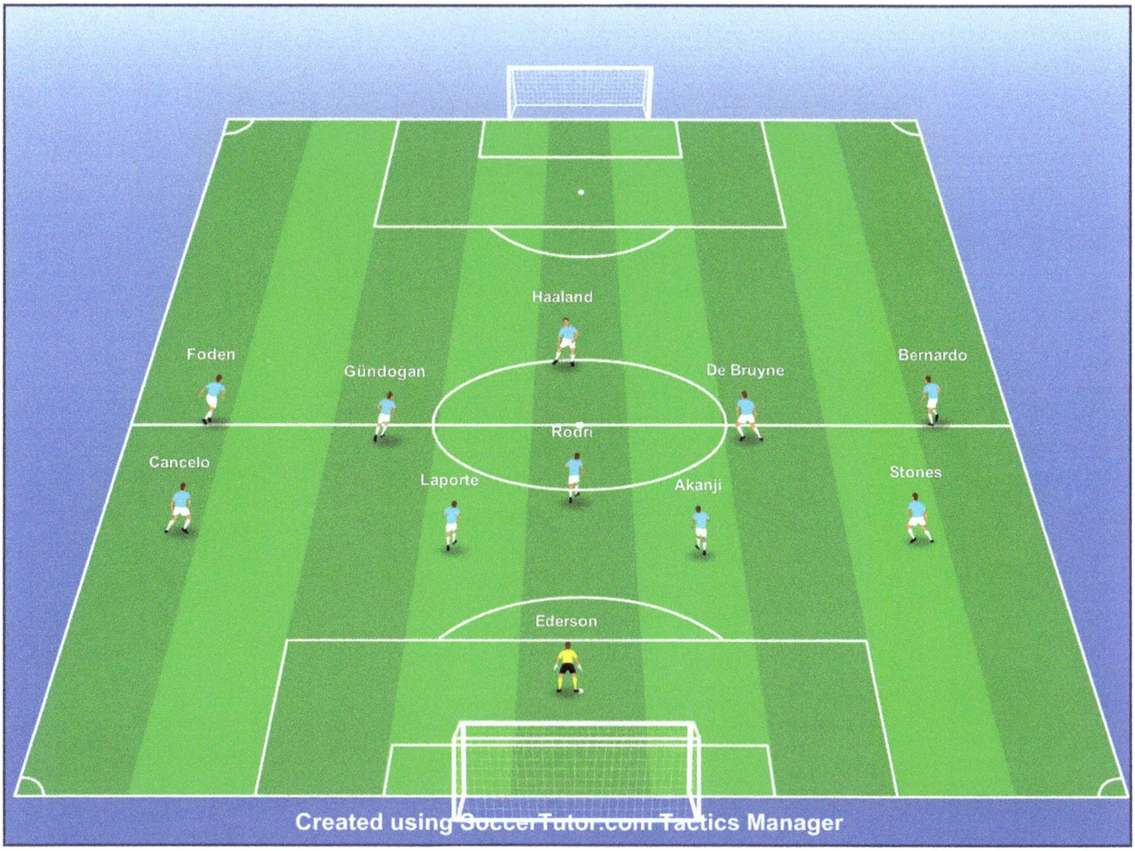

In his seventh season at Manchester City, Pep Guardiola's team won the Premier League, FA Cup, and Champions League to win a historic treble.

- **GK:** Ederson
- **LB:** Cancelo (or Aké)
- **LCB:** Laporte (or Aké)
- **RCB:** Akanji
- **RB:** Stones (or Walker)
- **DM:** Rodri
- **LAM:** Gündoğan
- **RAM:** De Bruyne
- **LW:** Grealish (or Foden)
- **RW:** Bernardo (or Mahrez)
- **F:** Haaland

Manchester City Seasons (2016-2024)

Option 2: **4-4-2 Diamond**

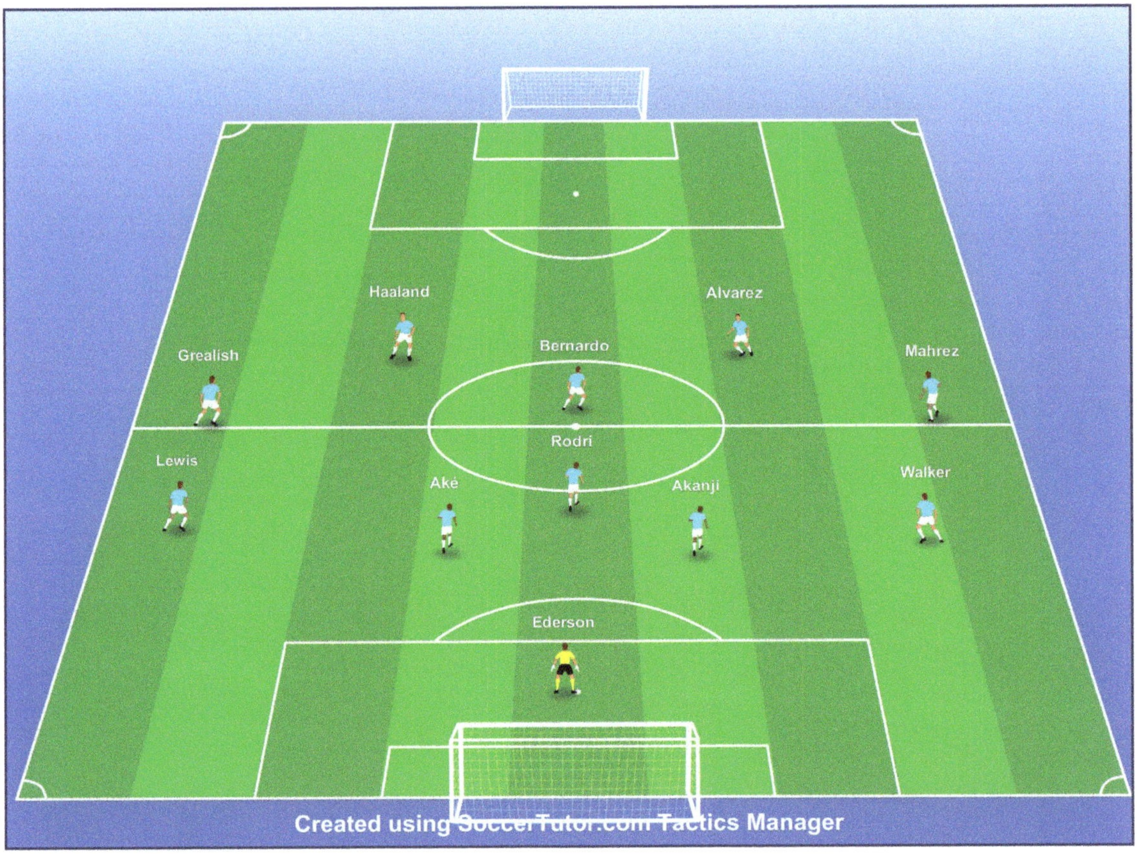

This diagram shows a formation variation Manchester City used during the 2022-23 treble winning season (**4-4-2 Diamond**).

The example is taken from a Premier League match against Tottenham Hotspur (5th February 2023), where Manchester City demonstrated their tactical flexibility.

In this game, Pep Guardiola removed one of the attacking midfielders from the usual 4-3-3 formation and introduced an **additional forward (Alvarez)** instead to partner **Haaland**. This provided **more direct attacking options** with the aim to better exploit the spaces left by their opponents' defensive structure.

Key Point: Pep Guardiola's team adjusted their shape to exploit key spaces and create tactical advantages against specific opponents.

Manchester City Seasons (2016-2024)

Manchester City Team During the 2023-24 Season

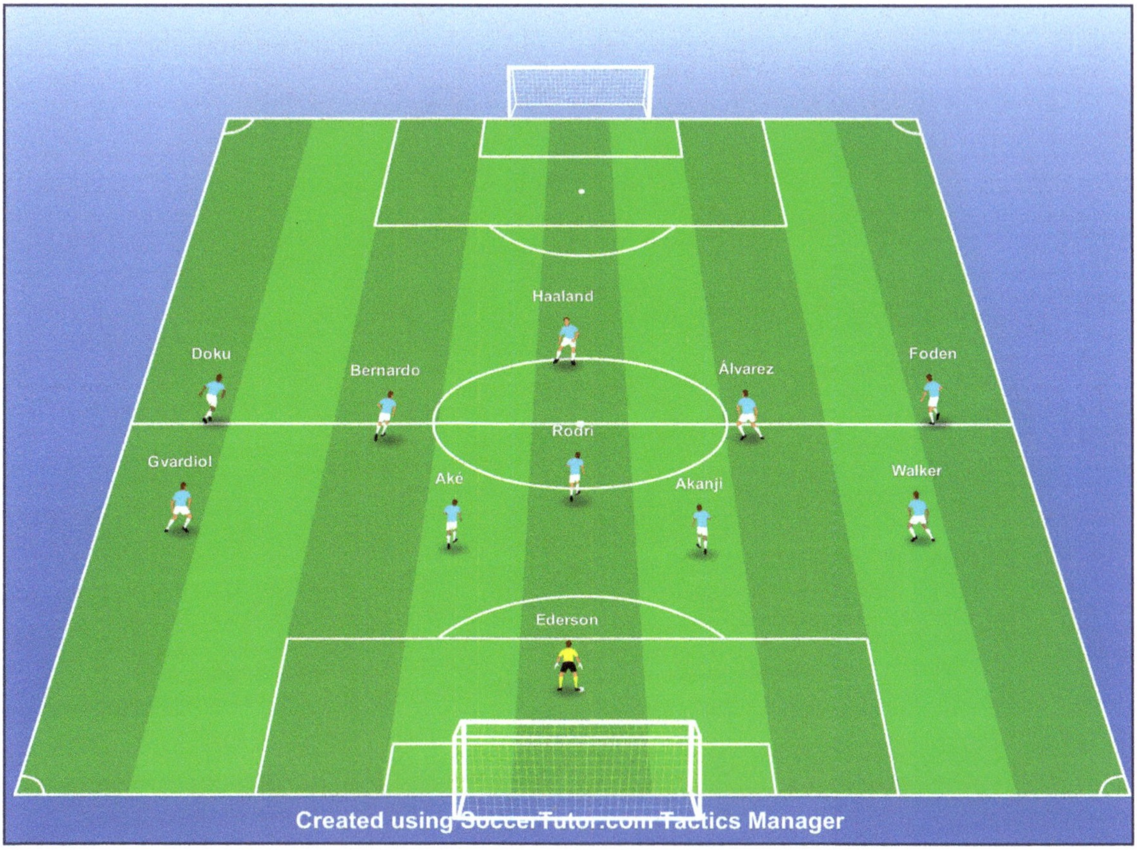

In his eight season at Manchester City, Pep Guardiola's team won their fourth consecutive Premier League title and reached the FA Cup final.

- **GK:** Ederson
- **LB:** Gvardiol
- **LCB:** Aké (or Stones)
- **RCB:** Akanji
- **RB:** Walker
- **DM:** Rodri
- **LAM:** Bernardo (or Kovačič)
- **RAM:** Álvarez (or De Bruyne)
- **LW:** Doku/Grealish (or Foden)
- **RW:** Foden
- **F:** Haaland

Foundations of Pep Guardiola's Game Model

Foundations of Pep Guardiola's Game Model at Manchester City

In this section of the book, we study the foundational principles of Manchester City's playing philosophy under Pep Guardiola, a philosophy that has redefined modern football. At its core lies an extraordinary adaptability, as the team does not rely on a rigid, predefined system of play. Instead, **City utilise various formations, adjusted meticulously to the opponent's setup, defensive approach, and the specific phase of play**, whether in the defensive third, middle third, or final third. This flexibility enables them to impose their game on any opposition, regardless of the challenges they face.

The cornerstone of this adaptability is the **players' remarkable ability to maintain compact distances between each other, combined with their masterful control of the ball**. This cohesion ensures that transitions between formations occur fluidly and with minimal disruption to the team's rhythm. Pep Guardiola's philosophy is deeply grounded in this cohesive framework, with the rhombus structure serving as the tactical cornerstone of his system. **The rhombus shapes are not just used as a framework for maintaining balance and cohesion but also as a powerful tool for ball circulation and positional play**. It binds players together, facilitates quick and precise passing, and allows Manchester City to adapt effortlessly to the various formations employed in different phases of the game.

We will break down these elements in detail, exploring how Manchester City's dynamic approach impacts their performance across all areas of the pitch. The **rhombus structure supports their tactical versatility and enables them to overcome even the most compact defensive blocks**.

Practical insights are provided, featuring training practices and sessions designed to improve individual technical skills, enhance spatial awareness, and develop the ability to read and respond to game situations. These practices form the foundation of the technical and tactical excellence required to execute Pep Guardiola's vision at the highest level.

Key Point: You, the coach, can learn and understand the intricate balance of structure, creativity, and fluidity that defines Pep Guardiola and Manchester City's dominance, with a deeper insight into one of football's most effective and revolutionary playing models.

Foundations of Pep Guardiola's Game Model

Pep Guardiola's Fluid Formations for Different Game Situations

1a. 4-1-4-1 Team Shape in the Defensive Third Against a High Press

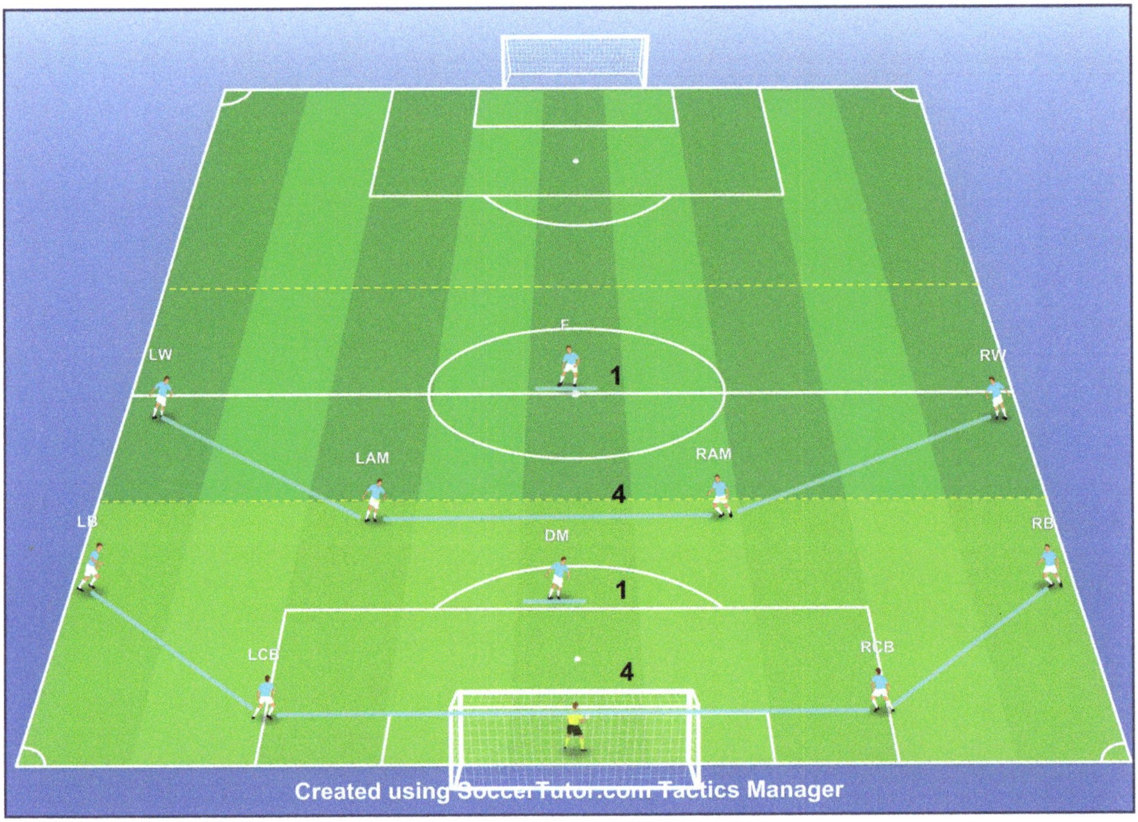

Pep Guardiola's Manchester City team do not rely on a fixed system of play during the possession phase. Instead, they use a dynamic approach tailored to the specific game situation. In our analysis of Manchester City's attacking phase game approach, we will break the study into three distinct situations:

1. **Team Shape in the Defensive Third Against a High Press**
2. **Team Shape in the Middle Third Against a Mid-Block**
3. **Team Shape in the Final Third Against a Deep Block**

The first situation focuses on the team's structure in the defensive third against opponents using high pressing strategies. In such instances, as we will explore, Manchester City most often use variations of the 4-1-4-1 or 4-2-2 formations, allowing them to effectively counteract and play through the pressure applied by their opponents. The diagram above shows the 4-1-4-1 structure.

Foundations of Pep Guardiola's Game Model

1b. 4-2-2 Team Shape in the Defensive Third Against a High Press

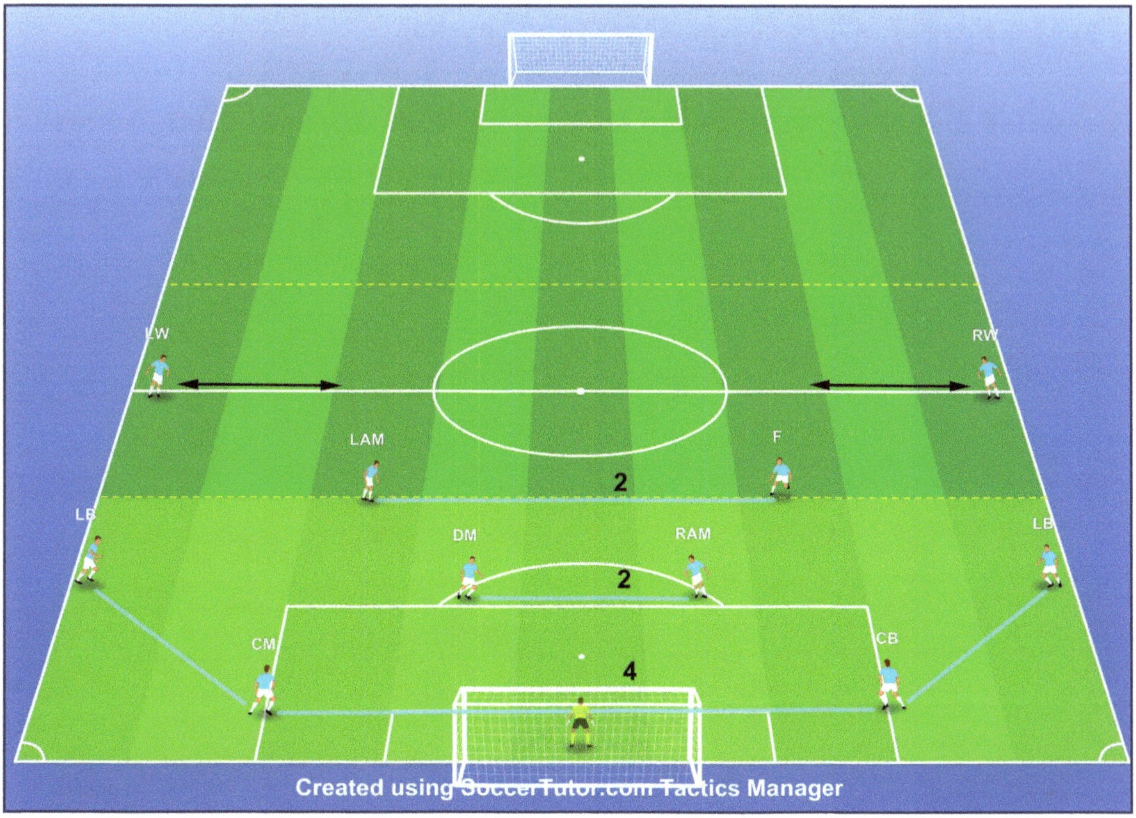

Diagram 1b shows a variation of the 4-1-4-1 shape shown on the previous page.

In this variation, Manchester City use a 4-2-2 shape to build up play from the back through an opponent's high press.

This setup provides added support in deeper areas, helping ball circulation and stability under pressure.

One of the attacking midfielders (**RAM**) drops back closer to the defensive line alongside the defensive midfielder (**DM**) to create a double pivot. This is done to create more passing options and assist in moving the ball forwards.

Key Point: This structure enables the team to bypass the press and progress effectively into more advanced areas of the pitch.

Foundations of Pep Guardiola's Game Model

2. 3-2-4-1 Team Shape in the Middle Third Against a Mid-Block

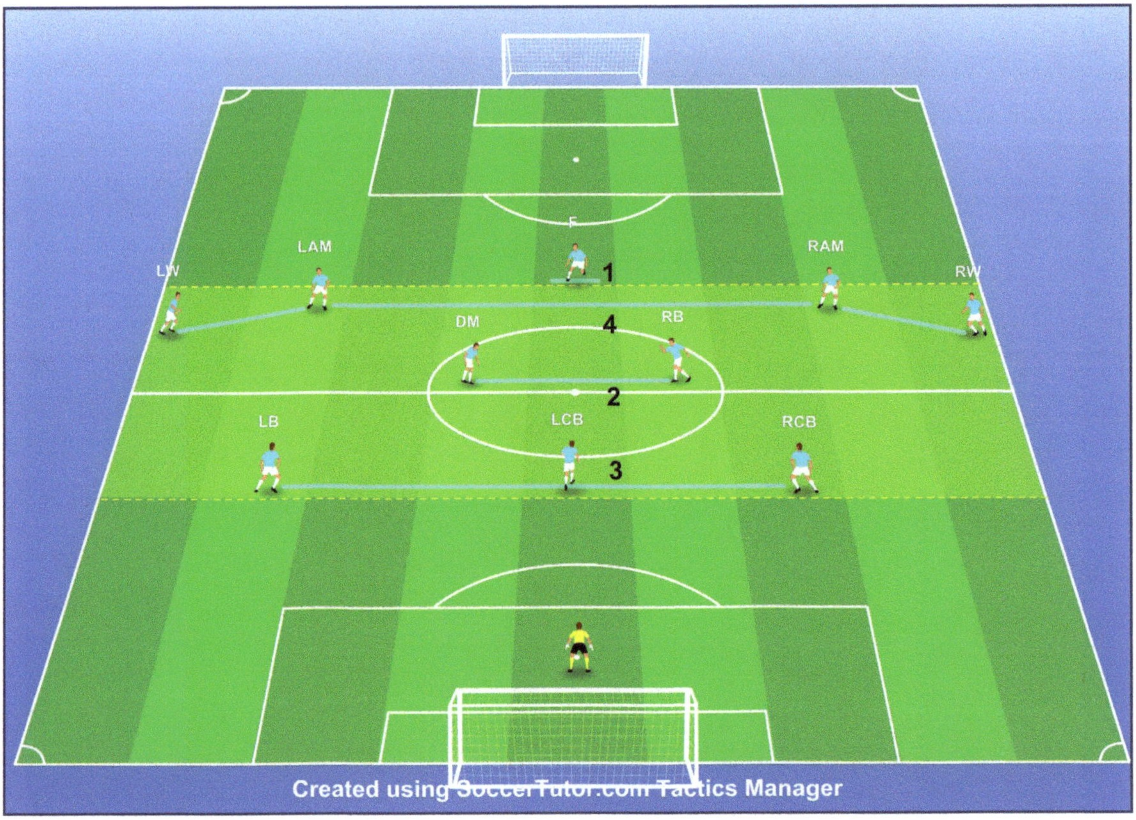

This second situation focuses on Manchester City's approach when playing against opponents positioned in the middle third of the pitch.

Pep Guardiola's team typically use a 3-2-4-1 shape, which creates a **structure designed to control the tempo of the game and dictate play**. This arrangement enables Manchester City to pin their opponents in place, using precise and repeated ball circulation along the perimeter to stretch the defensive shape.

Key Point 1: The aim is to maintain dominance in possession while probing for weaknesses in the opponent's structure.

When gaps begin to emerge within the opposition's formation, City's players are **well positioned to transition from horizontal ball circulation to forward penetrative passing**, effectively exploiting the spaces to create goal scoring opportunities.

Key Point 2: This dual approach of patient build up play and incisive forward play highlights the versatility and tactical intelligence of Pep Guardiola's system.

Foundations of Pep Guardiola's Game Model

3a. 2-3-5 Team Shape in the Final Third Against a Deep Block

The third situation focuses on when the opposition retreats into their defensive third, creating high density around the penalty box to block Manchester City's attacks. To counteract this, Pep Guardiola's team typically use a 2-3-5 formation.

This adjustment allows enables them to **maintain control of the ball and stretch the defensive block** horizontally, creating openings through patient ball circulation and precise positional play.

The **team's ability to adapt their shape ensures they can continue to create goal scoring opportunities**, even against compact and resolute defences.

Key Point: The tactical flexibility to fluidly transition between formations allows Pep Guardiola's Manchester City team to dominate possession and sustain a relentless attacking presence in the final third, regardless of the opposition's defensive strategy.

Foundations of Pep Guardiola's Game Model

3b. 1-3-6 Team Shape in the Final Third Against a Deep Block

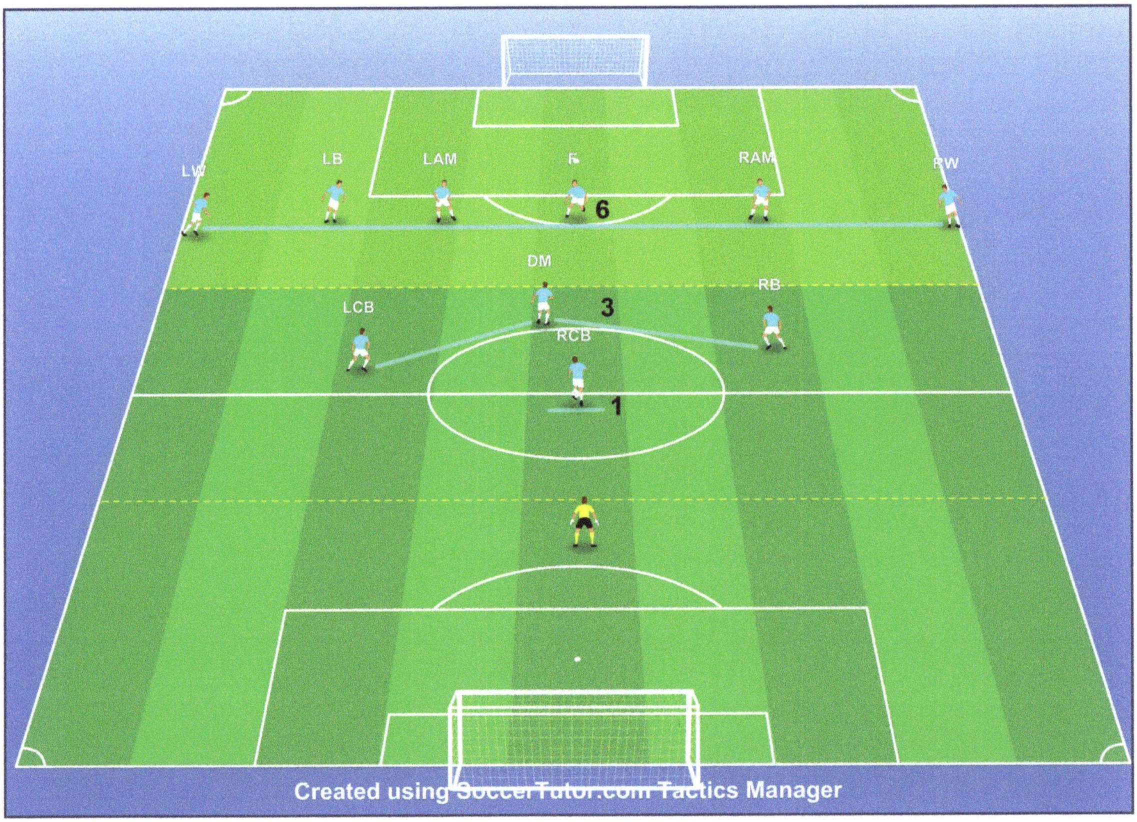

This diagram shows a tactical variation where Manchester City adjust their attacking shape to a 1-3-6 formation in response to their opponents reinforcing their defensive line with five players.

This tactical tweak helps the team to **overload the final third**, potentially create **numerical equality or superiority** in areas, and **stretch the opponent's defensive block**.

Key Point: The 1-3-6 shape increases attacking options in advanced areas, helping with movement, passing combinations, and opportunities to exploit small gaps against a deep defence.

Foundations of Pep Guardiola's Game Model

Tactical Solution 1 to Change Formations with Inverted Full Back

1a. Switch 4-1-4-1 to 3-2-4-1 with Left Back Moving into Midfield

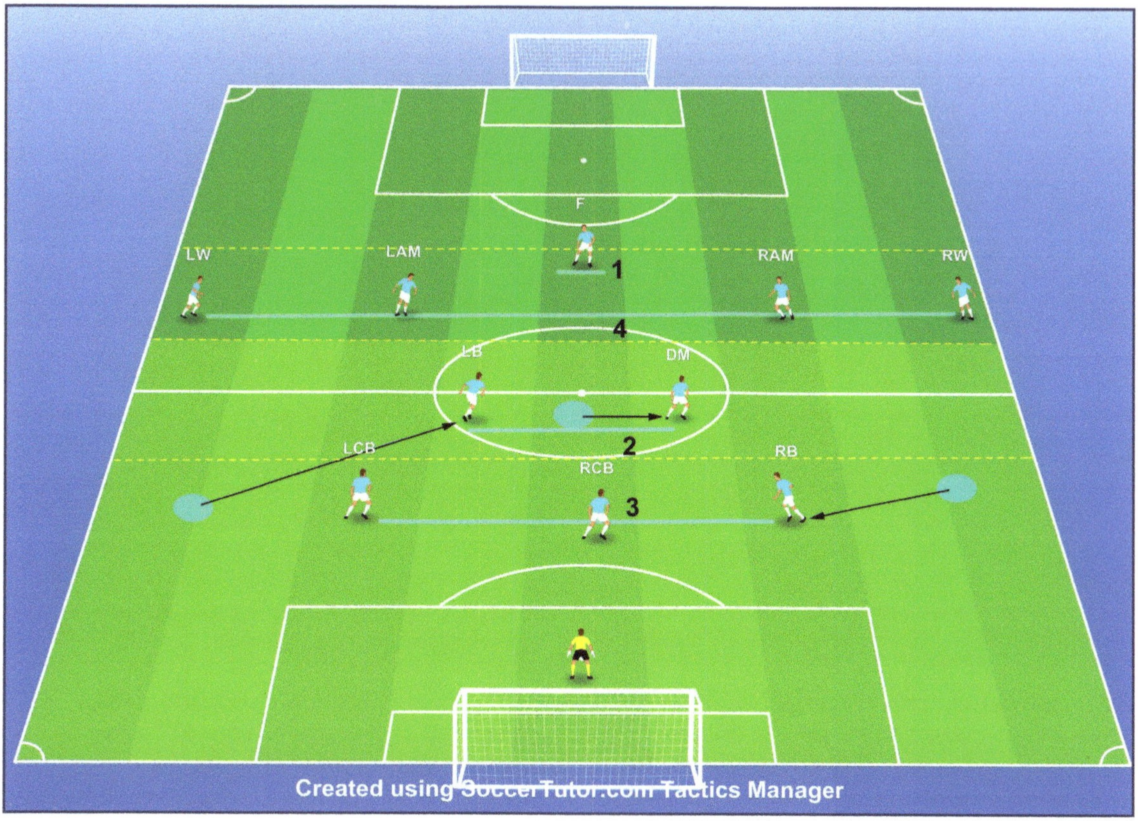

In the first tactical solution, **Manchester City switch from a 4+1 to a 3+2 structure at the back** with only the full backs changing their positioning.

The left back (**LB**) moves forward into midfield next to the defensive midfielder (**DM**) to create a double pivot. The right back (**RB**) shifts inside to tighten up the back line.

The centre backs (**LCB** and **RCB**) hold their positions and the defensive midfielder (**DM**) adjusts his position slightly, as shown.

This situation continues on the next page which shows you how Manchester City switch from their 3-2-4-1 shape into a 3-2-5 when the ball progresses into the attacking half of the pitch.

Key Point: The same can be replicated on the other side of the pitch with the right back (RB) moving forward instead, and the left back (LB) shifting inside.

Foundations of Pep Guardiola's Game Model

1b. Switch to 2-3-5 in Attacking Half with Right Back Moving Forward

From this situation, when the team advances into the opponent's half, the structure changes to a 2-3-5 (or 3-1-6) formation.

The right back (**RB**) moves forward into the midfield line alongside the left back (**LB**) and defensive midfielder (**DM**). The centre backs (**LCB** and **RCB**) converge and move forward as shown.

This setup is more suited to **managing possession effectively against an opponent defending deeper**. The shift allows Manchester City to **maintain control**, **dictate play**, and **create opportunities to break through** a compact defensive line.

These formations provide flexibility, enabling the team to adapt their positioning based on the opposition's defensive organisation.

The principles and patterns of play utilised in these phases of the game will be analysed later in the book.

Key Point: The 2-3-5 and 3-1-6 formations are essential for maintaining dominance in possession while applying pressure to teams defending deep in their own half.

Foundations of Pep Guardiola's Game Model

Tactical Solution 2 to Change Formations with Both Full Backs Inverted

2a. Switch 4-1-4-1 to 3-2-4-1 with Both Full Backs Inverted (DM Drops)

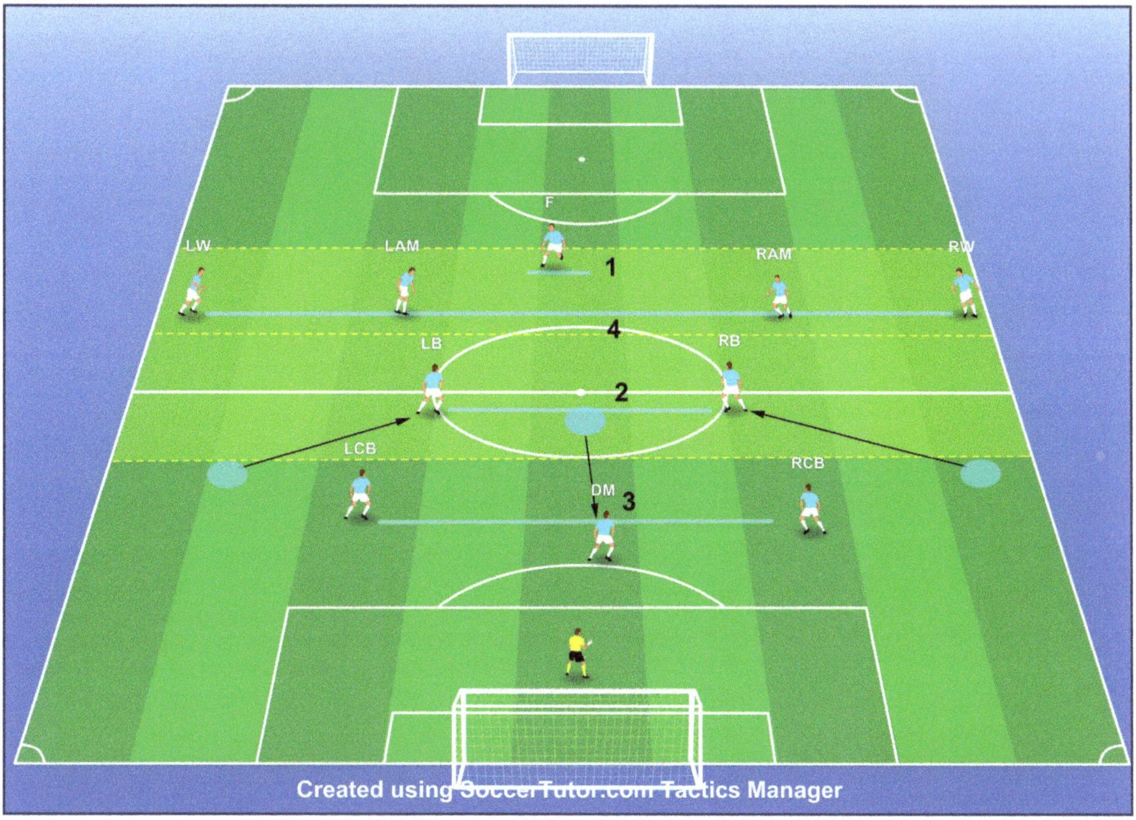

In this second tactical solution, both full backs (**LB** and **RB**) push forward and move inside to act as inverted midfielders, while the defensive midfielder (**DM**) drops back into the defensive line, forming a 3+2 structure at the back.

The full backs' advanced roles create additional passing options, linking midfield with attack.

The **DM's** deeper position secures the back line against counter attacks.

Key Point: This structure highlights Pep Guardiola's tactical flexibility, balancing defensive solidity with attacking fluidity.

Foundations of Pep Guardiola's Game Model

2b. Switch to 2-3-5 in Attacking Half with DM Moving Forward

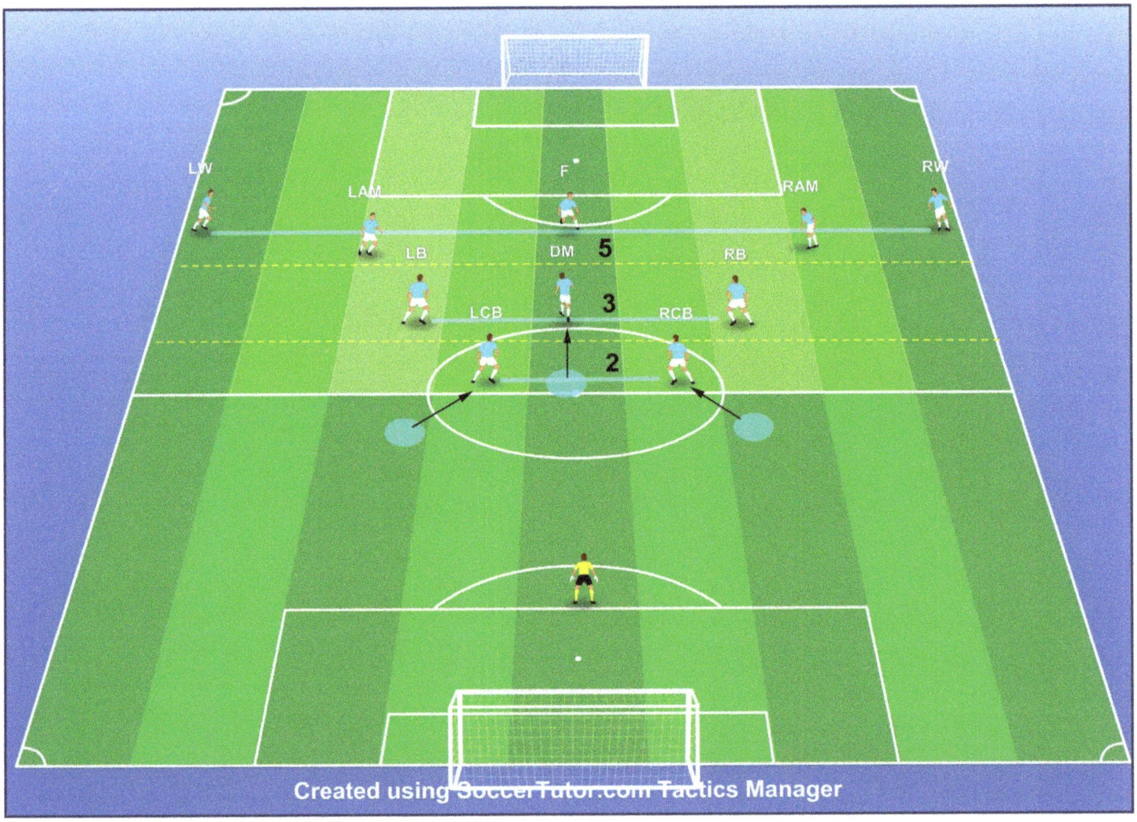

When Manchester City advance into their opponent's half, the structure changes to a 2-3-5 (or 3-1-6) formation. This shift is designed to **apply sustained pressure on the opponent's defensive block** while maintaining control of the game.

The defensive midfielder (**DM**) moves into the midfield line alongside both full backs (**LB** and **RB**). Both centre backs (**LCB** and **RCB**) converge and move forward.

In the 2-3-5 setup, 5 players position themselves high and wide, stretching the defence to create gaps and passing lanes.

The midfield 3 anchor the formation, ensuring **stability in possession** and using probing movements to exploit attacking opportunities.

Key Point: This structure enables Manchester City to dominate in the attacking half of the pitch, combining defensive solidity with attacking fluidity. Pep Guardiola's tactical fluidity is a key part of his ingenuity in breaking down compact defensive lines.

Foundations of Pep Guardiola's Game Model

Tactical Solution 3 to Change Formations with Centre Back Pushing into Midfield

3a. Switch 4-2-3-1 to 3-2-4-1 with Centre Back Moving Forward

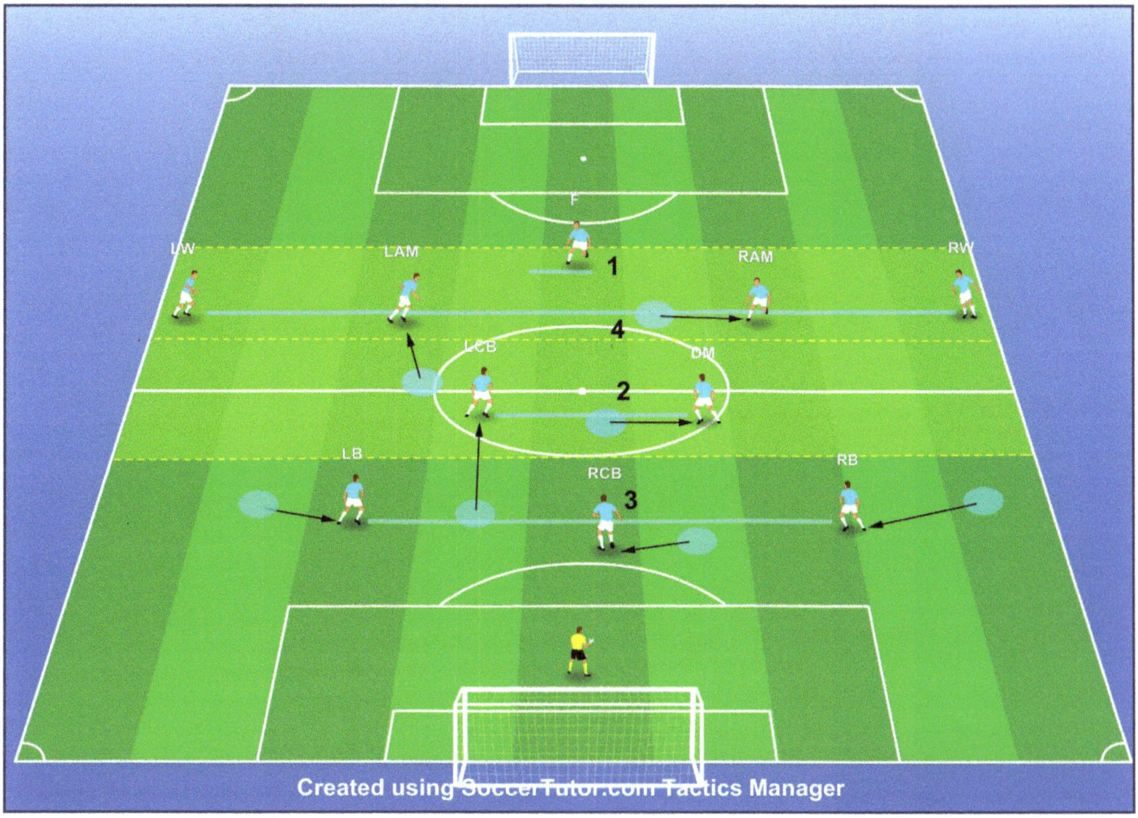

In this third tactical solution, Manchester City's team shape shifts with a centre back (**LCB**) moving into midfield to create a double pivot, and both full backs (**LB** & **RB**) shifting inside to form a back 3.

When there was a double pivot (4+2 at the back forming a 4-2-3-1), which happens in certain phases of the game, one of the attacking midfielders (**LAM in diagram example**) would move forward into the next line to accommodate the centre back's (**LCB**) movement and help create the same 3-2-4-1 shape.

Key Point: This structure strengthens midfield control, enhances possession, and helps with fluid ball progression against compact or pressing opponents.

Foundations of Pep Guardiola's Game Model

3b. Switch to 2-3-5 in Attacking Half with Left Back Moving Forward

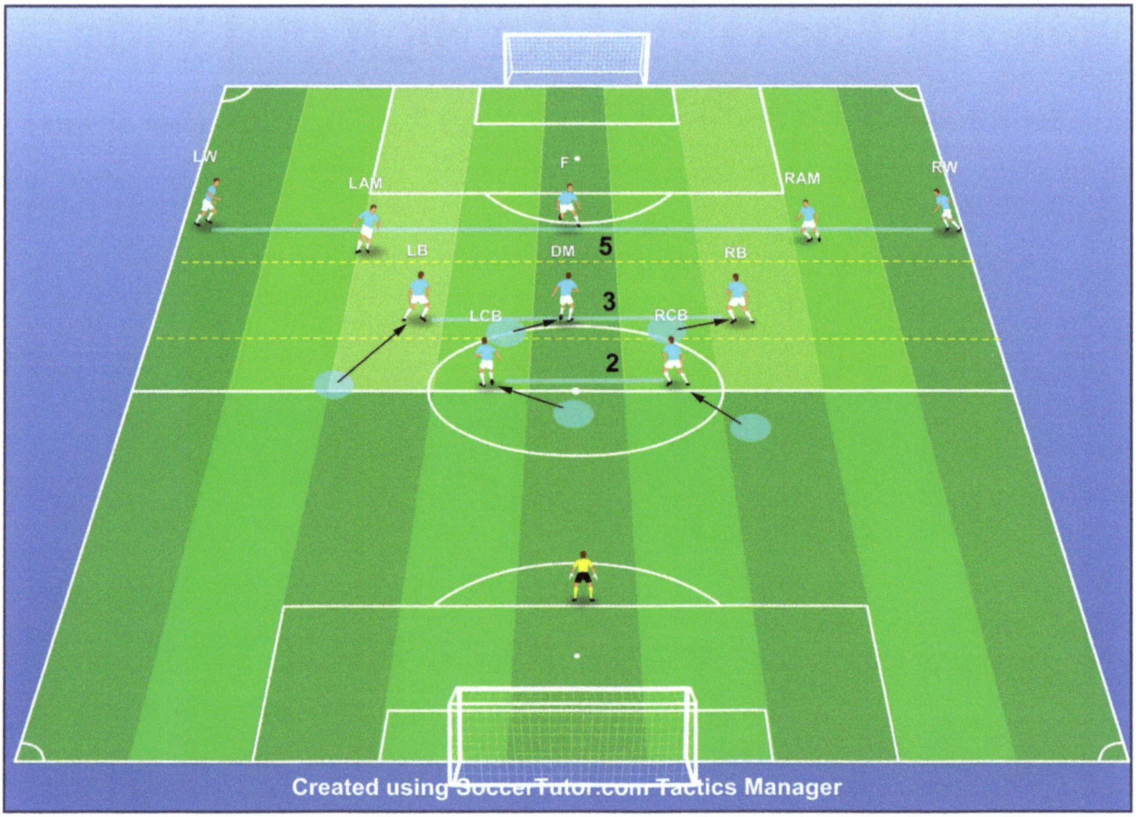

In the attacking half (during the possession phase), Manchester City change from their 3-2-4-1 shape to 2-3-5 with the left back (**LB**) moving forward into the midfield line to create a midfield 3.

This movement of **LB provides additional options for ball circulation and strengthens Manchester City's dominance in the attacking half**.

With technical security and a compact shape in case possession is lost, City can push both their wingers (**LW** and **RW**) high and wide.

Key Point: Both wingers' high positioning provides greater width and attacking presence high up the pitch to stretch the opposition's defensive block. This creates opportunities to play penetrating passes through the centre and into space in the wide areas.

Foundations of Pep Guardiola's Game Model

Tactical Solution 4 to Change Formations with Full Backs Pushing High and Wide

4a. Switch 4-3-3 to 3-2-4-1 with Full Backs Pushing High (DM Drops)

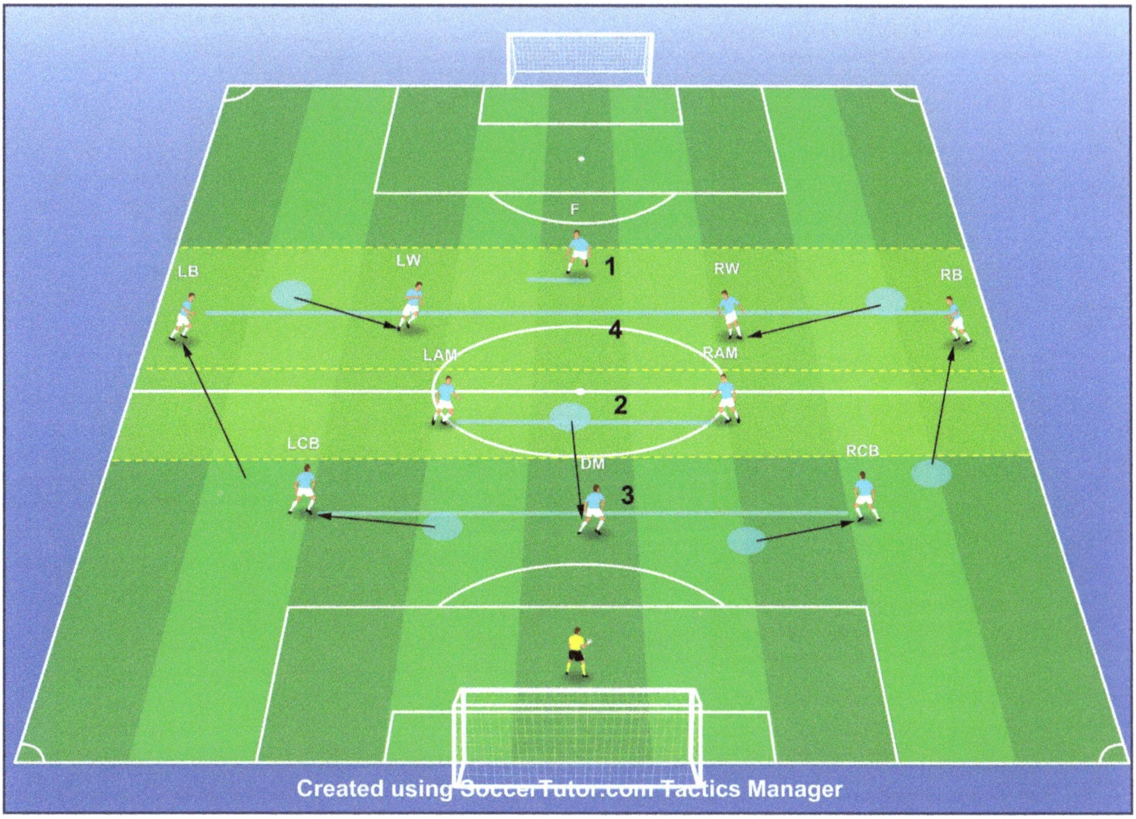

In this fourth tactical solution, Manchester City transition from an initial 4-3-3 shape into a 3-2-4-1 structure during the possession phase.

The 3+2 structure is created by the defensive midfielder (**DM**) dropping back to create a back 3.

Simultaneously, both full backs (**LB** and **RB**) move forward into high and wide positions. This **provides additional passing options at the same time as ensuring compactness** is retained in the central zones.

Attacking midfielders (**LAM** and **RAM**) function as a double pivot, acting as key connectors between the defensive and attacking lines. **LAM and RAM's positioning offers stability and enables fluid ball progression**, creating a platform for the team to dictate play, probe for openings, and prepare for a transition into the attacking phase.

Key Point: This formation not only reinforces control in the middle third but also sets up an effective structure for breaking down opposition lines.

Foundations of Pep Guardiola's Game Model

4b. Switch to 2-3-5 in Attacking Half with DM Moving Forward

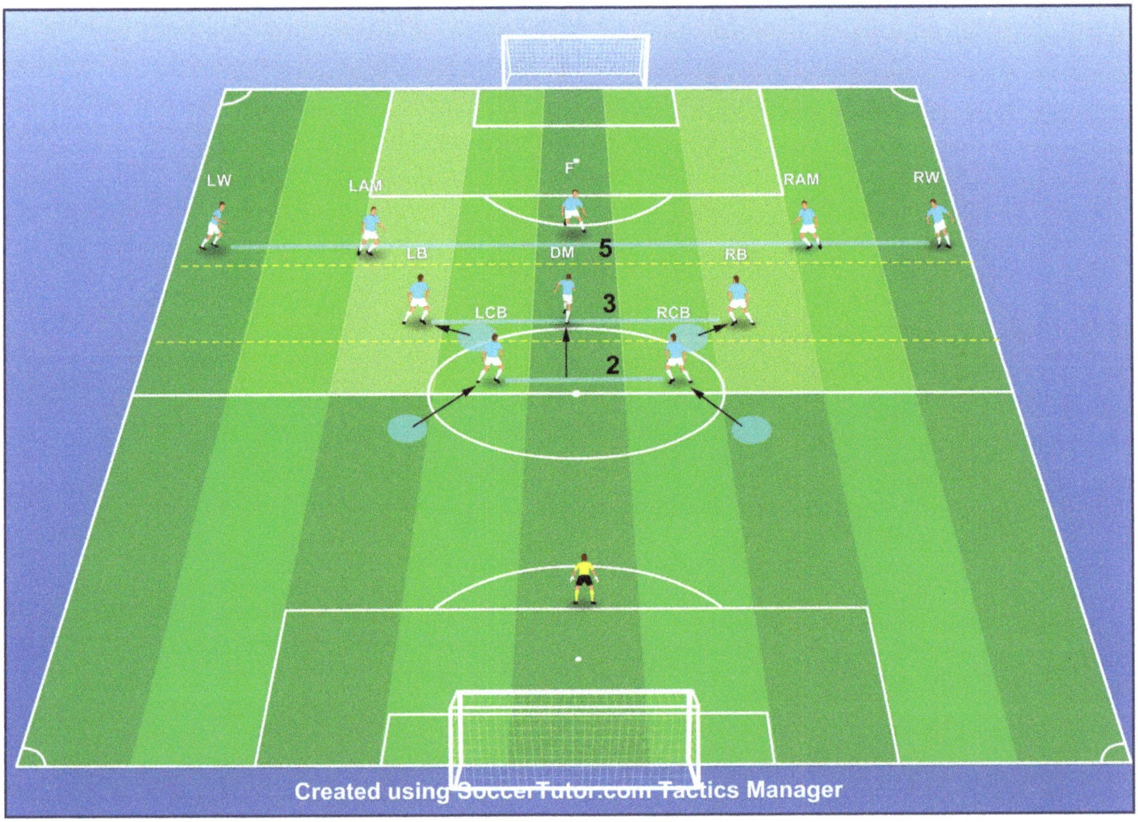

As the ball advances into the attacking half, Manchester City switch to a 2+3 central structure.

The defensive midfielder (**DM**) pushes forward into the midfield line, positioned centrally between the two full backs (**LB** and **RB**), who shifted slightly wider to occupy the half spaces.

Both centre backs (**LCB** and **RCB**) move up and inside as shown.

These movements allow Pep Guardiola's team to smoothly switch from a 3-2-4-1 to a 2-3-5 formation. This helps City to **maintain possession**, **stretch the opponent's defensive block**, and **create attacking opportunities**.

Key Point: The centre backs move closer together to form a compact pairing to provide support in possession, defensive stability, and prepare for any potential counter attacks.

Foundations of Pep Guardiola's Game Model

Tactical Solution 5 to Change Formations with a 3-Player Rotation

5a. Switch 4-1-4-1 to 3-2-4-1 (Full Back Up, Winger Inside, Att. Mid Drops)

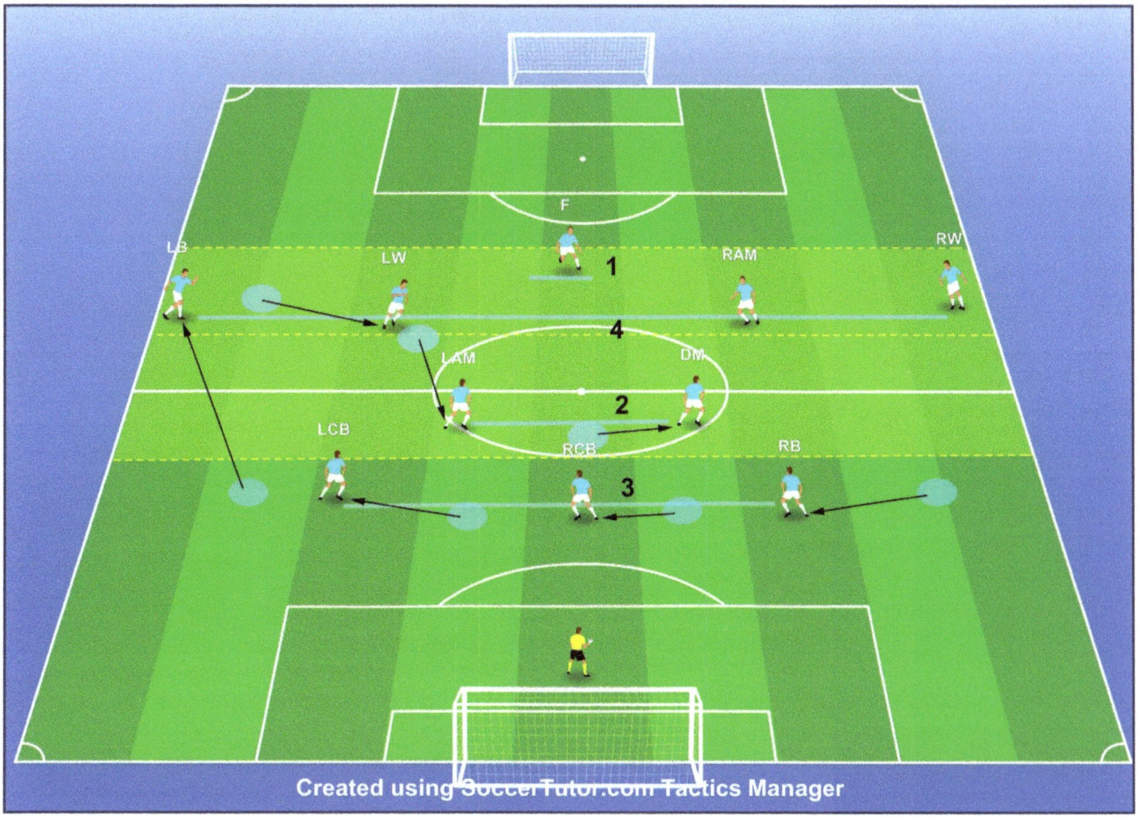

In this final tactical solution, Manchester City transition from an initial 4-1-4-1 shape into a 3-2-4-1 structure during the possession phase.

The attacking midfielder (**LAM**) drops back to create a 3+2 structure in the centre while the winger (**LW**) moves inside to take up his position, and the left back (**LB**) pushes forward into a high and wide position to take over **LW's** position (3-player rotation).

The right back (**RB**) shifts towards the centre to help provide defensive stability and the centre backs move across to create a structured back 3.

Key Point: All these movements happen at the same time and Manchester City are able to create a dynamic balance between exploiting the full width of the pitch and progressing the ball through the centre. The same can be replicated on the other side of the pitch with RB, RAM, and RW.

Foundations of Pep Guardiola's Game Model

5b. Switch to 2-3-5 in Attacking Half with Right Back Moving Forward

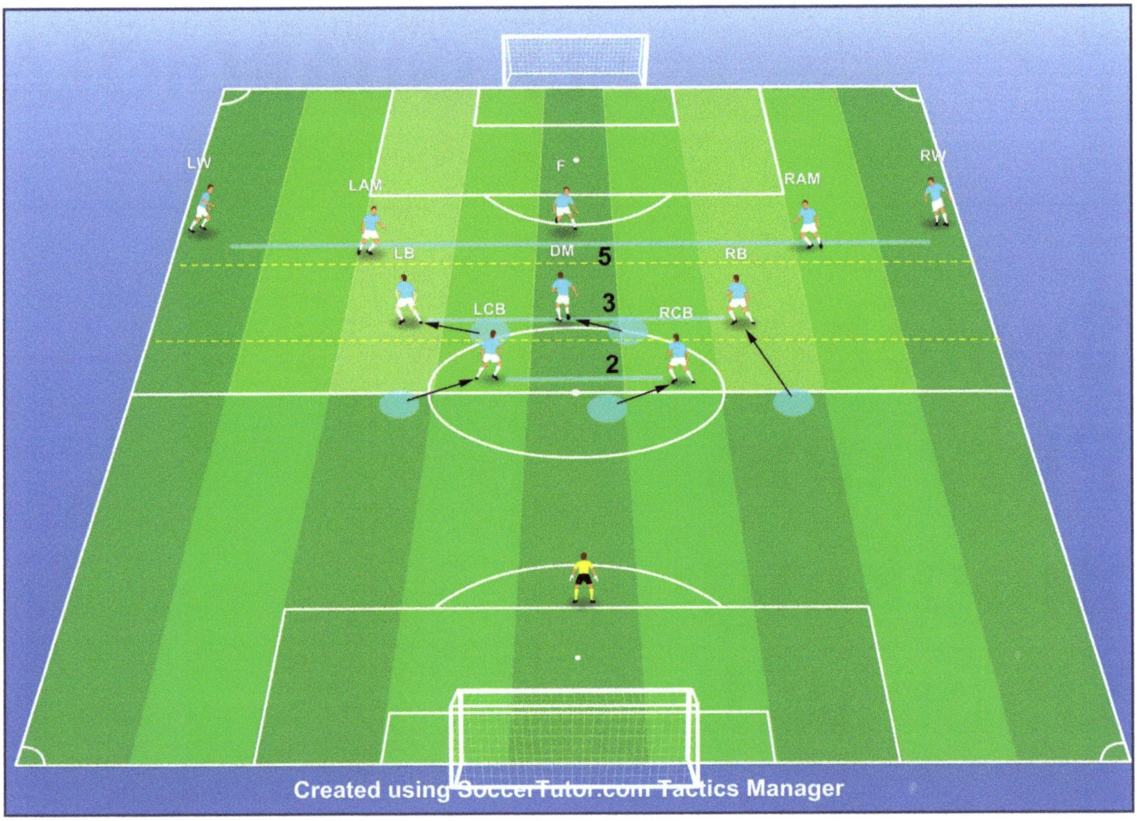

Once Manchester City progress the play into the attacking half, the formation adjusts to have a 2+3 structure in the centre.

The deeper full back (**RB**) advances into midfield and both centre backs (**LCB** and **RCB**) adjust slightly but maintain their positions to provide defensive stability.

Key Point: As is typical under Guardiola's system, which has been shown in all of the 5 tactical solutions presented, this progression sees the team switch fluidly from a 3-2-4-1 shape to 2-3-5, enhancing their ability to dominate possession and apply sustained pressure in the attacking half of the pitch.

SESSION BASED ON THE TACTICS OF PEP GUARDIOLA

Switching Play and Breaking Lines with Inverted Full Back

Session for PEP GUARDIOLA Tactics - **Switching Play and Breaking Lines with Inverted Full Back**

Positional Patterns of Play Setup with 4-1-4-1 Shape

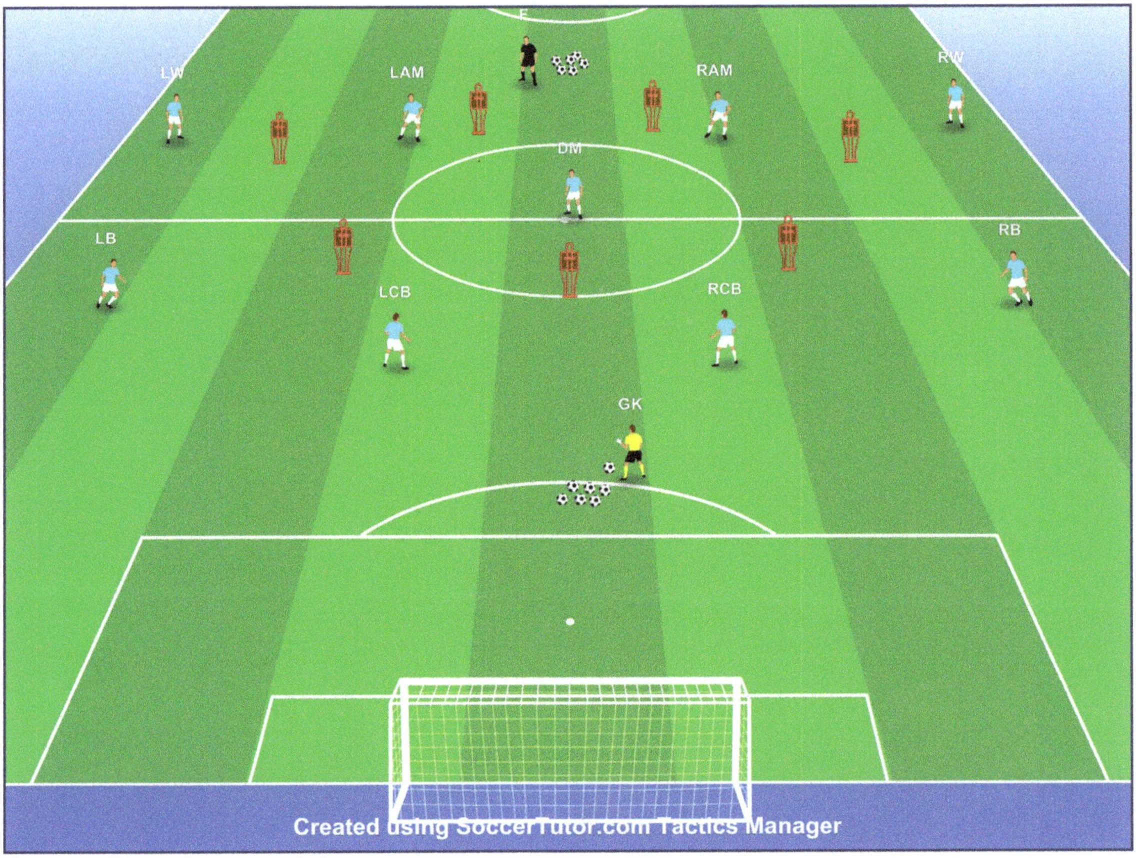

Here we show the setup for practicing **attacking positional patterns of play to coach the foundations of Pep Guardiola's game model**. The starting positions are from Manchester City's 4-1-4-1 possession phase formation.

The coach represents the forward (**F**) but when he feeds a ball in, it is as if the team have just won possession of the ball from the opposition. They play from there.

If the **GK** (or coach) at the bottom passes the ball in, it is as if the **GK** is playing out from the back.

The other players are 2 centre backs (**LCB** and **RCB**), 2 full backs (**LB** and **RB**), 1 defensive midfielder (**DM**), 2 attacking midfielders (**LAM** and **RAM**), and 2 wingers (**LW** and **RW**).

The **7 red mannequins represent likely opposition positions within a defensive organisation**. These serve as visual cues for players to understand spacing and positioning.

Throughout the training session, the players work on different patterns of play whilst changing the team shape.

Session for PEP GUARDIOLA Tactics - Switching Play and Breaking Lines with Inverted Full Back

SESSION FOR THIS TACTICAL SITUATION (5 PRACTICES)

1. Ball Circulation After Winning Possession + Break the Lines Pass (4-1-4-1 Shape)

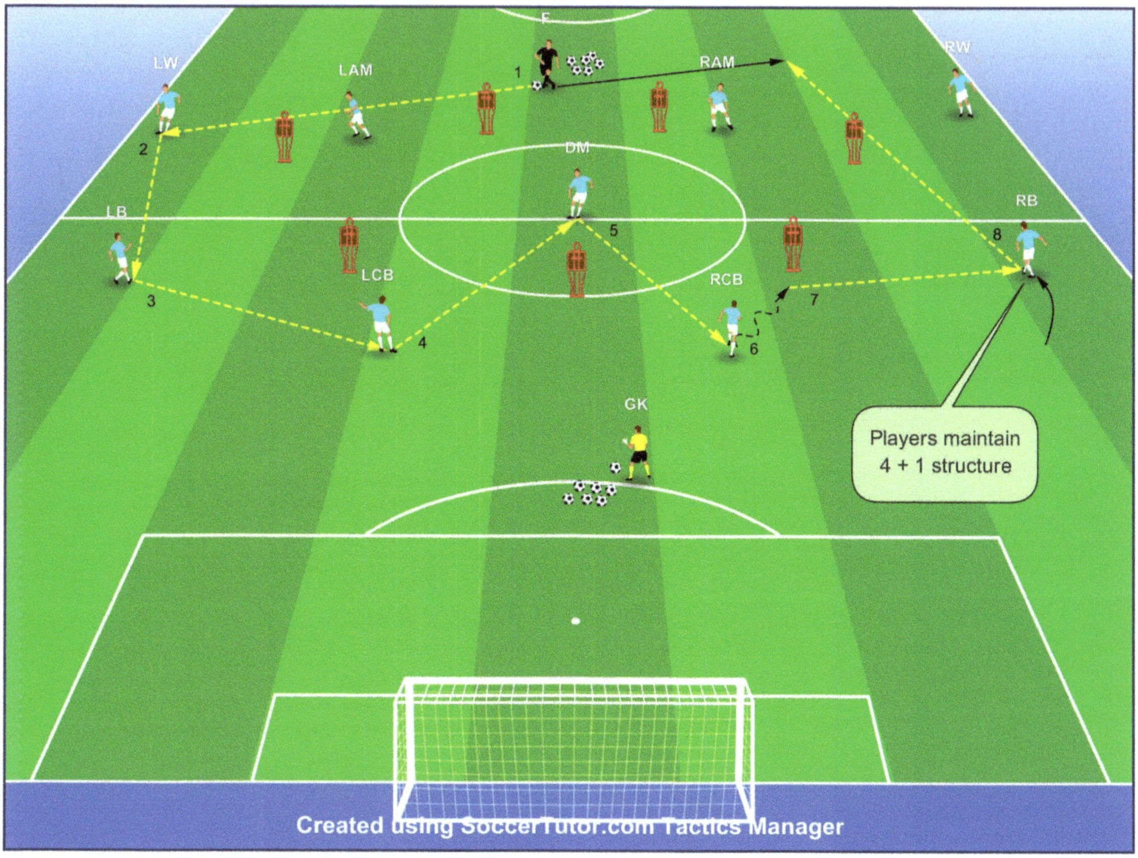

Players maintain 4 + 1 structure

Note: *Refer to page 38 for full explanation of the practice setup.*

Practice Description

- The coach starts the practice with a pass to the left winger (**LW**). This **pass represents winning the ball from the opposition**, and the team plays from there. The players circulate the ball from left to right and the coach then represents the forward (**F**).

- In this example, the players successfully switch the play and finish with a through pass to break the lines of the opposition.

- The final pass is a forward pass to the coach (**F**) from the right back (**RB**).

- With this first practice in the session, the players use a basic 4+1 structure for the defence and midfield lines, with the formation variations and positional changes to come on the following pages.

Coaching Point:

Ensure quality in technical execution, body shape, and positioning.

Session for PEP GUARDIOLA Tactics - Switching Play and Breaking Lines with Inverted Full Back

PROGRESSION

2. Switch Play + Break Lines while Changing Team Shape with Inverted Full Back

Phase 1/2: Switch + Change Defence/Midfield Structure from 4+1 to 3+2

Players change the structure as the ball moves from 4+1 to 3+2

Note: *Refer to page 38 for full explanation of the practice setup.*

Practice Description (Phase 1)

- This progression follows on from the practice on the previous page.
- This time, the players **switch the play while simultaneously changing the shape of the team**.
- The players adjust their structure during the ball movement, shifting from a 4+1 structure in the defence and midfield lines to 3+2, with the right back (**RB**) moving forward and inside to create a double pivot in midfield.
- The right winger (**RW**) drops back to receive and the practice continues with diagram 2b on the next page.
- **Note:** See the analysis of the team shape switch on <u>page 27</u> - "Tactical Solution 1 to Change Formations with Inverted Full Back."

Session for PEP GUARDIOLA Tactics - Switching Play and Breaking Lines with Inverted Full Back

Phase 2/2: Switch Back Again + Forward Pass to Break Lines

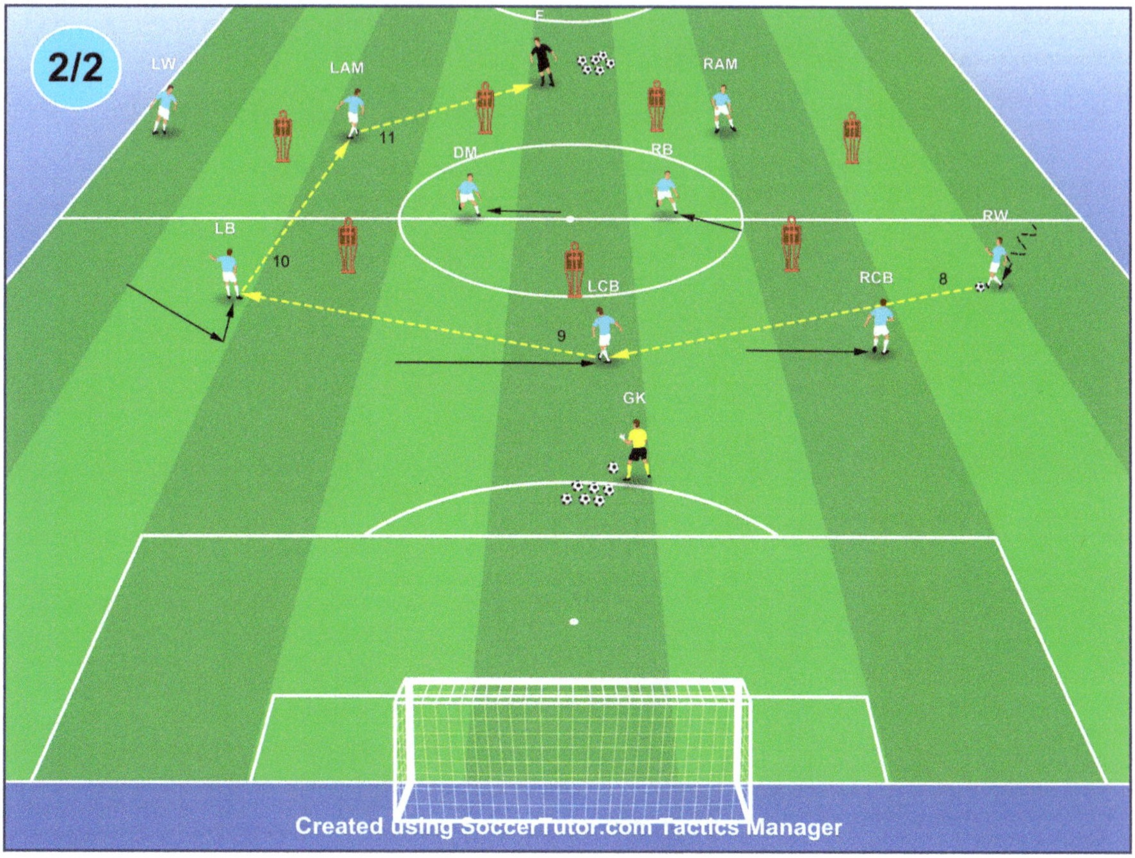

Practice Description (Phase 2)

- This diagram shows a continuation of the same phase on the previous page.
- The right winger (**RW**) has received in a deep position and starts the switch of play back from right to left.
- There is now a double pivot in midfield but these 2 players are not involved in this specific variation.
- When the left back (**LB**) receives, he looks up and plays a penetrating forward pass through the lines to the attacking midfielder on that side (**LAM**).
- The coach (**F**) represents the forward (target man teammate) and the sequence is completed once he receives the final pass.
- From there, either the coach (**F**) or the goalkeeper (**GK**) can feed in a new ball for a different variation (see the following pages).

Coaching Points

1. Ensure quality in technical execution, body shape, and positioning.
2. Emphasise the need for simultaneous movements (precise timing) when making structural changes to the team's formation.

VARIATION

3. Build Up Play + Break Lines while Changing Team Shape with Inverted Full Back (4-1-4-1 to 3-2-4-1)

Phase 1/2: Switch Play, Through Pass + Long Pass to Weak Side Winger

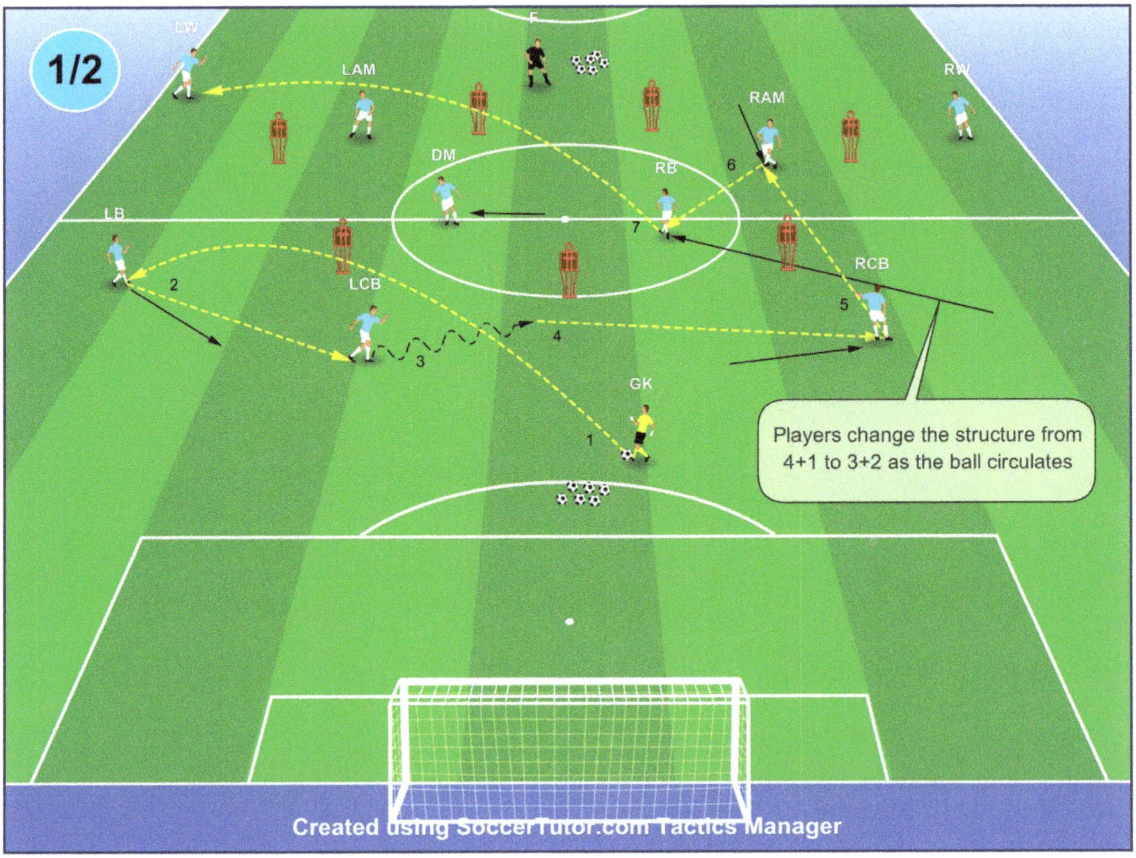

Players change the structure from 4+1 to 3+2 as the ball circulates

Practice Description (Phase 1)

- This is a variation of the previous practice which begins with the **GK's** pass. The team **build up play from the back while simultaneously changing the shape of the team from 4-1-4-1 to 3-2-4-1**.

- The structure changes during the ball movement, shifting from a 4+1 structure in the defence and midfield lines to 3+2, with the right back (**RB**) moving to create a double pivot in midfield.

- **Note:** See the analysis of the team shape switch on page 27.

- In this pattern of play example, the left back (**LB**) receives from the **GK**, the ball is moved to the centre back (**RCB**) on the opposite side who passes forward to the attacking midfielder (**RAM**).

- **RAM** sets the ball for the right back (**RB**), who is now in midfield, to switch the play with a long pass to the left winger (**LW**). The phase continues on the next page.

Session for PEP GUARDIOLA Tactics - Switching Play and Breaking Lines with Inverted Full Back

Phase 2/2: Switch Play Back Again + Play Through Midfield to Forward

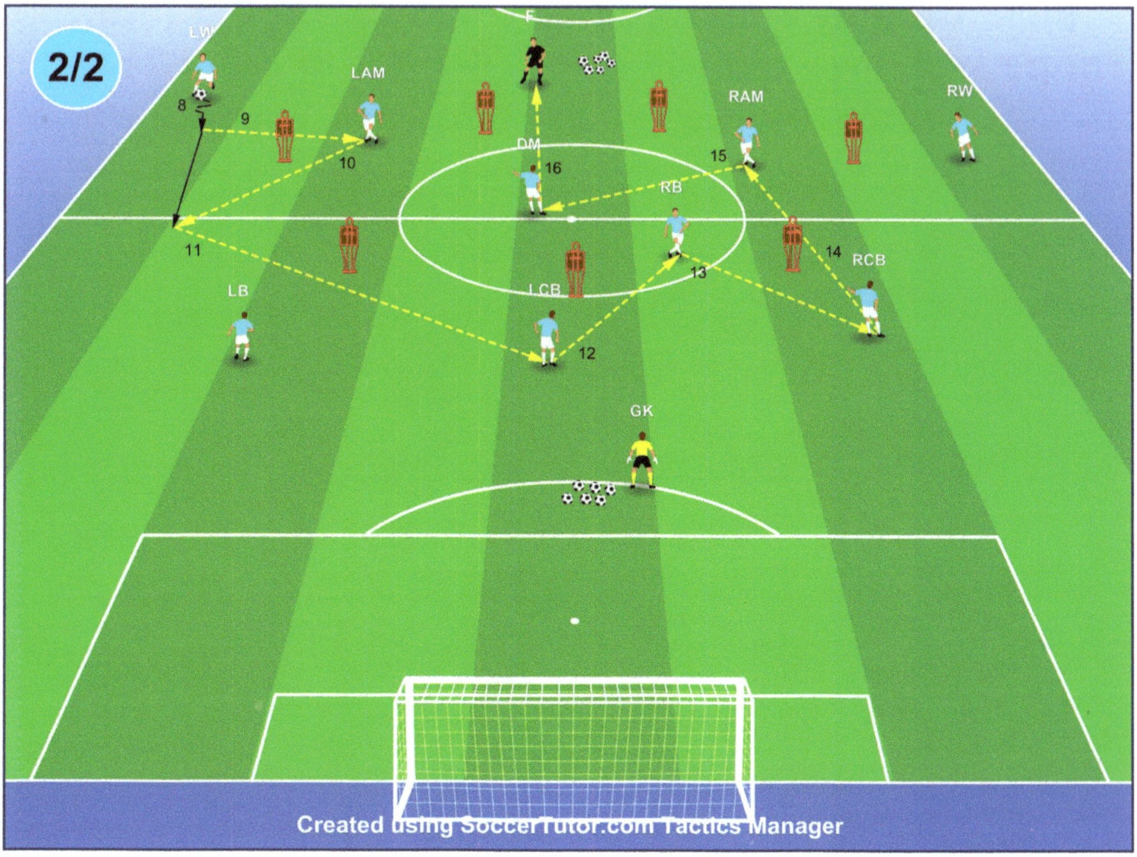

Practice Description (Phase 2)

- This diagram shows a continuation of the same phase on the previous page.
- There is now a **double pivot in midfield after the right back inverted**, so the team are in a 3-2-4-1 shape.
- The left winger (**LW**) has received a long pass and starts the switch of play back from left to right.
- When the right side centre back (**RCB**) receives, he looks up and plays a penetrating forward pass in between the lines to the attacking midfielder on that side (**RAM**), who sets the ball back to the defensive midfielder (**DM**).
- **DM** passes forward to the coach (**F**), who represents the forward (target man teammate), and the sequence is completed with this final pass.
- From there, either the coach (**F**) or the **GK** can feed in a new ball for a different variation (see the following pages).

Coaching Points

1. Ensure quality in technical execution, body shape, and positioning.
2. Emphasise the need for simultaneous movements (precise timing) when making structural changes to the team's formation.

Session for PEP GUARDIOLA Tactics - Switching Play and Breaking Lines with Inverted Full Back

VARIATION

4. Switch Play while Changing Shape from 4-1-4-1 to 3-2-4-1 + Attack with 2-3-5 Shape

Phase 1/2: Play Across Back Line to Switch Play with DM Dropping Back

Practice Description (Phase 1)

- The coach starts the practice with a pass to the left back (**LB**). This **pass represents winning the ball from the opposition**, and the team plays from there. From that point, the coach then represents the forward (**F**).

- The players circulate the ball from left to right as both full backs (**LB** and **RB**) invert into midfield and the defensive midfielder (**DM**) drops into defence.

- The defence and midfield line structure changes from 4+1 to 3+2.

- **Note:** See the analysis of the team shape switch on page 29 - "Tactical Solution 2 to Change Formations with Both Full Backs Inverted."

- In this pattern example, the ball is played all the way along the back line via the **DM** in his new position, and passed to the right winger (**RW**), who drops to receive. The phase continues on the next page.

45

PEP GUARDIOLA - COACHING FLUID POSITIONAL ROTATIONS

Session for PEP GUARDIOLA Tactics - Switching Play and Breaking Lines with Inverted Full Back

Phase 2/2: Switch + Play Through Centre while Changing Shape to 2-3-5

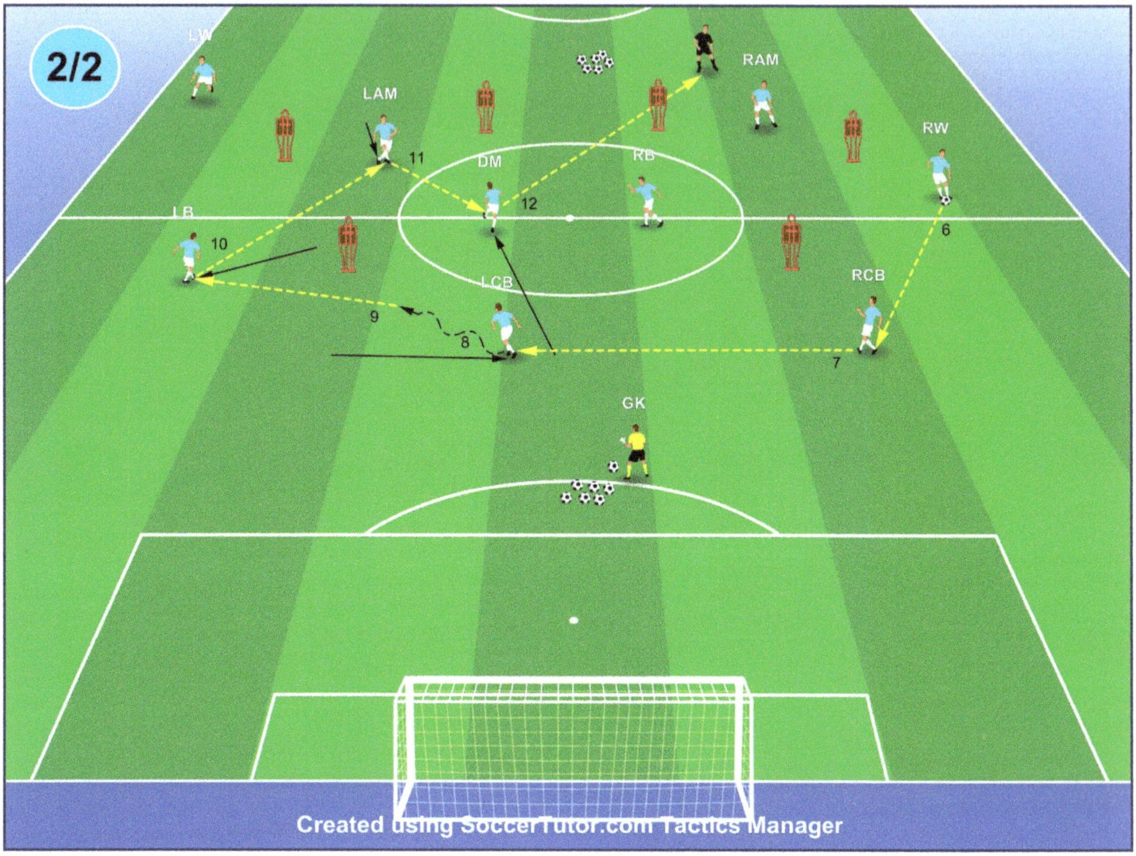

Practice Description (Phase 2)

- This diagram shows a continuation of the same phase on the previous page. The winger (**RW**) starts the switch of play back from right to left.

- As the attacking pattern progresses, the team changes shape again. The left back (**LB**) moves into a wider position to receive from the centre back (**LCB**), and the **defensive midfielder** (**DM**) **pushes forward into midfield again to create a 3-2-5 attacking phase shape**.

- Note: See the analysis of the team shape switch on page 30 - "Switch to 2-3-5 in Attacking Half with DM Moving Forward."

- **LB** passes to the attacking midfielder (**LAM**) on that side between the lines, who sets the ball back for **DM**.

- The coach (**F**) represents the forward (target man teammate) and the sequence is completed once he receives the final pass.

Coaching Points

1. Ensure quality in technical execution, body shape, and positioning.

2. Emphasise the need for simultaneous movements (precise timing) when making structural changes to the team's formation.

Session for PEP GUARDIOLA Tactics - Switching Play and Breaking Lines with Inverted Full Back

PROGRESSION

5. Build Up Play + Finish while Changing Shape with Inverted Full Back Positional Possession Game

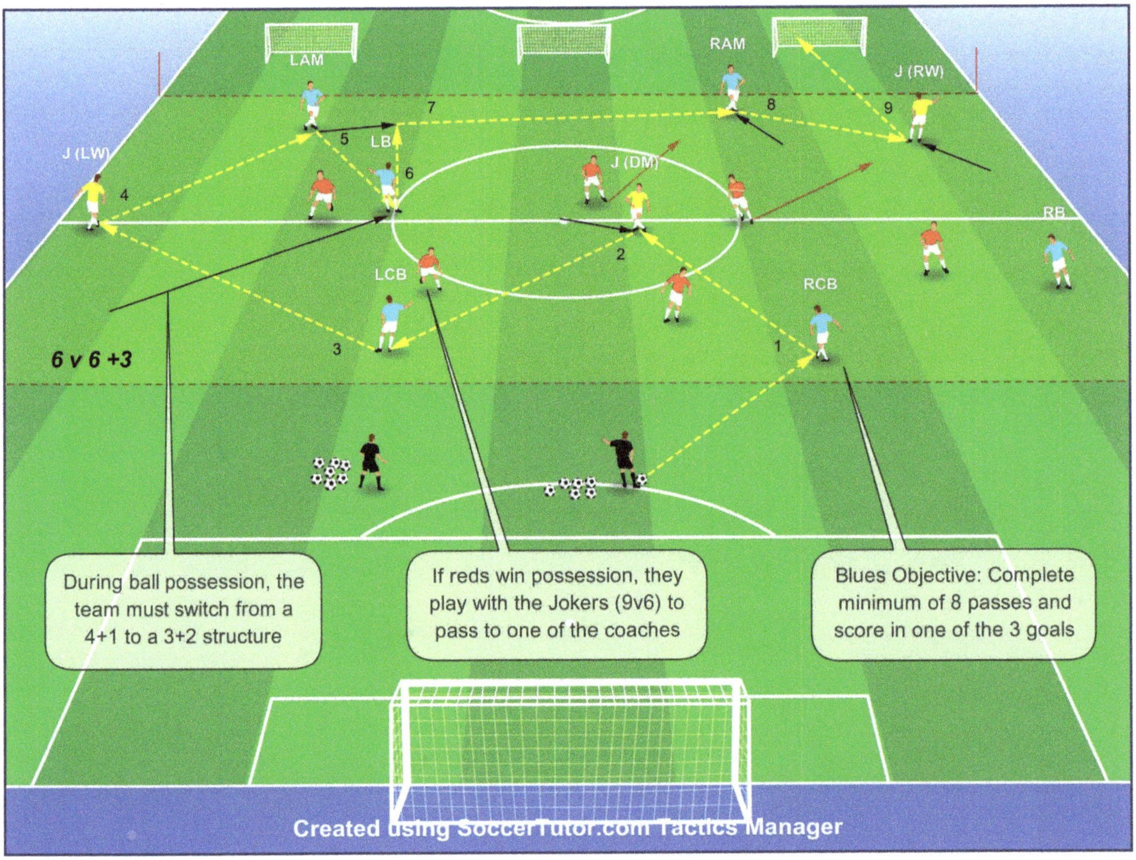

During ball possession, the team must switch from a 4+1 to a 3+2 structure

If reds win possession, they play with the Jokers (9v6) to pass to one of the coaches

Blues Objective: Complete minimum of 8 passes and score in one of the 3 goals

Practice Description

- This 6v6 (+3) game is played in the middle third of a full pitch. The 3 Jokers support the team in possession.
- The game starts with the coach's pass to a blue centre back (**RCB** in diagram example). With the Jokers, the blues start in a 4-1-4 formation.
- **Possession Team Objective:** Complete a minimum of 8 passes while **changing the defence and midfield line structure from 4+1 to 3+2 (4-1-4 to 3-2-4)**, and then score in one of the 3 goals.

- **Defending Team Objective:** Win the ball, complete 5 passes (9v6 with 3 Jokers), and pass to a coach. The teams then switch roles and positions, and the game continues. Most goals wins.

Coaching Points

1. Focus on precise technical execution and correct body shape.
2. Accurate timing during team shape changes.
3. Optimal spacing between players and lines.

Pep Guardiola's Passing Structures with Rhombus Shapes

Pep Guardiola's Pep Guardiola's Passing Structures with Rhombus Shapes

Rhombus Shapes in Different Areas and Phases of the Game

1a. 4-1-4-1 Build Up Phase Shape from Goal Kicks

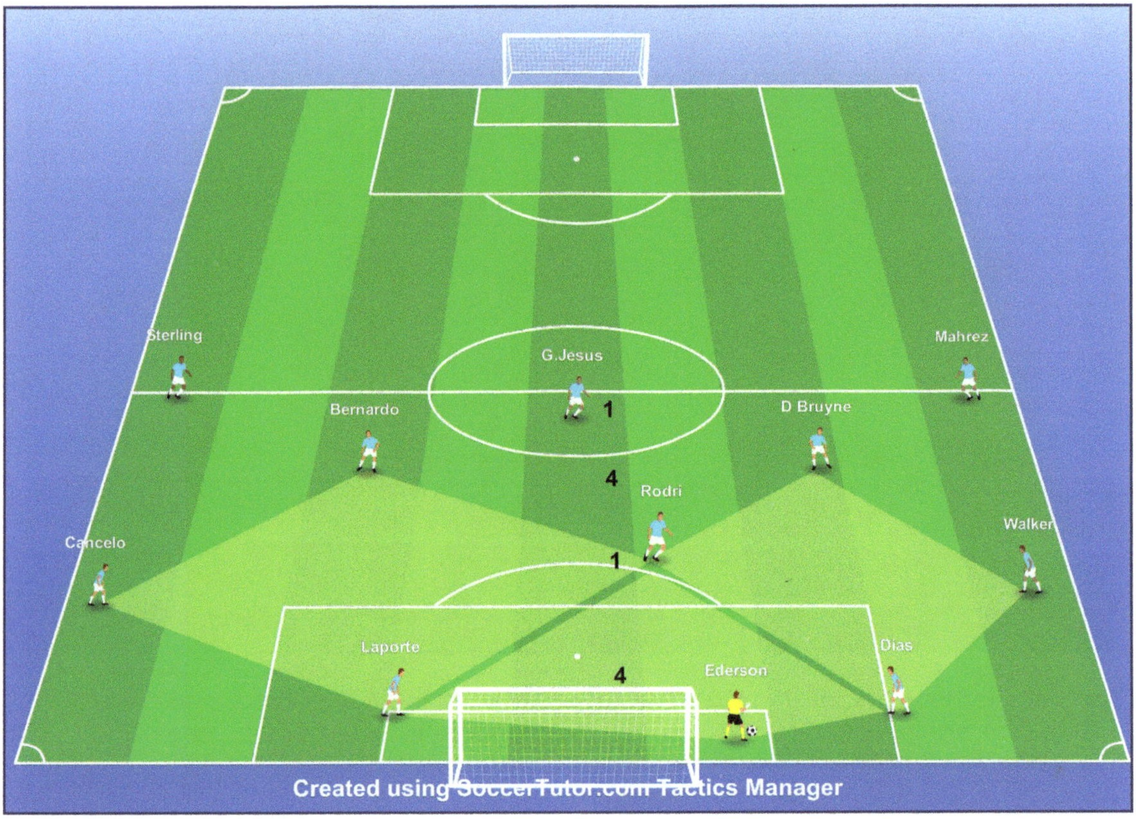

Manchester City's model of play under Pep Guardiola is characterised by **fluid structures, with the rhombus as a central feature**. This shape provides a dynamic framework for **maintaining control and progressing the ball** up the pitch.

In the diagram above, we show Guardiola's 4-1-4-1 build up shape, which creates 3 distinct rhombuses (highlighted) within the team's defensive structure.

These **interconnected rhombus shapes form the foundation for building up play** from the back and adapting to different types of opposition pressing.

The rhombuses play a crucial role in moving the ball forward (playing through) against teams using high pressing tactics.

Key Point: By ensuring numerical superiority in the defensive areas, Manchester City bypass the opposition's pressing effectively while maintaining composure and control.

Pep Guardiola's Passing Structures with Rhombus Shapes

1b. 4-2-2 Build Up Phase Shape from Goal Kicks (Variation)

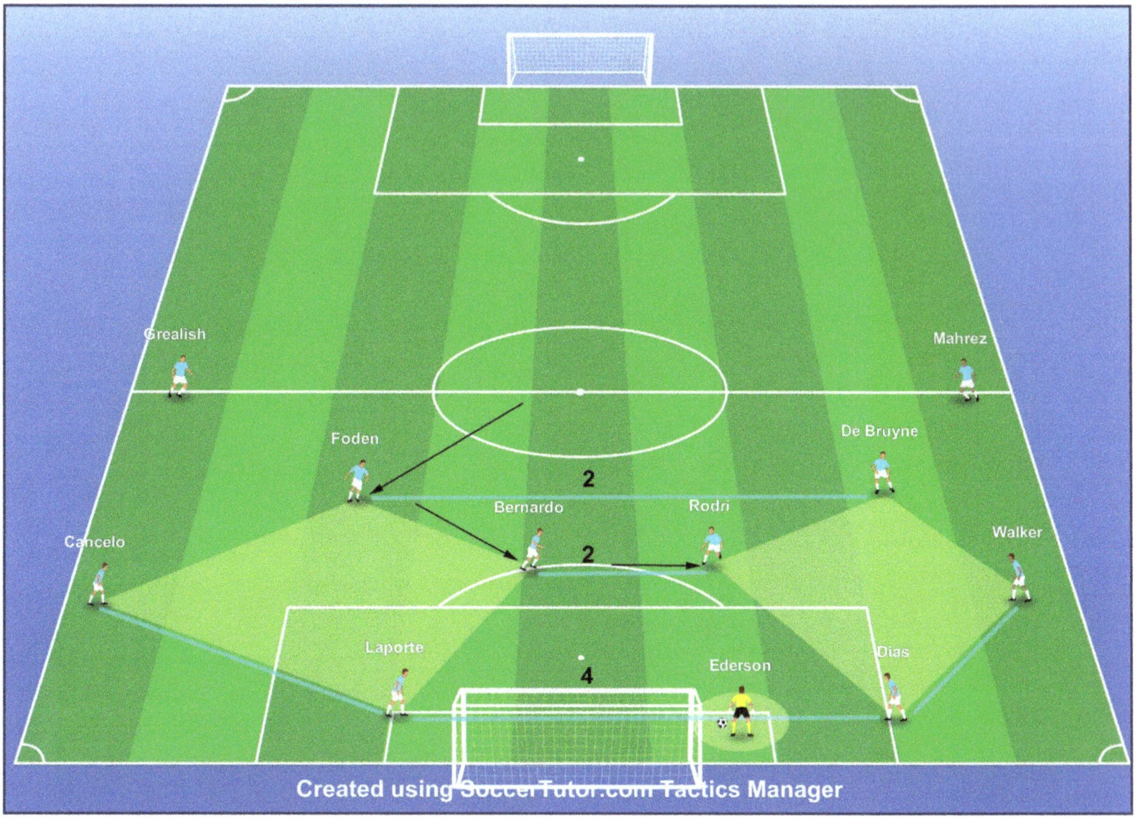

Two key rhombus shapes (highlighted) are created within Manchester City's alternative 4-2-2 build up shape.

This formation is **frequently used by Pep Guardiola's team to play through teams that press high** with 6 advanced players.

The rhombus structures provide multiple passing options and ensure that City control the spaces, making it challenging for opponents to isolate players or disrupt their possession.

Deploying a player adept at linking play as a **"False 9"** (**G. Jesus**) increases the functionality of this setup. This role helps the team with seamless ball circulation within the rhombuses, allowing them to bypass pressing efficiently while maintaining control and creating opportunities to progress the play.

Key Point: These build up play tactics underscore the importance of positional awareness and technical ability in Pep Guardiola's approach to breaking down high pressing teams.

Pep Guardiola's Passing Structures with Rhombus Shapes

2. 3-2-4-1 Possession Phase Shape in the Middle Third

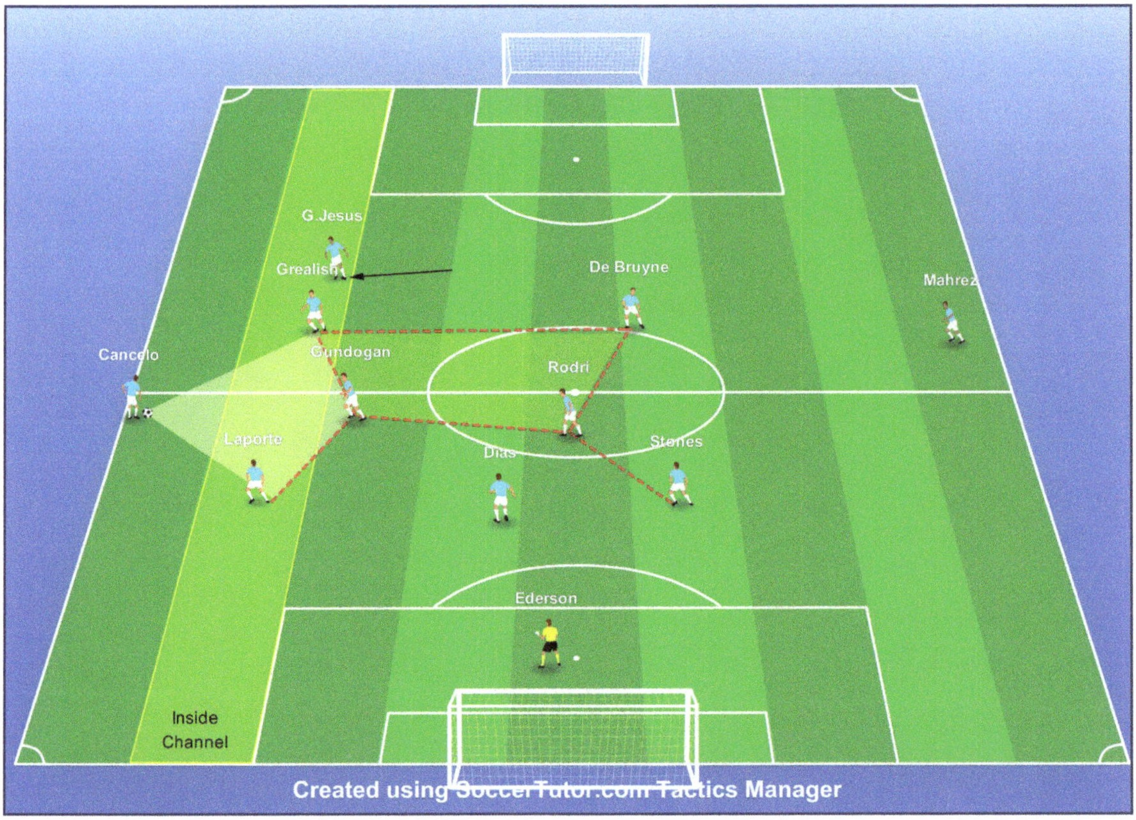

Pep Guardiola's Manchester City often use a 3-2-4-1 shape when positioned in the middle third of the pitch.

This shape provides **balance and fluidity**, allowing the team to **maintain control and dictate play**.

The rhombus shape remains a crucial part of this setup, as highlighted in the diagram, and the specific dynamics will be fully analysed later in the book. The red lines show how 3 players, supported by the forward (**G. Jesus**), effectively operate within the inside channel.

This **structure is vital for moving the ball** forwards, backwards, and inside, **creating multiple passing options**, to **disrupt the opposition's defensive block**.

Key Point: These tactical features underpin Pep Guardiola and Manchester City's ability to manage transitions and sustain possession.

3. 2-3-5 Attacking Phase Shape in the Opposition's Half

The 2-3-5 structure became a prominent attacking phase shape for Pep Guardiola's Manchester City team during the early stages of the 2022/23 season.

This team shape emphasises the use of rhombuses to **create connections and integrate players effectively in the final (attacking) third** to create goal scoring opportunities.

As shown in the diagram, **every player participates in multiple overlapping rhombuses**, enhancing the team's positional dynamics.

For the player in possession, the correct decision making relies on engaging with teammates within these sub-structures based on the desired direction of play.

For instance, the right centre back (**Dias**), when in possession, operates within 3 rhombus shapes, giving him the option to pass forward, diagonally to the right, or simply circulate the ball to the left.

Key Point: The choice of action for the player in possession is dictated by the opposition's defensive organisation and the passing lanes they leave open. From there, the team can exploit spaces and maintain their attacking rhythm.

Pep Guardiola's Passing Structures with Rhombus Shapes

Rhombus Shapes in the Final Third with the Right Centre Back in Possession

1a. Exploiting Right Side Rhombus Against Compact Defensive Block

In this example, the **opposition are focusing their defensive efforts centrally with a compact defensive block**.

The **wide right rhombus is left open and provides an opportunity for Manchester City to progress the ball forward** by exploiting this sector effectively.

The play develops through a quick forward pass into the right rhombus to the attacking midfielder (**De Bruyne**). He quickly passes wide to the right winger (**Mahrez**), who is free of marking.

Key Point: This passing sequence bypasses the opposition's compact central defensive block and redirects the attack to an area where there is more space, creating options for further progression or a potential crossing opportunity.

Pep Guardiola's Passing Structures with Rhombus Shapes

1b. Play to Left Side Rhombus when the Forward Pass is Blocked

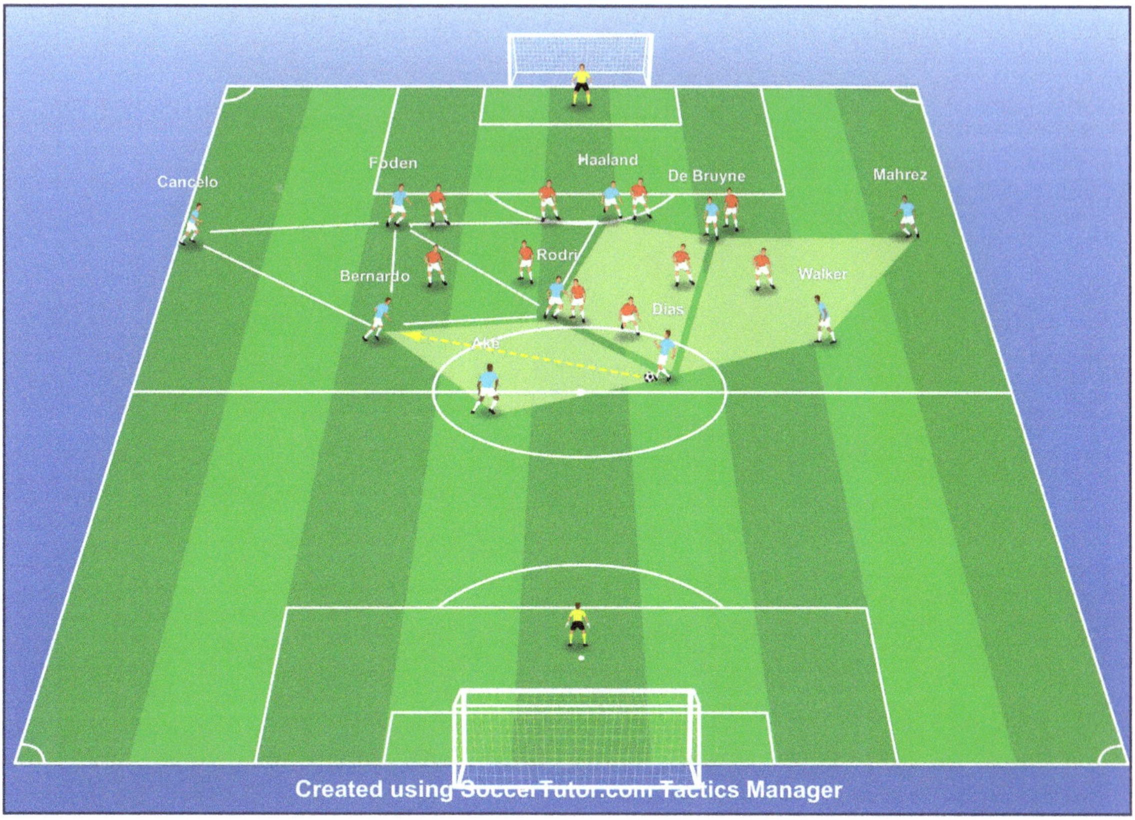

In this variation of the previous page (1a), **the opposing midfielders block the forward pass towards the right attacking midfielder** (**De Bruyne**), so the centre back in possession (**Dias**) redirects play to the left rhombus.

Dias' pass is along the perimeter to the left attacking midfielder (**Bernardo**), who receives successfully.

From this position, **Bernardo** can choose to progress the Manchester City attack via 2 different rhombus shapes:

1. The **Inside Rhombus**
   (Bernardo → Foden → Haaland → Rodri).

2. The **Outside Rhombus**
   (Bernardo → Cancelo → Foden → Rodri).

Key Point: This adaptability ensures Manchester City can respond effectively to defensive adjustments, retaining control while seeking openings to advance the attack.

Pep Guardiola's Passing Structures with Rhombus Shapes

1c. Pass to the Winger when the Forward Pass is Blocked

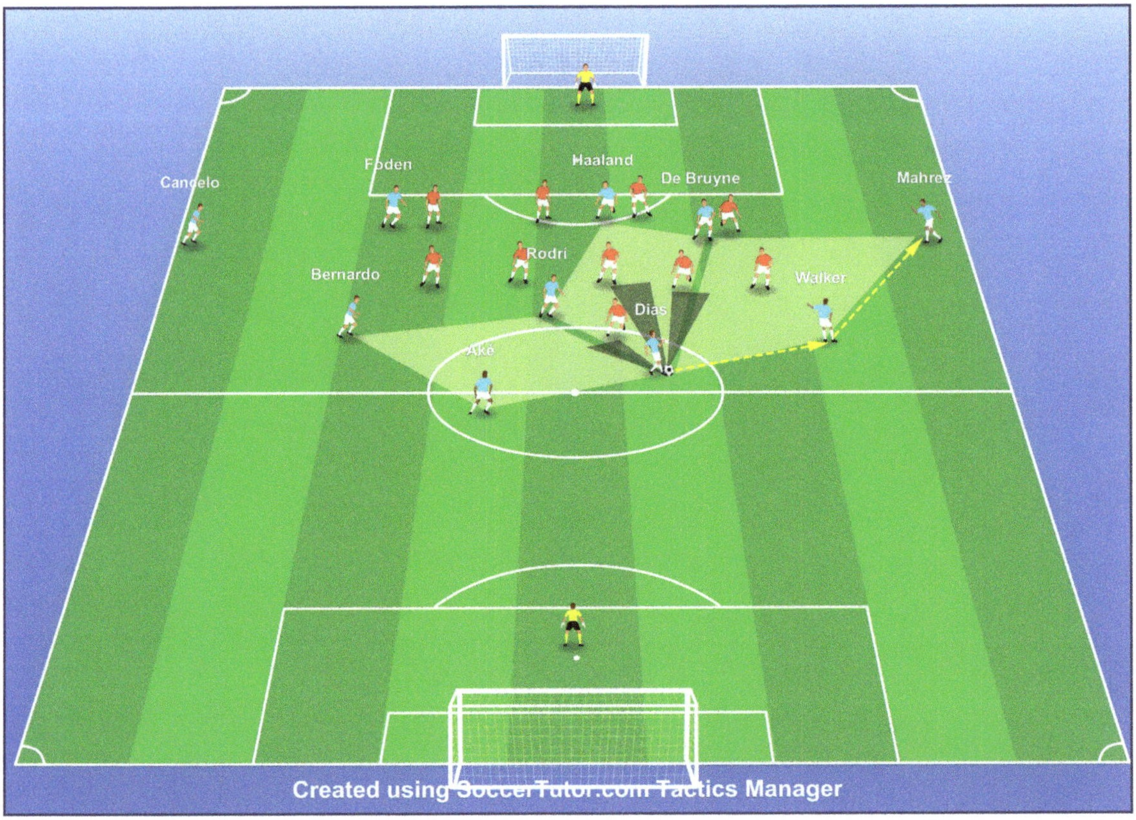

As was the situation in the previous example (1b), **the forward pass to the attacking midfielder (De Bruyne) is blocked** (as shown in the diagram), an alternative option is to direct the ball around the perimeter of the right side rhombus to the right flank where the winger (**Mahrez**) is positioned.

Manchester City bypass the opposition's central defensive block with the right centre back's (**Dias**) pass to the right back (**Walker**). He passes wide to **Mahrez**, allowing the attack to progress while maintaining fluidity and control.

2. Options when the Opposing Midfielders Press Aggressively

In this example, the **opposing midfielders apply aggressive pressing, marking key players and limiting immediate forward options**. However, this strategy leaves a forward passing option (winger - **Mahrez**) open within the right rhombus. The right centre back is in possession (**Dias**) and can take advantage of this gap to play the ball through the available channel.

If the opponents react quickly and succeed in closing off the right rhombus passing lane, **Dias** can adapt by switching the play to the left side rhombus with a pass back to the other centre back (**Aké**). This pass bypasses the pressure, helps maintain momentum, and opens up opportunities to advance in a less congested area, keeping the opponent on the back foot.

Key Point: Reacting to defensive adjustments by switching rhombus channels ensures sustained attacking fluidity and tactical adaptability.

3a. Playing Through the Opposition's Aggressive Pressing

In this example, the **opposing midfielders apply aggressive pressure on the perimeter players, successfully cutting off forward and diagonal passing lanes**. However, the centre back in possession (**Dias**) retains the option to pass to the defensive midfielder (**Rodri**), forcing the opponents into a tactical decision - they can either shift their focus to the central area or maintain their pressure on the perimeter.

Alternatively, **Dias** can pass back to his centre back partner (**Aké**) positioned in the left side rhombus, as shown in the previous example.

Key Point: Having 2 options provides flexibility, enabling the team to adapt to the opposition's defensive tactics while maintaining control of the play and finding opportunities to advance.

Pep Guardiola's Passing Structures with Rhombus Shapes

3b. Forcing Defensive Decisions with the Full Back Dropping Deeper

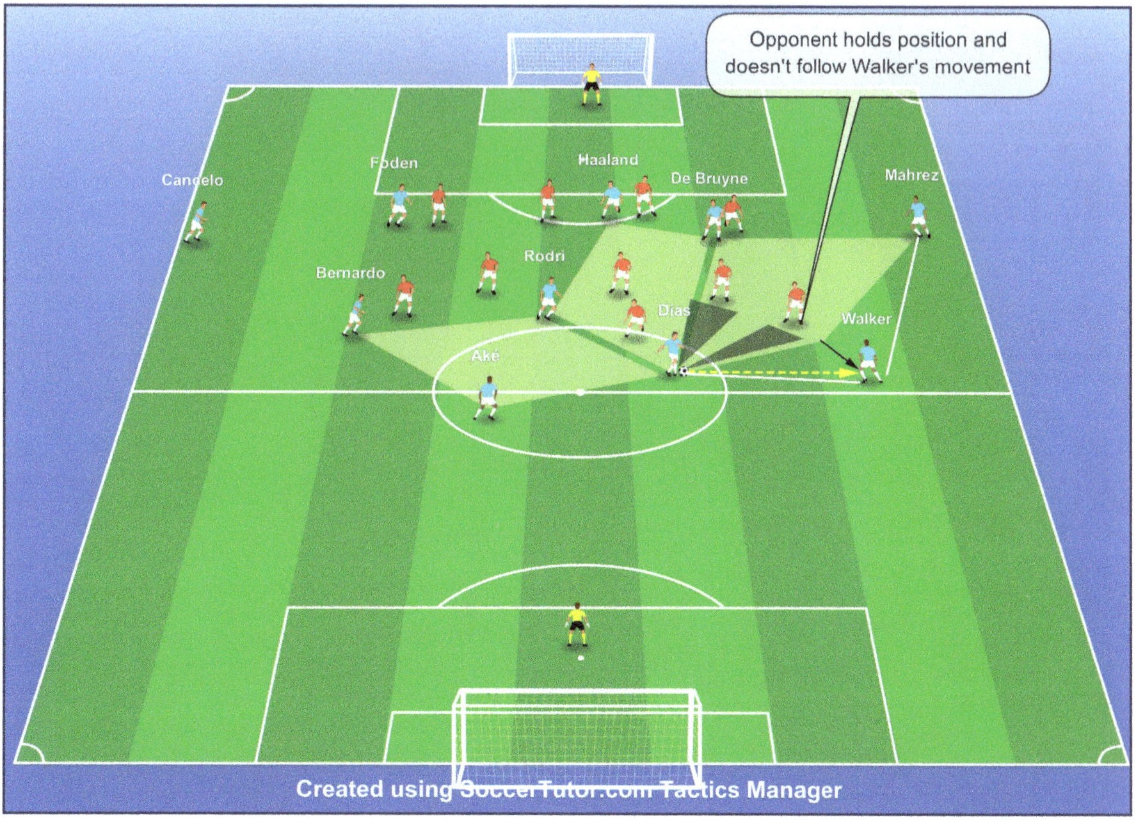

In this variation of the previous example, the opposing midfielders apply aggressive pressure on the perimeter players again, successfully cutting off Manchester City's forward and diagonal passing lanes.

This tactical solution is simple - the right back (**Walker**) **drops into a deeper position to provide an easy angle for a pass, and this movement expands the size of the right side rhombus**.

By doing this, **Walker forces the opposing wide player into make a decision** to hold his position or move to mark him.

If the red left sided midfielder/winger holds their position within the team's defensive organisation, as shown in the diagram, they are then unable to prevent the ball from being circulated along the perimeter. Therefore, in this situation, the ball can easily be moved to the right winger (**Mahrez**) via the link player **Walker**.

Alternatively, if the red player did step out of the defensive organisation to mark City's right back (**Walker**), a gap would be created for **Dias** to play a diagonal pass directly to **Mahrez** instead.

SESSION BASED ON THE TACTICS OF PEP GUARDIOLA

Pep Guardiola's Passing Structures with Rhombus Shapes

Session for PEP GUARDIOLA Tactics - Pep's Passing Structures with Rhombus Shapes

SESSION FOR THIS TACTICAL SITUATION (8 PRACTICES)

1. 4v2 Rhombus Shape Positional Passing Practice in Different Areas of the Pitch

1a. Playing Out from the Back with the Right Side Rhombus

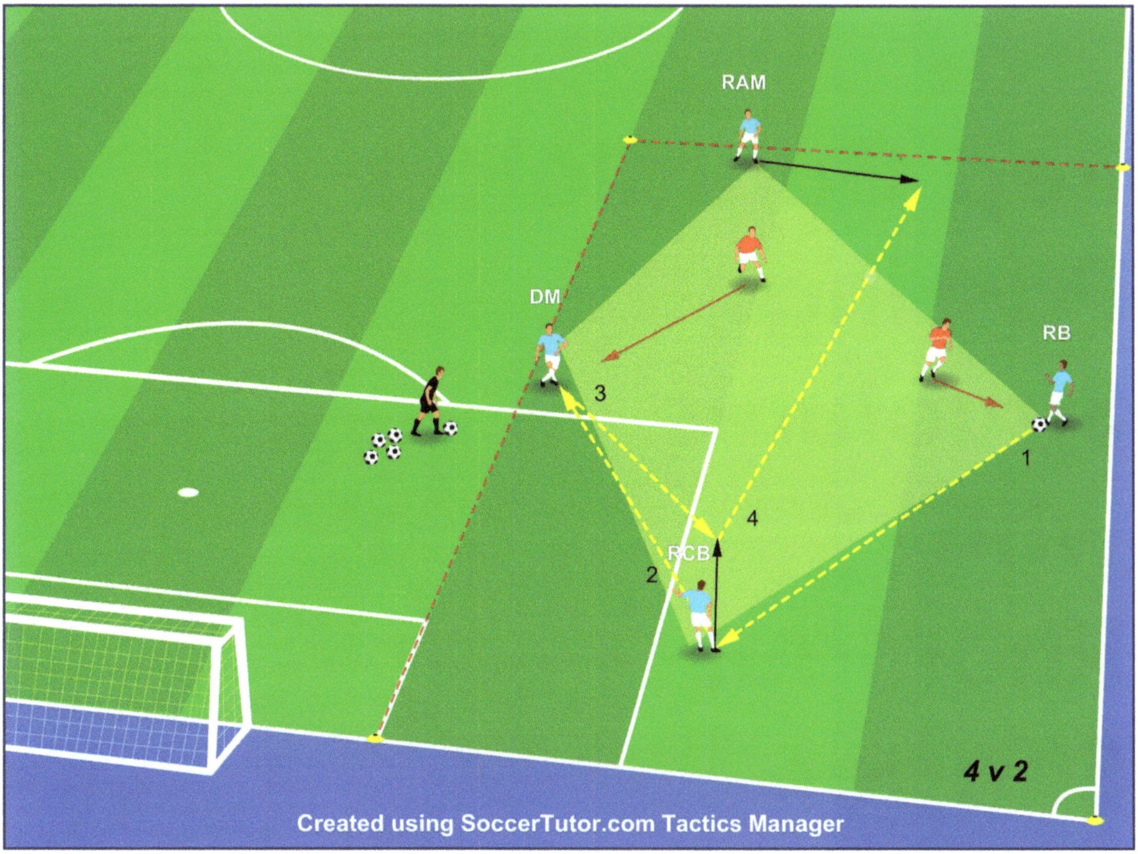

Practice Description (Variation 1a)

- Diagram 1a shows the first variation in the right corner of the pitch, which should be replicated on the left.

- The blue centre back (**RCB**), right back (**RB**), defensive midfielder (**DM**), and attacking midfielder (**RAM**) play against 2 red opponents.

- The 4 blue players **focus on maintaining composure under defensive pressure and providing constant passing options**.

- The player in possession reads the opponents' positioning to decide between a forward pass when perimeter lanes are blocked or a diagonal pass when forward passing lanes are closed.

- **Blue Objective:** As shown, the aim is to play forward to the **RAM**, and then back again (continuous).

- **Red Objective:** Intercept passes. The practice is in timed intervals, so make sure to rotate these players often.

Session for **PEP GUARDIOLA Tactics** - **Pep's Passing Structures with Rhombus Shapes**

1b. Playing Out from the GK in the Box with a Central Rhombus

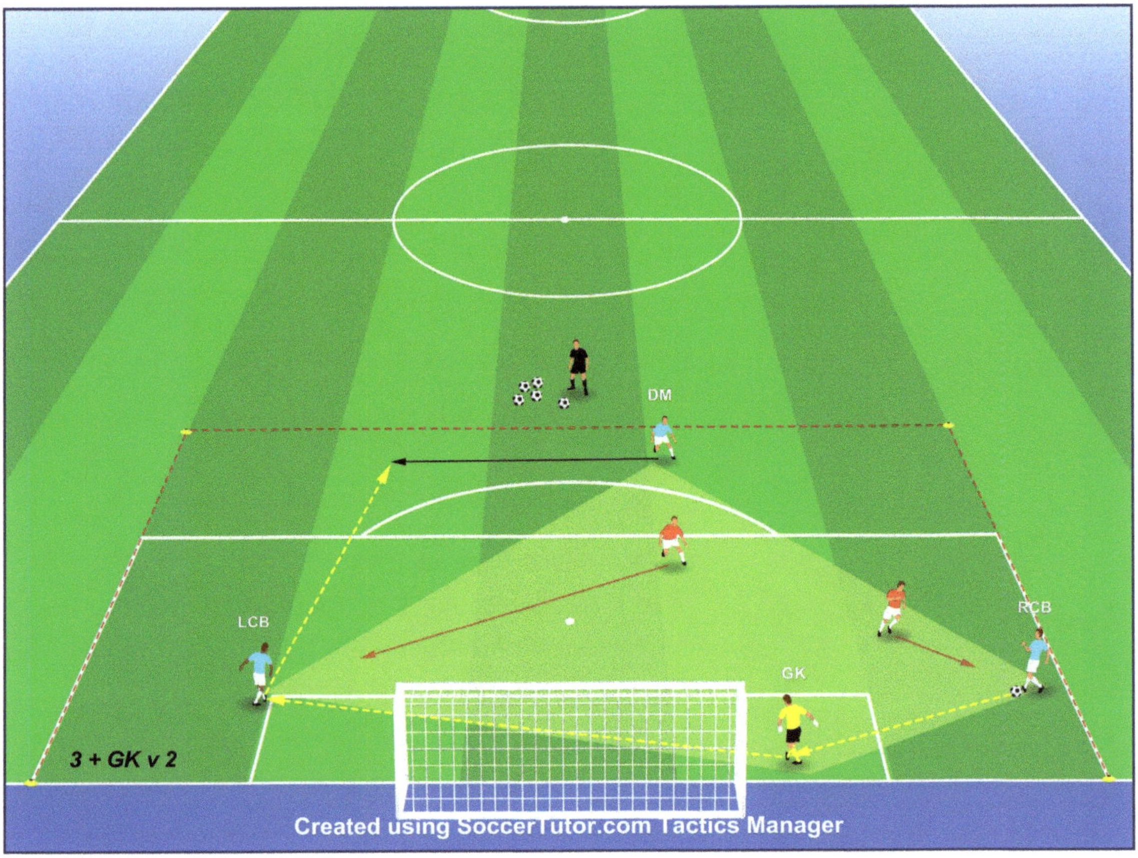

3 + GK v 2

Practice Description (Variation 1b)

- Diagram 1b shows the second variation with the goalkeeper (**GK**), 2 centre backs (**LCB** and **RCB**), and defensive midfielder (**DM**) play against 2 red forwards.

- The size of the area used is the penalty box plus an extra 10 yards.

- The 4 blue players again focus on **maintaining composure under defensive pressure and providing constant passing options** to progress the play forward.

- The player in possession reads the opponents' positioning to decide what the best passing option is, to either maintain possession or progress the ball.

- **Blue Objective:** As shown, the aim is to play forward to the **DM**, and then back again (continuous).

- **Red Objective:** Intercept passes. The practice is in timed intervals, so make sure to rotate these players often.

- The third and last variation is shown on the next page.

Session for **PEP GUARDIOLA Tactics** - Pep's Passing Structures with Rhombus Shapes

1c. Playing Through Midfield with a Central Rhombus

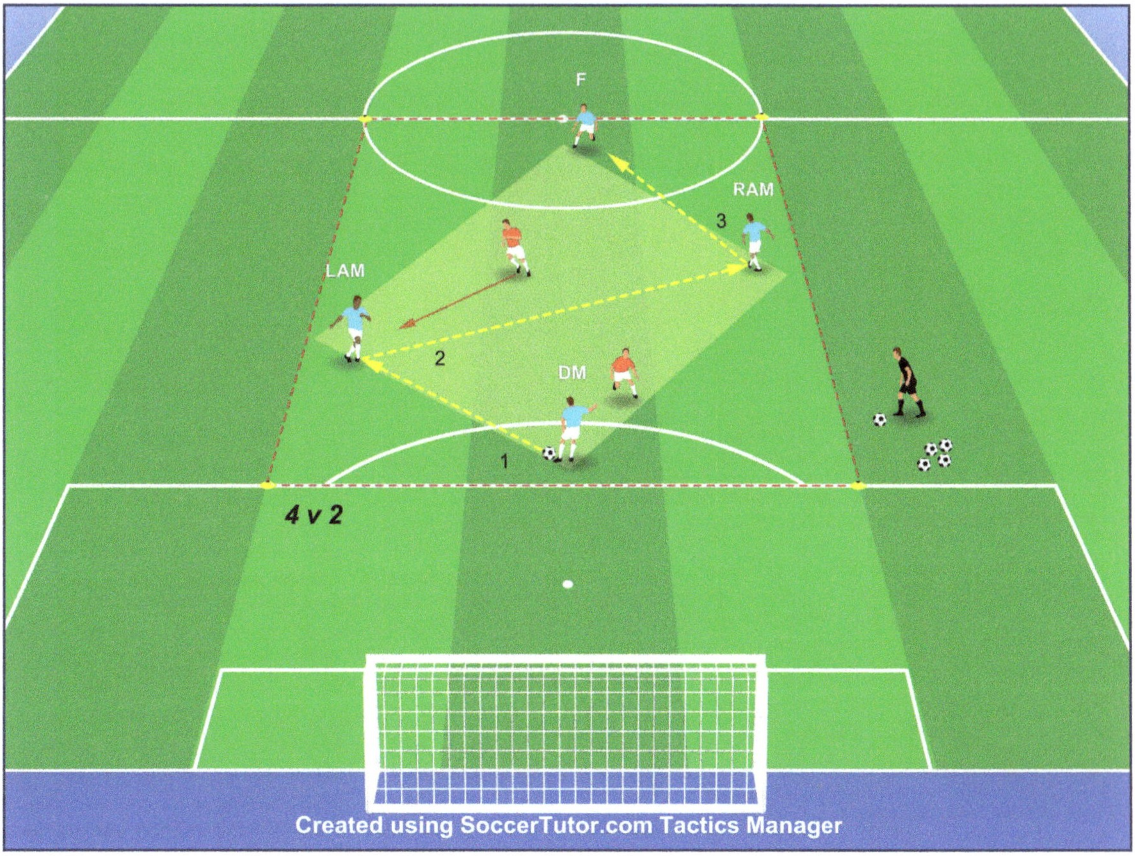

Practice Description (Variation 1c)

- Diagram 1c shows the third variation with the defensive midfielder (**DM**), 2 attacking midfielders (**AM**), and the forward (**F**) against 2 red opponents. The area used is the central zone of the pitch between the edge of the penalty box and the halfway line.

- The 4 blue players again focus on maintaining composure under defensive pressure and providing constant passing options to progress the play forward.

- The player in possession reads the opponents' positioning to **decide between a forward pass when perimeter lanes are blocked or a diagonal pass when forward passing lanes are closed**.

- **Blue Objective:** As shown, the aim is to play to the forward (**F**), and then back again (continuous).

- **Red Objective:** Intercept passes. Rotate these players often.

Coaching Points

1. Focus on precise ball control to maintain possession.
2. Accuracy and purpose in passing.
3. Constantly provide open options for the player in possession.
4. Quick and intelligent decision making under pressure.

Session for PEP GUARDIOLA Tactics - Pep's Passing Structures with Rhombus Shapes

PROGRESSION

2. 5 (+GK) v 3 Positional Build Up Play Against High Press with TWO Rhombus Shape Structure

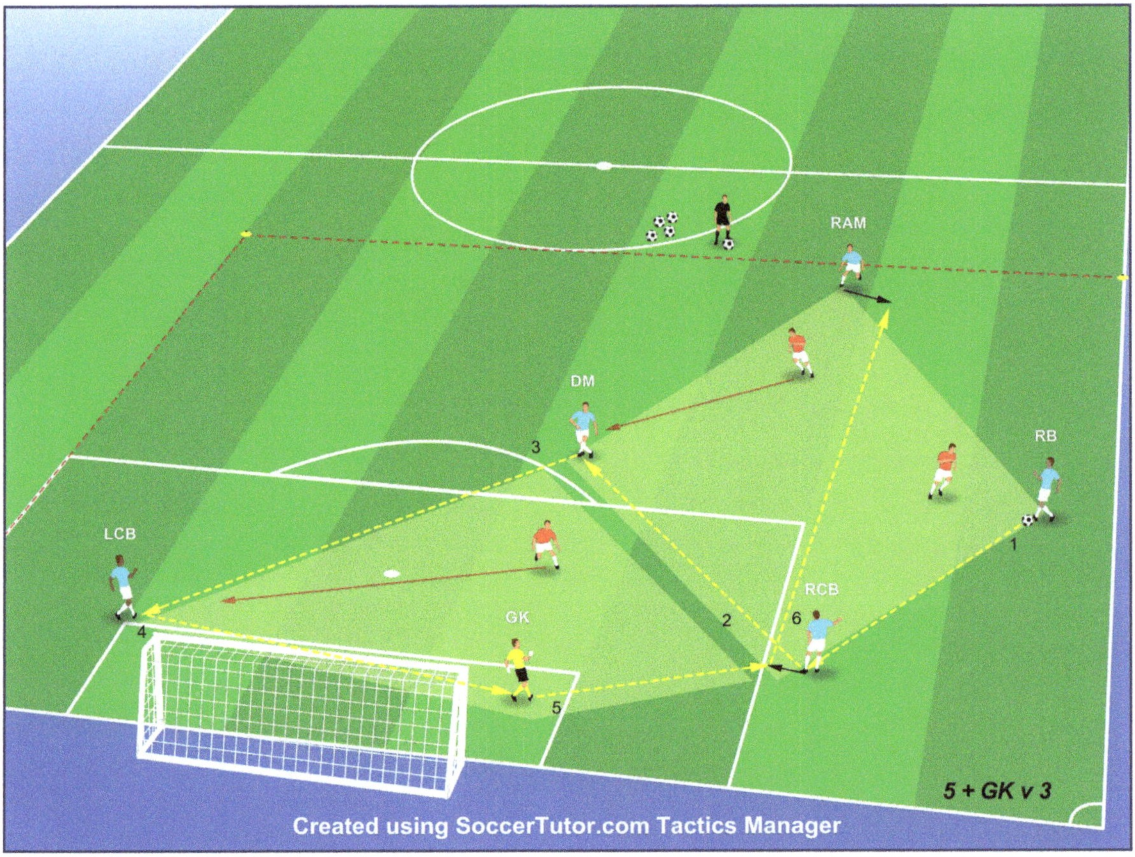

Practice Description

- This practice operates within 2 match specific connected rhombus structures. There is the goalkeeper (**GK**), 2 blue centre backs (**LCB** and **RCB**), right back (**RB**), defensive midfielder (**DM**), and attacking midfielder (**RAM**) versus 3 red pressing opponents.

- **Blue Objective:** Maintain control under pressure, move the ball efficiently between the rhombuses, select the best passing lanes, ultimately aiming to play to **RAM**, and back again (continuous).

- **Red Objective:** Disrupt the build up and win the ball with interceptions.

- Play in set intervals of time and rotate the 3 defending players each time.

Coaching Points

1. Precise ball control to keep possession.
2. Accuracy and purpose in passing.
3. Constantly provide open options for the player in possession.
4. Quick and intelligent decision making under pressure.

Session for **PEP GUARDIOLA Tactics** - Pep's Passing Structures with Rhombus Shapes

PROGRESSION

3. 7 (+GK) v 4 Positional Build Up Play Against High Press with THREE Rhombus Shape Structure

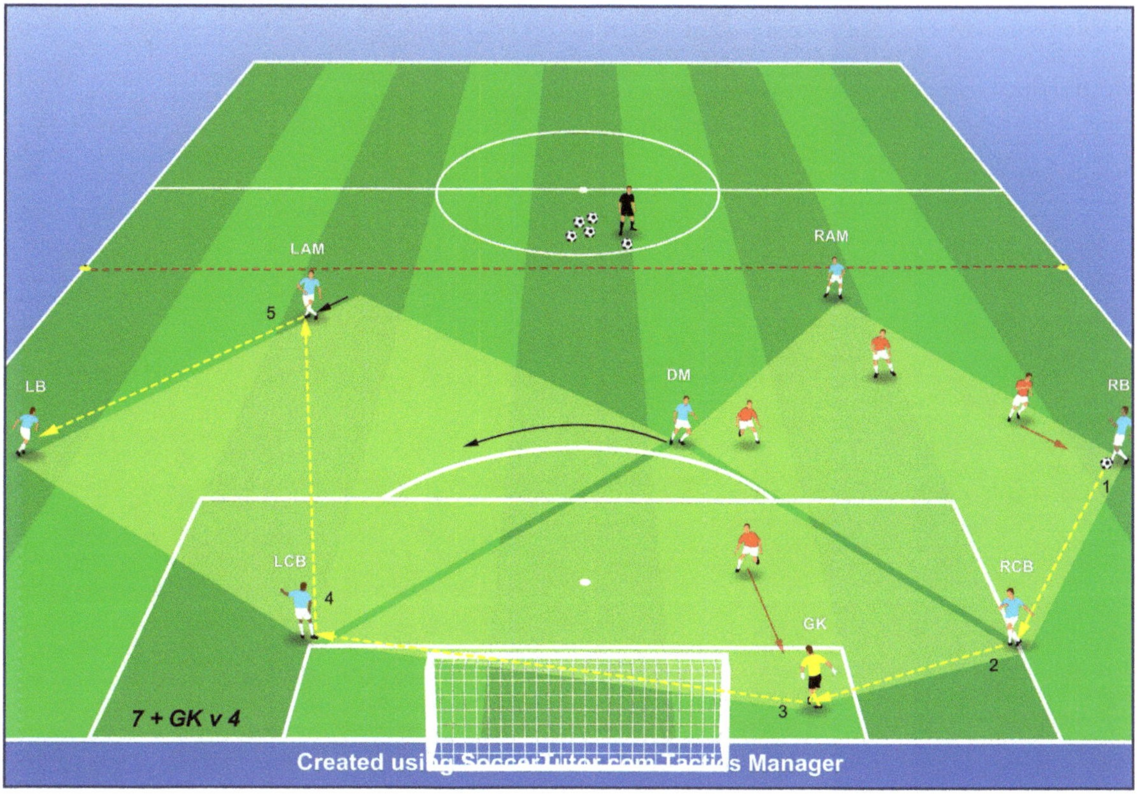

Practice Description

- In this practice, 7 blue players and the goalkeeper (**GK**) maintain possession against 4 red players who are positioned on one side to implement a high press.

- The **blue players' positioning forms 3 interconnected rhombuses**, designed to simulate realistic match conditions.

- **Blue Objective:** A full back starts and the blues maintain possession under pressure, circulate the ball through the rhombuses, and exploit spaces to progress the play. They switch play from one side to the other, and vice versa continuously.

- In this example, the blues successfully switch play from the right back (**RB**) to the left back (**LB**) via the **GK**.

- **Red Objective:** Disrupt the blue team's possession play and try to win the ball.

- Play in set intervals of time and rotate the defending players each time.

- **Coaching Point:** Quick ball movement and intelligent positioning are essential to maintaining control and bypassing the opposition's press.

Session for PEP GUARDIOLA Tactics - Pep's Passing Structures with Rhombus Shapes

PROGRESSION

4. Positional Build Up Play Against High Press with FOUR Rhombus Shape Structures

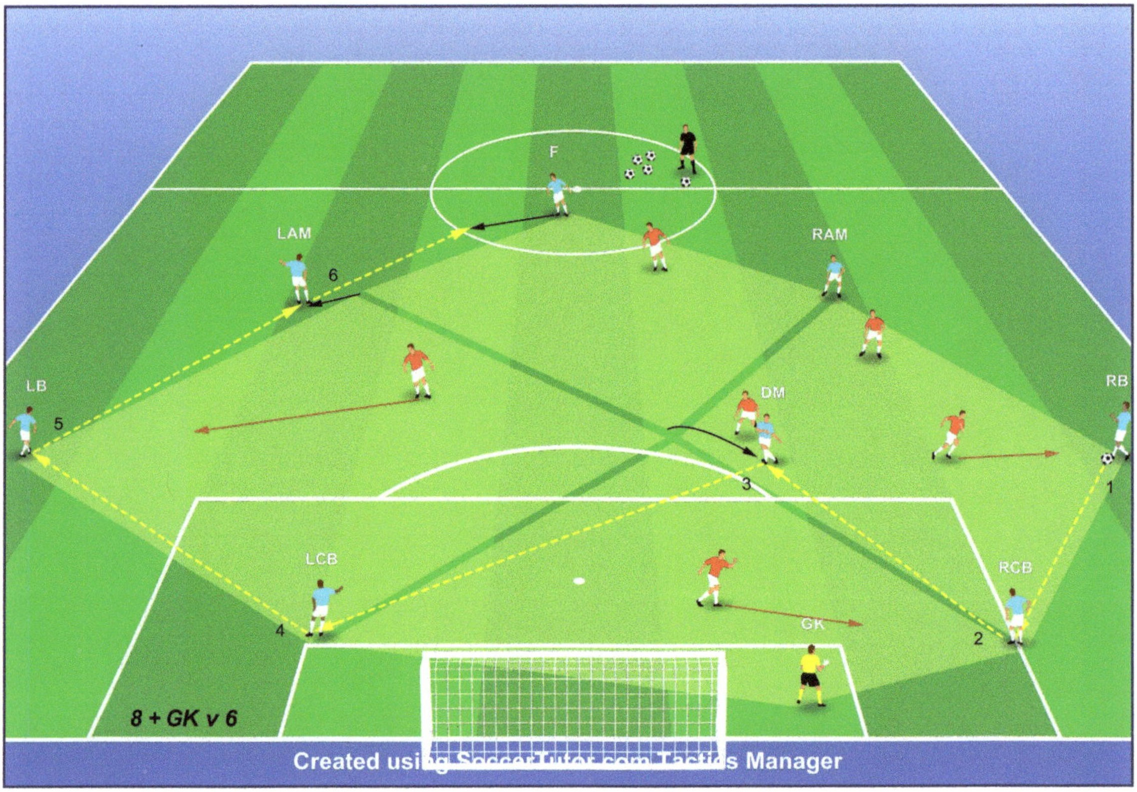

Practice Description
- In this progression of the previous practice, there are now 9 blue outfield players, with only the wingers excluded. They play against 6 reds.
- The **blue players' positioning forms 4 interconnected rhombuses**, designed to simulate realistic match conditions, that guide the team's structure.
- **Blue Objective:** Circulate the ball quickly to play around or through the red's pressing and exploit free spaces.
- **Red Objective:** Disrupt the blue team's possession play and try to win the ball.
- Play in set intervals of time and rotate the defending players each time.

Coaching Points
1. Maintain positional discipline and balance within the rhombus shapes.
2. Quick ball circulation to exploit the numerical advantage.
3. Use the goalkeeper (GK) as an outlet when under pressure.
4. Adapt passing and movement to the defensive setup.

Session for PEP GUARDIOLA Tactics - Pep's Passing Structures with Rhombus Shapes

VARIATION

5. Positional Build Up Play Against High Press with THREE Rhombus Shape Structures Using a "False 9"

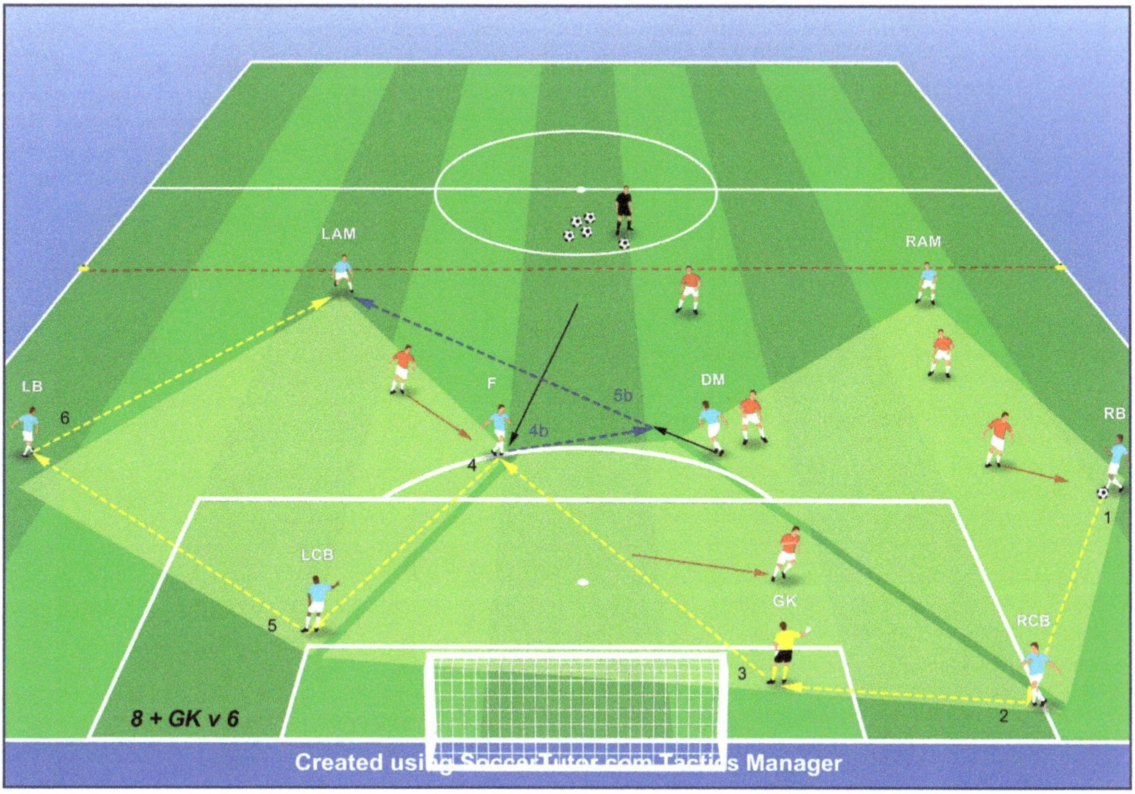

Practice Description

- In this variation, we play in a shorter area and the advanced forward is replaced with a **"False 9" (F)**, **who's role is to drop deep and assist in midfield combination play**. He drops near the edge of the box to receive from the **GK** and acts as a link player to help the blues circulate the ball or progress the play forward.

- The yellow arrows example shows **F** playing back to the centre back (**LCB**), who can then play wide. An alternative is shown with the blue arrows where **F** plays a short first time pass to the defensive midfielder (**DM**), who then passes forward to the attacking midfielder (**LAM**).

Coaching Points

1. Maintain composure to circulate the ball horizontally under pressure.
2. Exploit gaps in the defensive structure through precise passing.
3. Ensure proper spacing to maximise passing options.

Key Point: This tactic improves the team's options to switch play effectively, a key factor in bypassing pressure and disrupting the opposition's defensive structure.

Session for PEP GUARDIOLA Tactics - Pep's Passing Structures with Rhombus Shapes

PROGRESSION

6. 10 v 6 Positional Play in the Middle Third with Rhombus Shapes

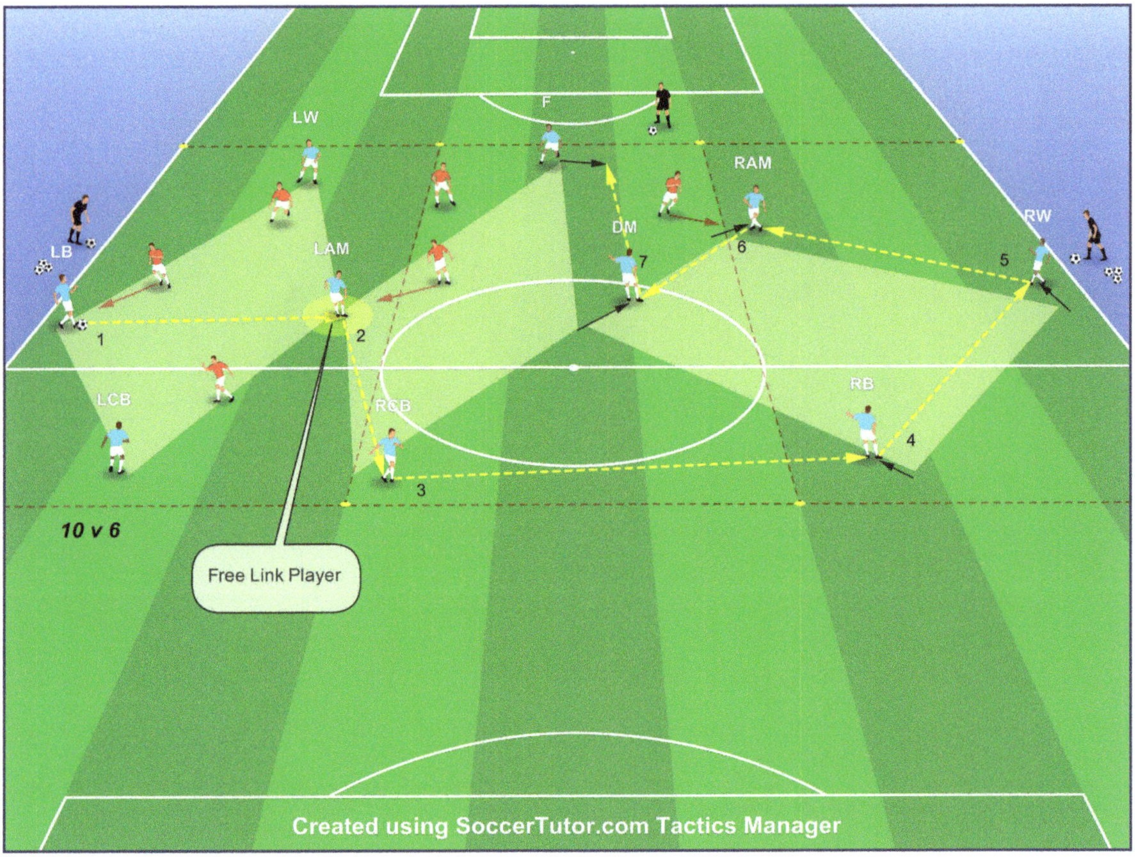

(Diagram: 10 v 6 — Free Link Player)

Practice Description

- This practice is played across 3 channels in the middle third of the pitch, as shown. **Only 3 red players are allowed in the same channel**, ensuring the player in possession always has a passing option.

- In each channel, a rhombus shape is created with 4 blue players against 3 red defenders. In this example, the left back (**LB**) has 3 teammates within his channel.

- If the red defenders stick tightly to these 3 potential receivers, **LB** will have space and can easily switch the play.

- Alternatively, if a red defender steps out to press **LB** (as shown in the diagram example), at least 1 player will be left unmarked, and able to receive the ball directly or indirectly via a link player. Here, **LB** is able to pass inside to the attacking midfielder (**LAM**).

- **Blue Objective:** The aim for the blue team is to circulate the ball effectively and progress the play to the attacking players, while moving the ball from left to right and vice versa continuously.

- **Red Objective:** Intercept passes.

PROGRESSION

7. Integrated and Dynamic Possession Play in the Defensive and Middle Thirds

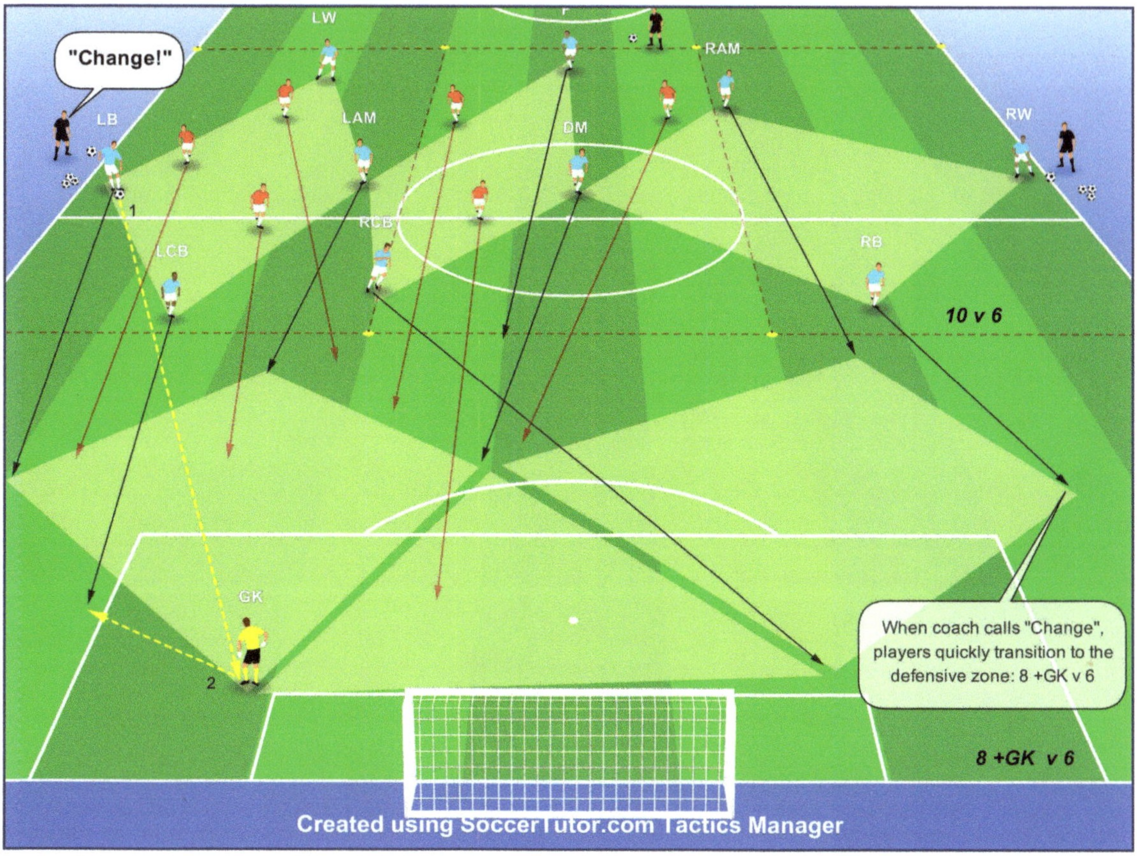

Practice Description

- Once the players can manage possession in the defensive and middle thirds of the pitch, this combined practice can be introduced, incorporating elements from previous practices in the session.

- The **practice starts with 10v6 in the middle third**. See Practice 6 on page 66 for full instructions.

- On the **coach's call "Change"**, the player in possession passes back to the GK for an **8 (+GK) v 6 situation in the defensive third**. See Practice 5 on page 65.

- When the ball is in the defensive third, the wingers (**LW** & **RW**) stay in the middle third waiting for the coach to call again, and the ball is played forward.

Coaching Points

1. Circulate the ball efficiently between the defensive and middle thirds.
2. Precise passing in transitions.
3. Adapt positioning dynamically to maintain balance across both thirds.
4. React quickly to defensive pressure by creating passing angles.

PROGRESSION

8. 10 v 6 Positional Play in the Final Third with Rhombus Shapes

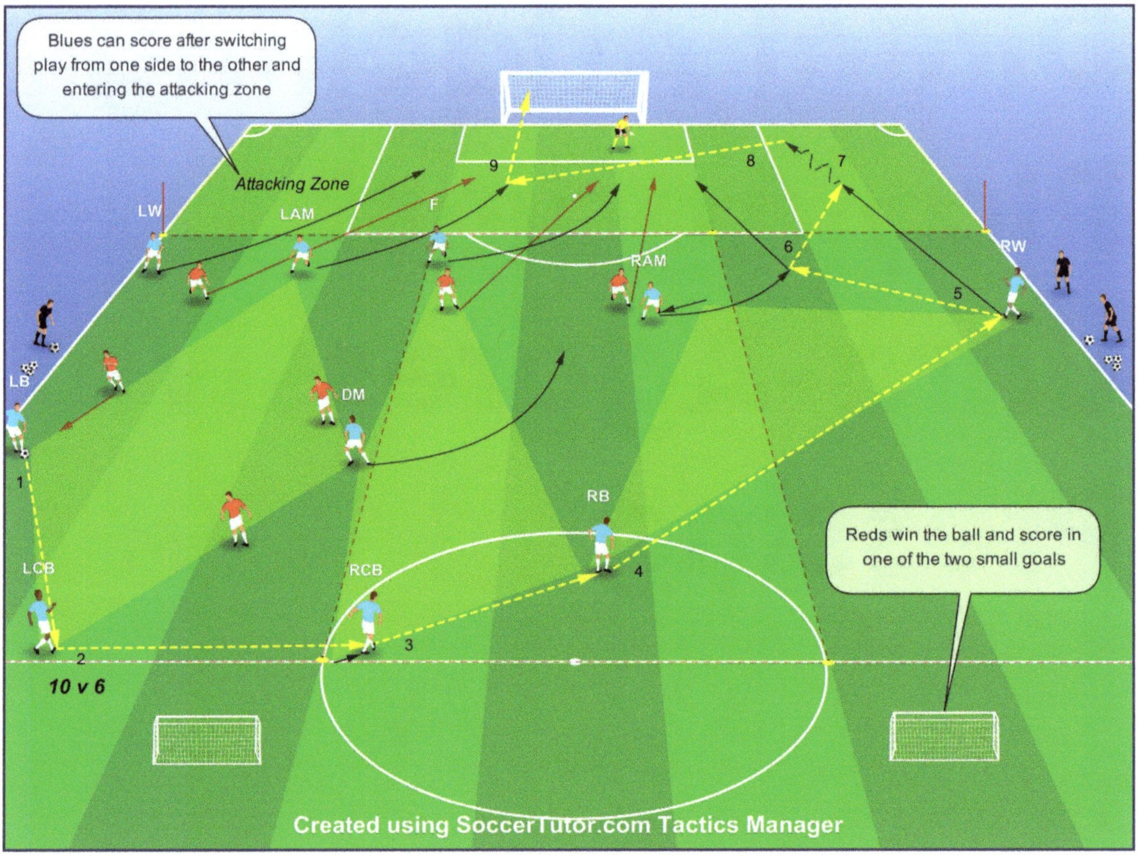

Practice Description

- The final practice of the session is played in the attacking half of the pitch (10 v 6), across 4 channels. Only 4 red players are allowed in the same channel at a time.
- **Blue Objective:** Circulate the ball to maintain possession and switch play or pass forward to break lines, depending on the red team's pressing decisions.
- Once the blues have broken through the red's pressing, they can then play into the **"Attacking Zone"** to try and score past the goalkeeper.
- **Red Objective:** Win the ball and counter to score either small goal.

Coaching Points

1. Maintain composure in possession while under pressure in the final third.
2. Create space by varying the tempo and switching play.
3. Use off-the-ball runs to disrupt the red team's defensive block.
4. Focus on quality and timing of final passes to maximise attacking speed and efficiency.

Direct Attacking Play Against Ultra-Aggressive Pressing

Direct Attacking Play Against Ultra-Aggressive Pressing

Direct Attacking Play Against Ultra-Aggressive Pressing Tactics

1. Direct Attack from Goalkeeper's Long Pass (Goal Kick)

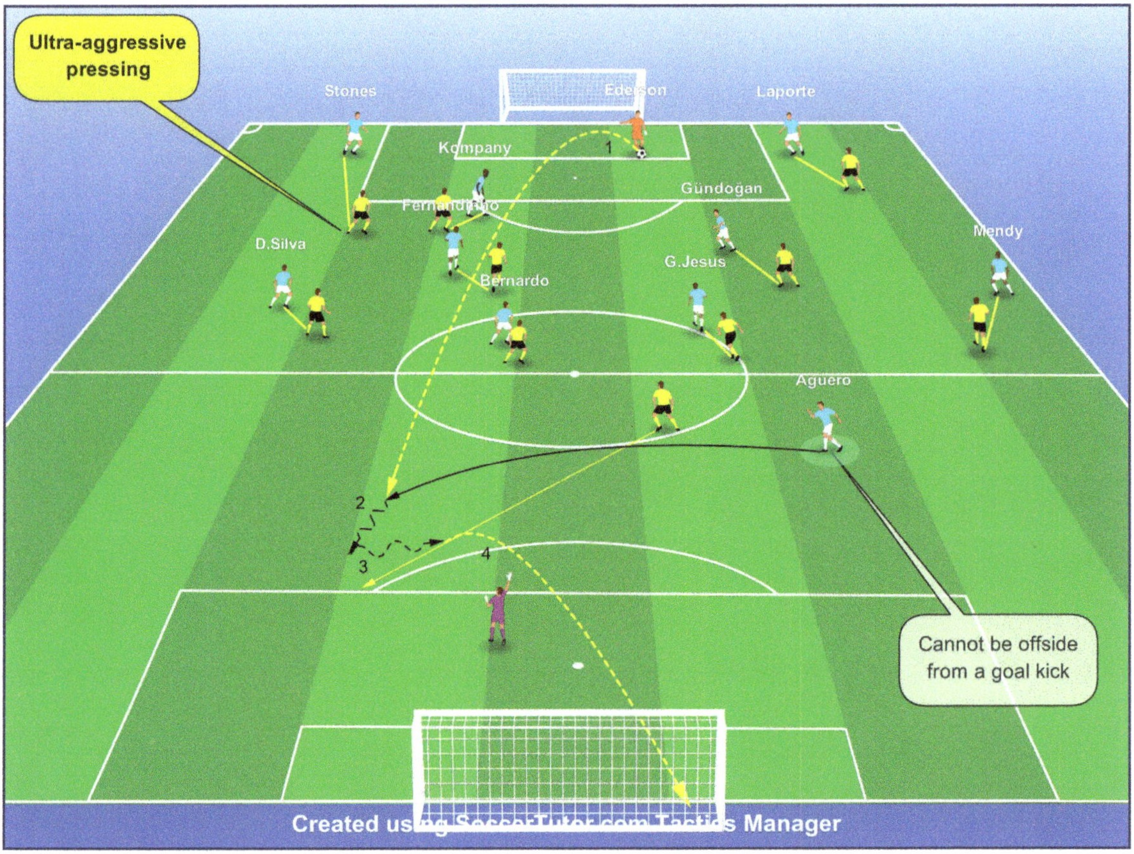

Pep Guardiola's teams are not known for long passing. However, in certain situations, Manchester City have effectively utilised direct attacking play to initiate attacks against opponents using ultra-aggressive high line pressing. This first example was against Huddersfield (Premier League, 19th August 2018).

Huddersfield used a man-to-man pressing tactic across the pitch, with the deepest defender left in a one-on-one situation against City's forward (**Agüero**).

From a 3-1-4-2 shape, one of the forwards (**G. Jesus**) dropped into midfield and the other one (**Agüero**) positioned himself beyond the last defender as you cannot be offside from a goal kick. **Ederson** (**GK**) played a direct pass over the defensive line, finding **Agüero**, who controlled the ball, beat his marker, and scored.

Key Point: This example highlights a tactic designed to exploit teams that press man-to-man with an aggressive high line.

Direct Attacking Play Against Ultra-Aggressive Pressing

2. Direct Attack from Goalkeeper's Long Pass (Open Play)

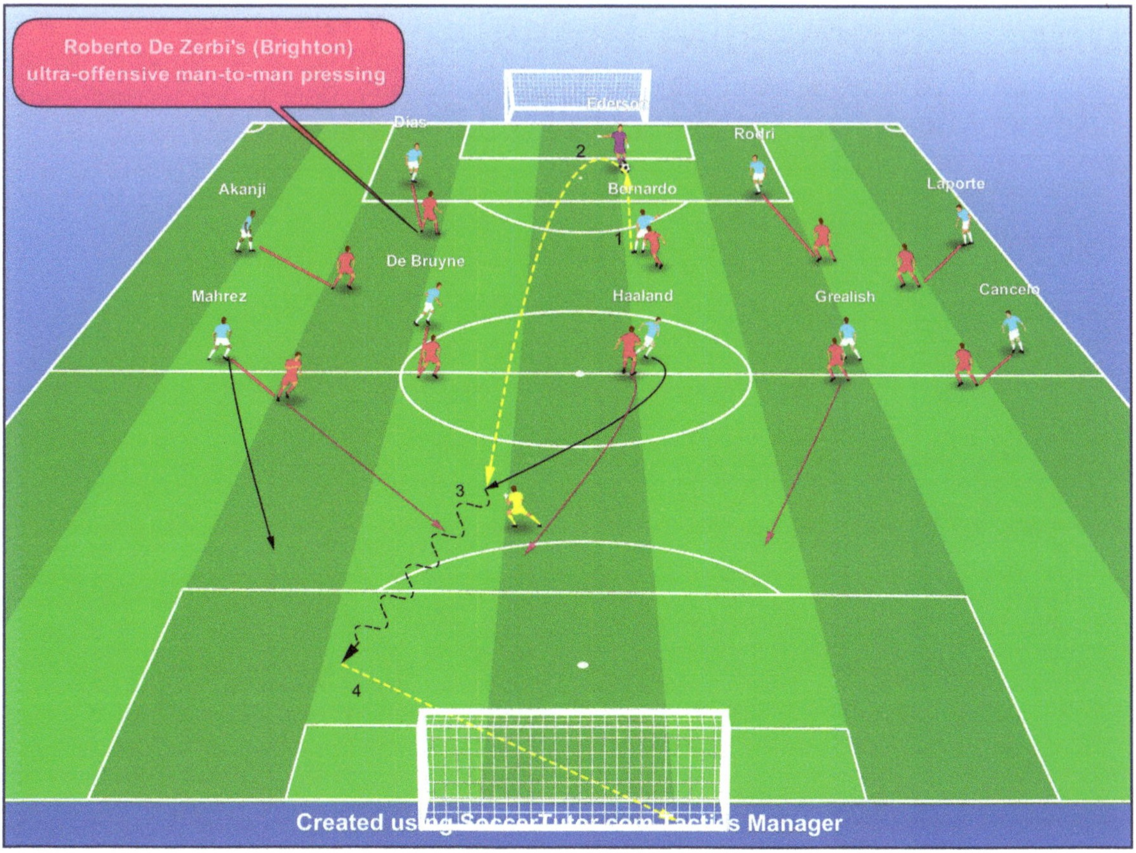

This second example was against Roberto De Zerbi's Brighton (Premier League, 22nd October 2022). Manchester City again utilise **Ederson's (GK) great technical ability to bypass the opposition's ultra-aggressive man-to-man pressing with long accurate passing**.

Manchester City play short initially, drawing Brighton's players forward, which creates space behind their defensive line.

The attacking midfielder (**Bernardo**) had received from the defensive midfielder (**Rodri**). After passing, **Rodri** moved into a centre back's position, and the left centre back (**Laporte**) shifted wide, while **Bernardo** dropped into a deeper position.

The forward (**Haaland**) also moved back. **Bernardo** passes back to **Ederson**.

With all of the Manchester City players marked within their own half, **Haaland** made a curved run into the space in behind. **Ederson** delivered a precise long pass, allowing **Haaland** to control the ball, beat his marker, and score.

Key Point: This showcases Manchester City's ability to draw pressure forward and exploit the space in behind, relying the Ederson's passing accuracy and Haaland's movement and technical execution.

Direct Attacking Play Against Ultra-Aggressive Pressing

3. Direct Attack from Centre Back's Breaking Lines Pass

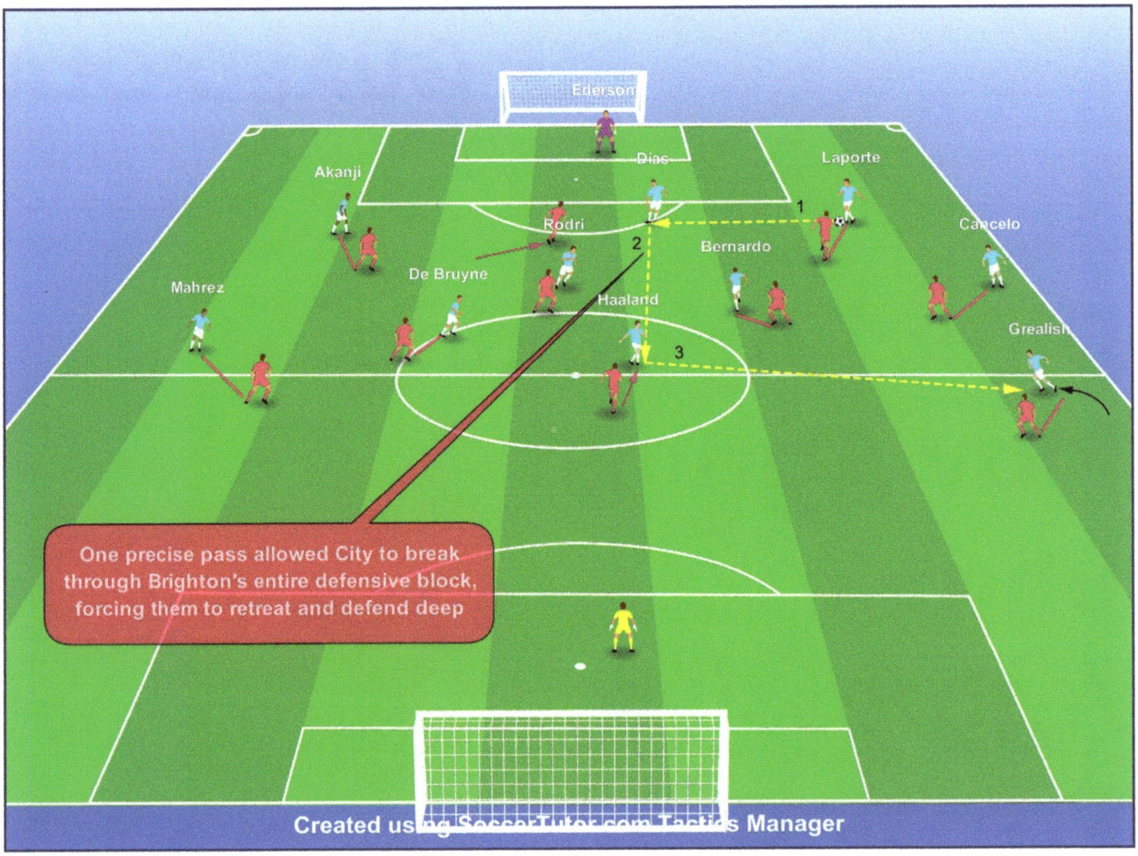

One precise pass allowed City to break through Brighton's entire defensive block, forcing them to retreat and defend deep

From the same match as the example on the previous page, here is another key situation which demonstrates **Pep Guardiola and Manchester City's response to Roberto De Zerbi's (Brighton) aggressive man-to-man pressing tactics**.

Brighton's defensive setup consistently involved advancing forward to mark players tightly. Manchester City would often react by trying to **play passes to break multiple lines of pressure**. This approach **exploits gaps left by defenders who fail to balance marking and covering spaces correctly**.

In this example, the centre back (**Dias**) received with enough time to control and look up before pressure arrived. The closest midfield passing options (**Rodri**, **Bernardo**, and **De Bruyne**) were closely marked as Brighton anticipated short passes to be played.

Dias identified the available passing lane to **Haaland**, who made a well-timed movement, controlled the ball, and played it wide to the left winger (**Grealish**).

Key Point: This single pass bypassed Brighton's entire defensive block, forcing them to track back so they could attempt to defend deeper. The resulting attack led to the penalty that gave Manchester City a two goal lead in the match.

PRACTICES BASED ON THE TACTICS OF PEP GUARDIOLA

Direct Attacking Play Against Ultra-Aggressive Pressing

Practices for PEP GUARDIOLA Tactics - Direct Attacking Play Against Ultra-Aggressive Pressing

PRACTICES FOR THIS TACTICAL SITUATION (2 PRACTICES)

1. Direct Attack from Goal Kicks 7 (+GK) v 8 Functional Multi-Zone Practice

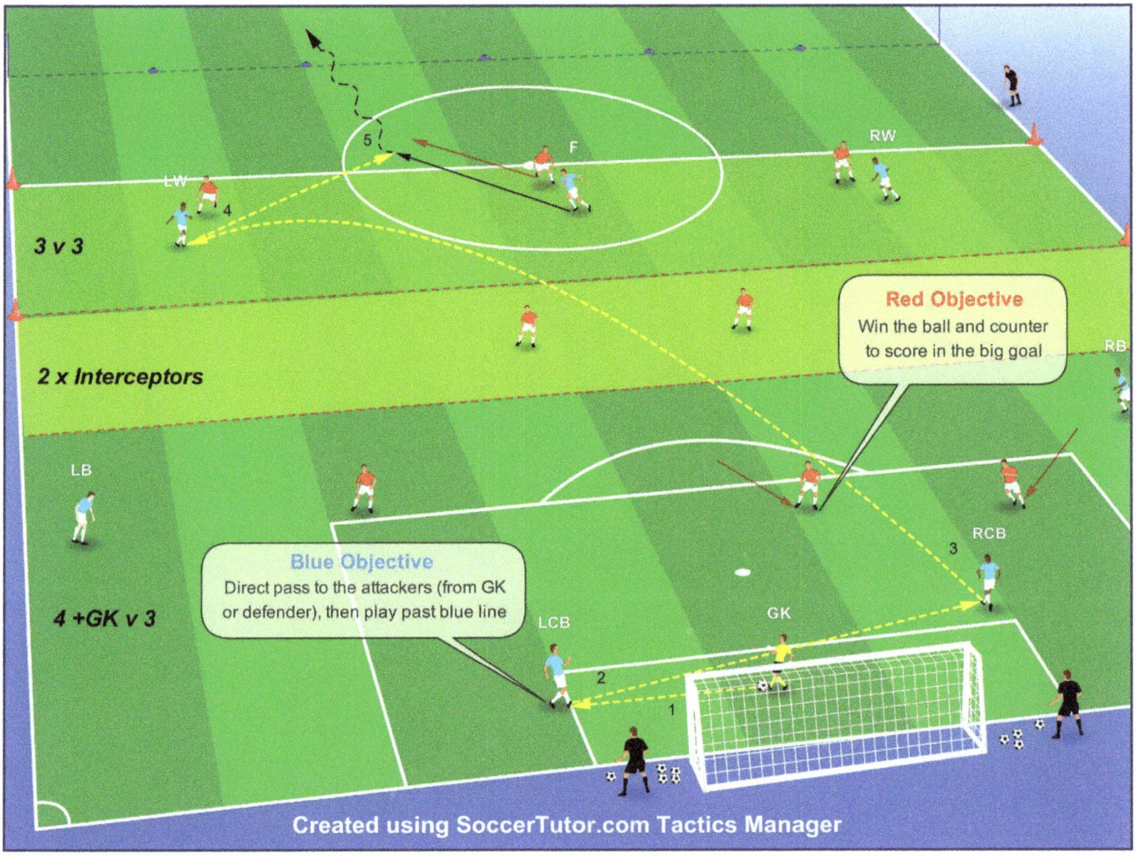

Practice Description

- The playing area is divided into 4 zones with the players restricted to their zones.
- The blue team have 4 defenders and 3 attackers from Manchester City's 4-3-3. They play against 8 opponents in a 3-2-3.
- **GK's Objective:** Take long direct goal kick or pass short for defender.
- **Blue Objective:** Progress the ball to the 3v3 Zone (long pass) and use individual actions or combinations to progress the ball past the blue end line.
- **Red Objective:** Win the ball and then counter attack (5 v 4 +GK) to score.
- **Rule:** Both teams must advance play forward, with no backward passes allowed into deeper zones.

Coaching Points

1. Precision and quality long passing for forward ball progression.
2. Strength and skill in winning duels.
3. Execute quick and effective attacking combinations.

Practices for PEP GUARDIOLA Tactics - Direct Attacking Play Against Ultra-Aggressive Pressing

VARIATION

2. Direct Attack with Breaking Lines Passes 7 (+GK) v 8 Functional Multi-Zone Practice

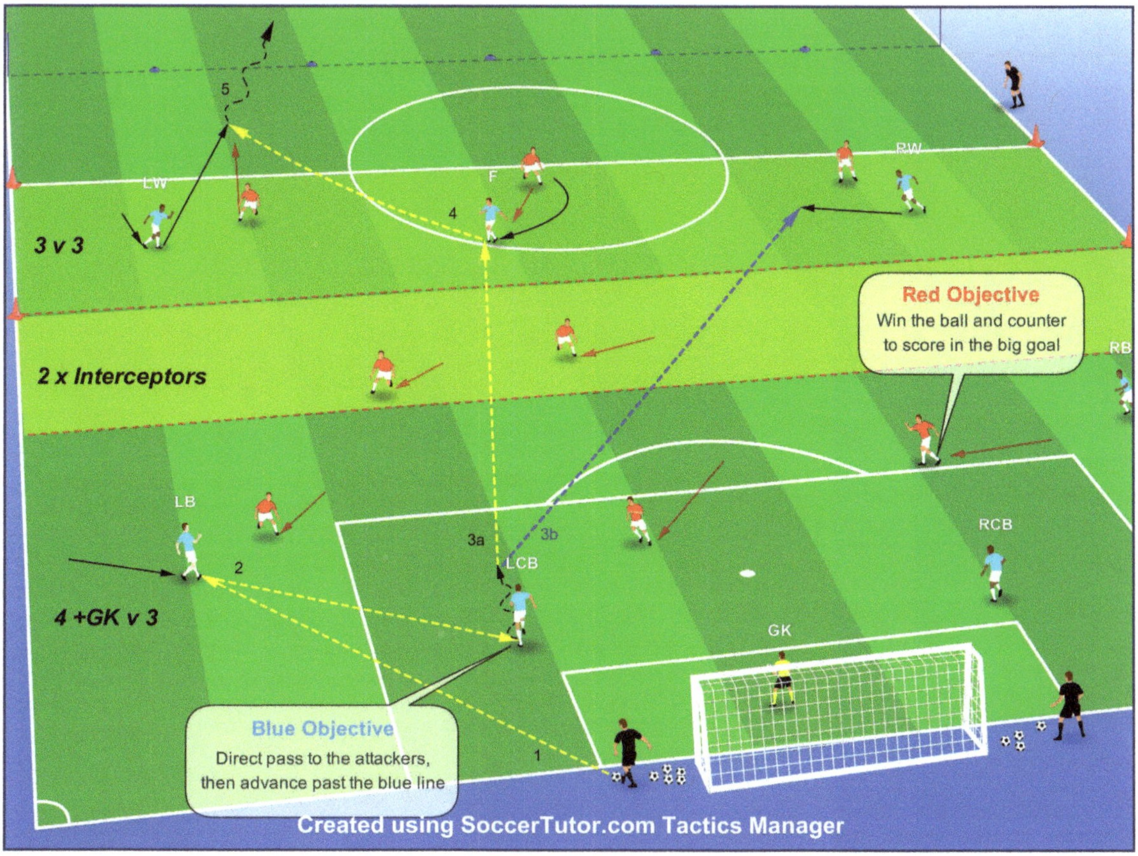

Practice Description

- This is a variation of the previous practice. Instead of starting from a goal kick, now a coach positioned beside the goal passes the ball in to a blue defender.
- The practice focuses on forward ground passes to break the lines to play into the attackers.
- **Blue Objective:** The receiver (**LB**) protects the ball under pressure and either plays a long pass to break the lines himself or passes short for a teammate to do so instead (**LCB** diagram).

- **Red Objective:** Win the ball and then counter attack (5 v 4 +GK) to score.
- **Rules:** Both teams must advance play forward, with no backward passes allowed into deeper zones. All passes must be along the ground.

Coaching Points

1. Firm and precise ground passes.
2. Strength and skill in winning duels.
3. Quick attacking combinations.
4. Manage transitions effectively.

Build Up Play to Break Lines Against High Pressing

Tactical Solutions for Build Up Play Against High Pressing

When opponents press Manchester City in their half, the team responds with these primary strategies:

1. **Long Passing:** Bypass man-to-man pressing with a long pass or break the lines pass, as outlined in the previous section of the book.

2. **Play Through Press:** Penetrate the defensive block by exploiting passing connections and advancing the ball forward with combination play.

3. **Ball Circulation Around the Perimeter:** Evading the press through effective ball circulation along the perimeter.

This section of the book focuses on how **Pep Guardiola's Manchester City tactics effectively counter high pressing through precise positioning and well-coordinated combination play**.

A prime example of this was Manchester City's Champions League match against Lyon on 19th September 2018, for which the analysis presented in this section has been drawn from. Lyon's structured pressing approach with their 4-1-1 formation involved 6 players, deliberately avoiding numerical equality (7v7) to maintain a compact defensive shape. The 2 Lyon attackers (forward and attacking midfielder) alternated roles, which were pressing the ball carrier and marking City's defensive midfielder (**Fernandinho**). Behind them, Lyon's 4 midfielders compressed the central areas, each shadowing a specific opponent. This strategy aimed to force Manchester City toward the flanks, where pressing could be intensified against Pep Guardiola's attacking full backs.

Manchester City responded by using a **rhombus shape to build up play** formed by the goalkeeper (**Ederson**), both centre backs (**Laporte** and **Stones**), and the defensive midfielder (**Fernandinho**). There would therefore be an **initial 4v2 advantage for the build up phase**. This helped **disrupt Lyon's press and opened up passing lanes behind the pressing block**.

By circulating the ball quickly within the rhombus shape, Pep Guardiola's team:

- Maintained composure.
- Moved opponents out of position.
- Created opportunities to progress the ball forward.

Key Point: Pep Guardiola is able to organise his teams for maximum effectiveness, even under intense pressure. His detailed tactical adjustments not only neutralise the opposition's high pressing system but also allow Manchester City to dictate the game and exploit spaces in the next phase of play.

Build Up Play to Break Lines Against High Pressing

1/7. Short Goal Kick with Rhombus Shape at the Back

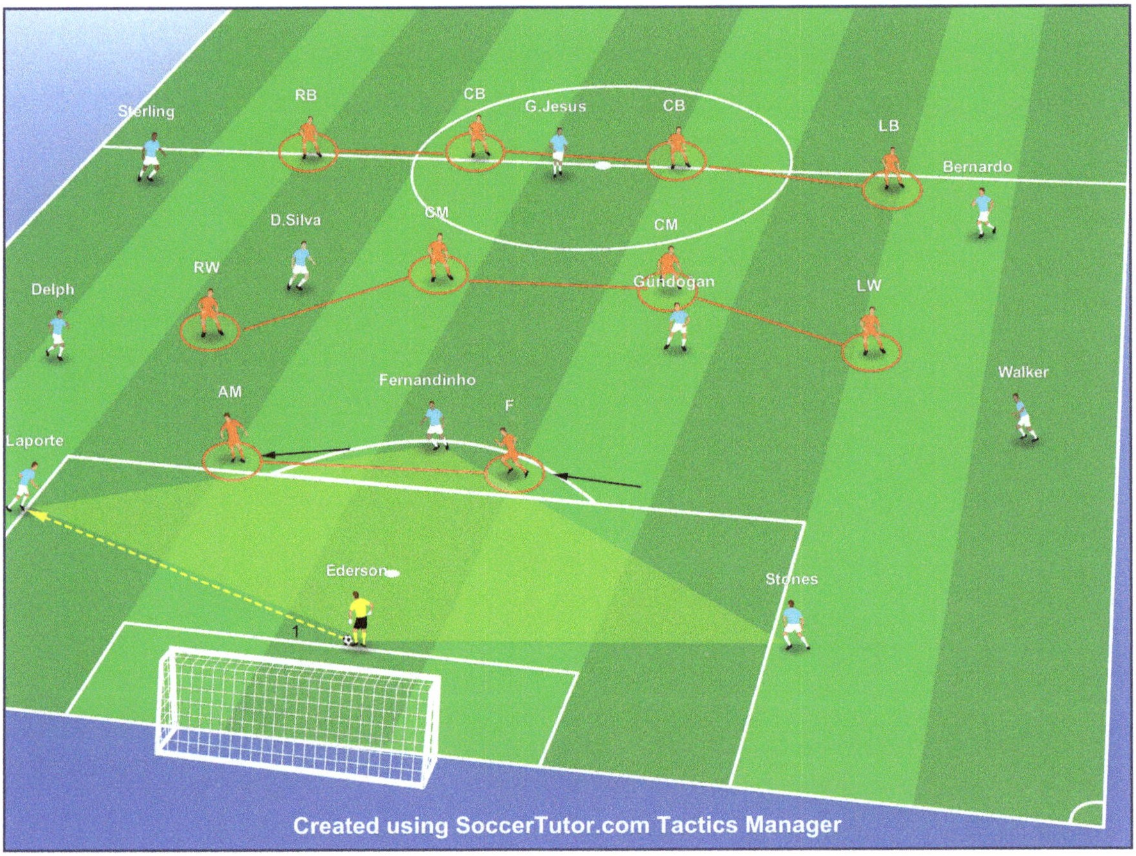

For the goal kick, the centre backs (**Stones** and **Laporte**) are positioned wide on either side of the box, with the defensive midfielder (**Fernandinho**) occupying a central position near the edge of the box.

Lyon's pressing strategy encouraged the goalkeeper (**Ederson**) to pass the ball to **Laporte** to the left, with one of their 2 attackers positioned to mark **Fernandinho**, and the other tasked with pressing **Stones** if he received.

As **Laporte** received the ball, the Lyon attacking midfielder (AM) moved to press him, while the forward (F) shifted across towards the centre.

Key Point: This movement activated Pep Guardiola and Manchester City's tactical plan, which relied on the rhombus shape to create space and utilise combination play. It allows them to bypass the opposition's pressing block efficiently with a 4v2 advantage and progress the ball into more advanced areas.

The same phase continues on the next page.

Note: *Before the goal kick rule change in 2019, the ball had to leave the box before being played after a goal kick. The analysis shown reflects a match before this adjustment was made.*

Build Up Play to Break Lines Against High Pressing

2/7. Centre Back Passes Back to GK and a Forward Moves to Press

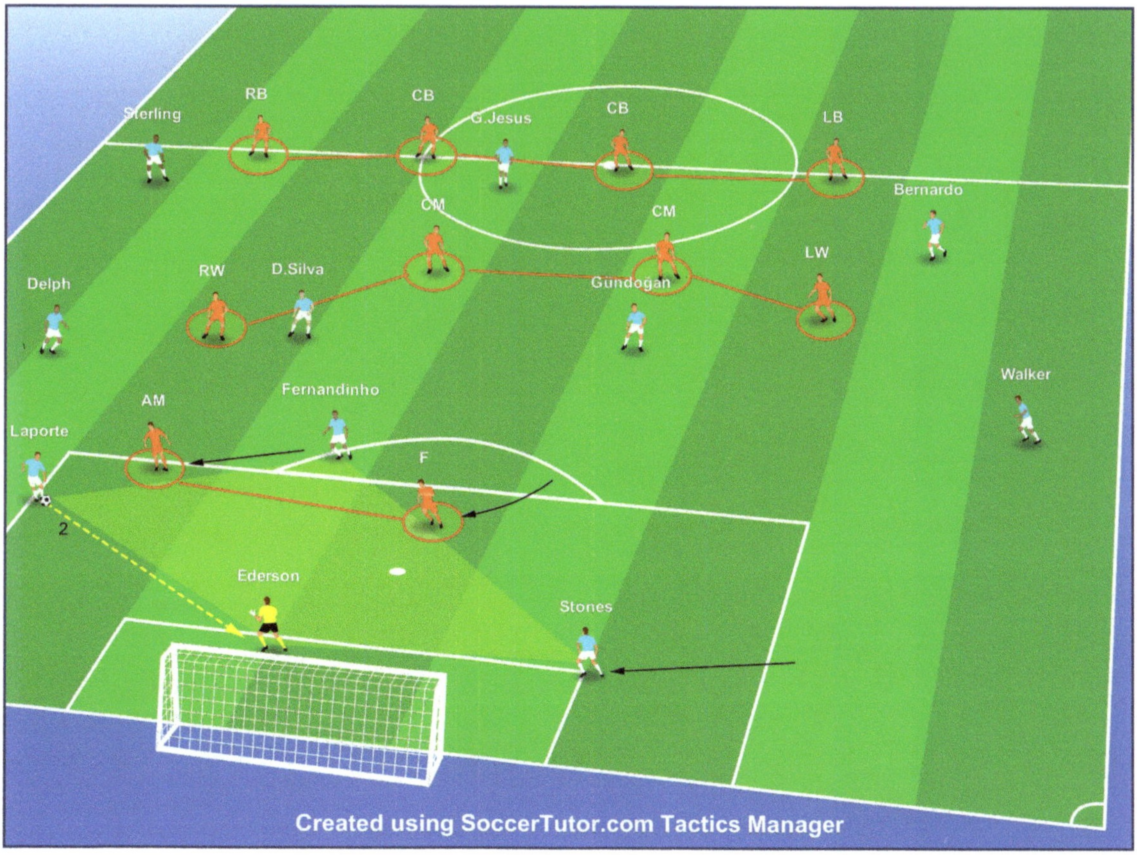

Continuing from the previous diagram, the left centre back (**Laporte**) passes back to the goalkeeper (**Ederson**), which prompts Lyon's forward (F) to move forward and press **Ederson**.

This adjustment aimed to disrupt Manchester City's build up play at the source, forcing the goalkeeper to make a quicker decision in the hope of causing a mistake.

However, **Manchester City's rhombus structure and positional discipline ensured they maintained passing options to bypass the pressing line effectively**.

The same phase continues on the next page.

Build Up Play to Break Lines Against High Pressing

3/7. Goalkeeper's Quick Pass to Other Centre Back to Play Forward

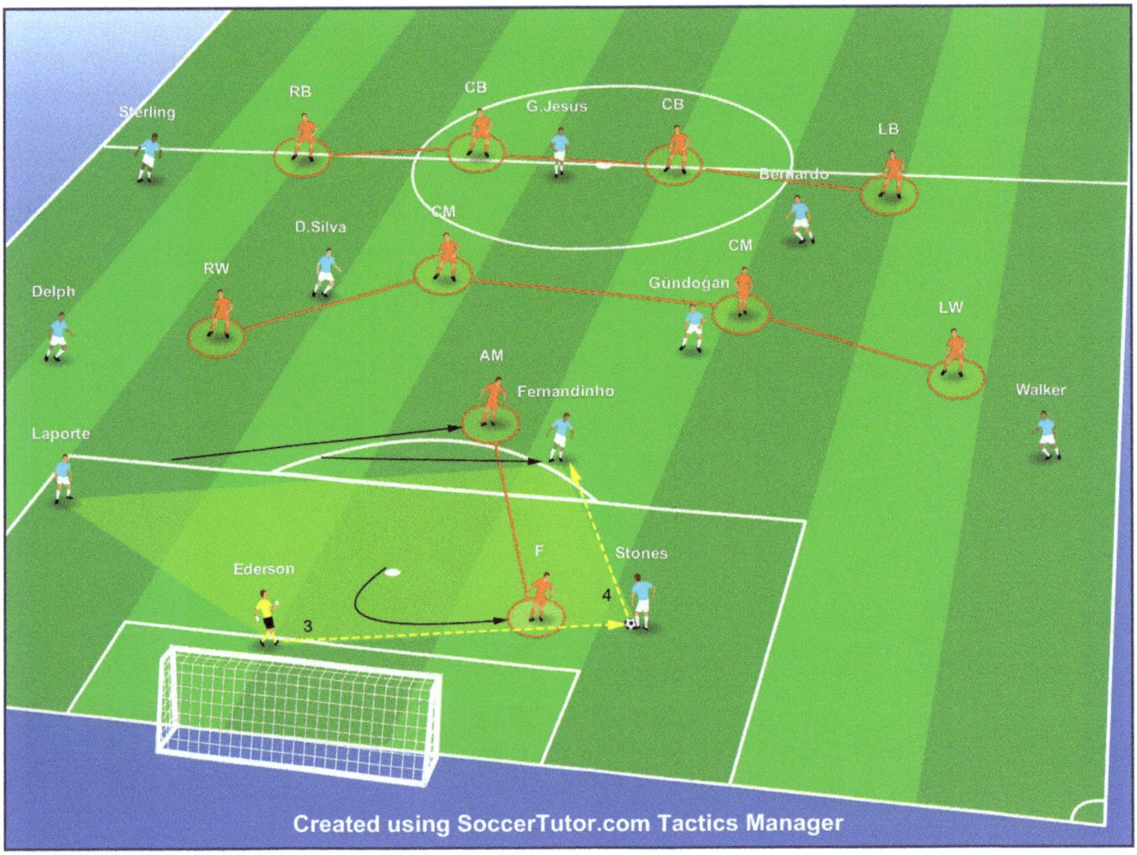

This continues on from the previous page after the left centre back's (**Laporte**) pass back to the goalkeeper (**Ederson**).

Ederson passes to the right centre back (**Stones**). After pressing the goalkeeper, the Lyon forward (F) continued his run to press **Stones** immediately after receiving the pass.

Recognising that playing to the right back (**Walker**) would invite pressure, **Stones** avoided that option. He identified that **Ederson** was the free man behind Lyon's front pressing line. To return the ball to the goalkeeper, **Stones** used the defensive midfielder (**Fernandinho** - top of rhombus), who had shifted across, as a link player.

Fernandinho's marker (AM) was unable to close the distance in time to prevent him from being able to play back safely to the goalkeeper, which is shown in the diagram on the next page as the same phase continues.

Build Up Play to Break Lines Against High Pressing

4/7. DM Passes Back to GK and Both Forwards Move to Press

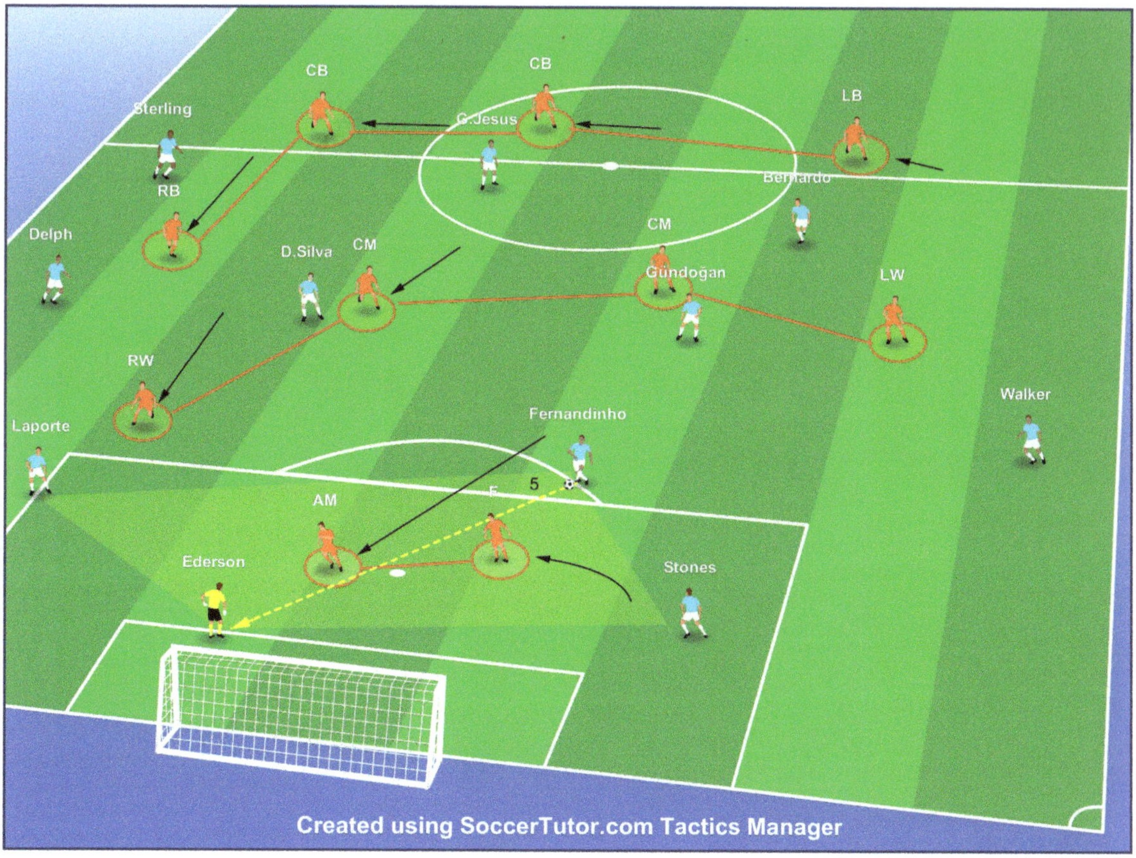

This continues on from the previous page and the defensive midfielder (**Fernandinho**) safely redirected the ball back to the goalkeeper (**Ederson**), making sure to maintain Manchester City's control of the ball.

Lyon's attacking midfielder (AM) pressed **Ederson**, who is positioned at the base of the rhombus behind Lyon's front line of pressure.

At the same time, Lyon's right winger (RW) moved forward to close down Manchester City's left centre back (**Laporte**). Lyon's right back (RB) also moves forward to mark the right back (**Delph**) and was poised to move further forward.

Meanwhile, Lyon's 2 central midfielders (CM) prepared to press City's attacking midfielders (**Silva** and **Gündoğan**) in case they dropped deeper to help with the build up and create space for progressing the play forwards.

The same phase continues on the next page.

Build Up Play to Break Lines Against High Pressing

5/7. GK's Dummy Pass to Left Centre Back + Pass to Right Centre Back

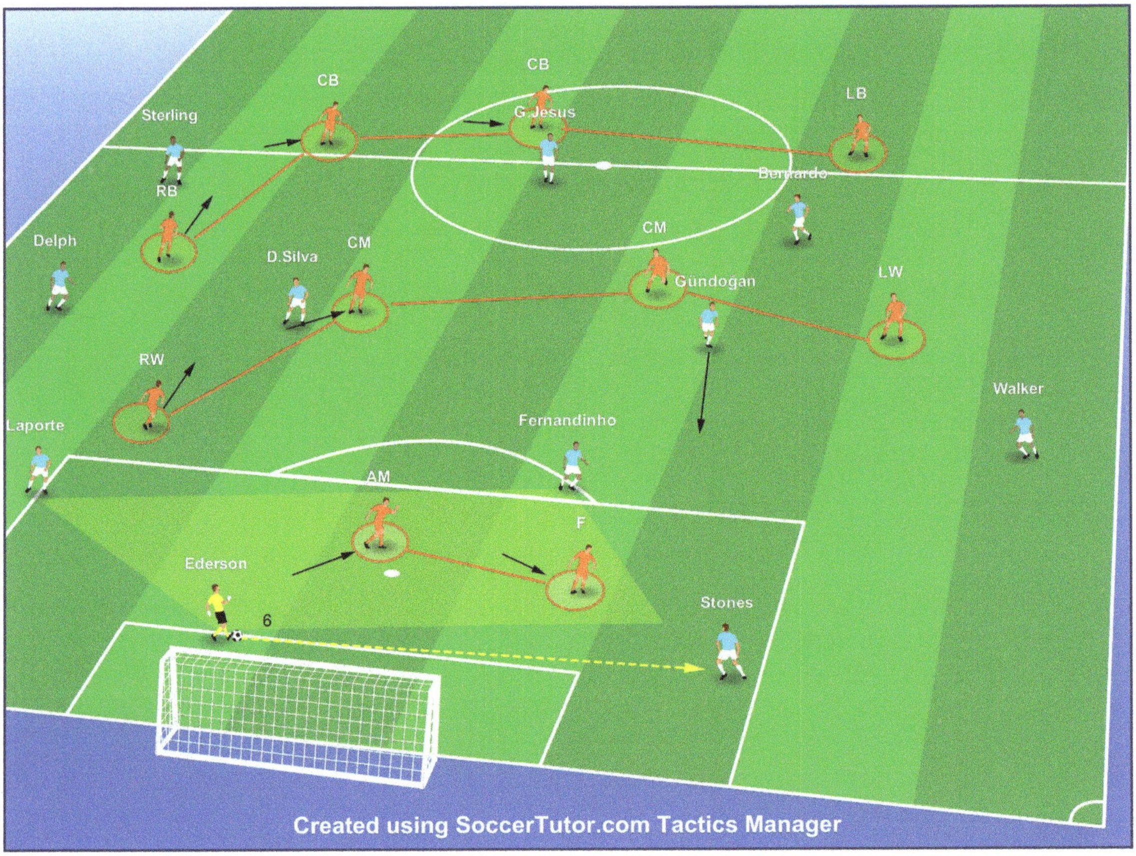

With Lyon pushing players forward on Manchester City's left side (see previous page), the goalkeeper (**Ederson**), under pressure from Lyon's attacking midfielder (AM), faked a pass towards the left (to **Laporte**) before quickly directing the ball to the opposite side, to the right centre back (**Stones**).

Stones was temporarily unmarked as the Lyon forward (F) was covering the Manchester City defensive midfielder (**Fernandinho**).

Stones received the pass from **Ederson** and is immediately pressed by the forward (F), which in turn, leaves **Fernandinho** unmarked.

Key Point: With the defensive midfielder unmarked, Manchester City had the opportunity to progress the ball forward and would look to exploit this situation to play out from the back successfully.

The same phase continues on the next page.

Build Up Play to Break Lines Against High Pressing

6/7. Combination Play Through the Press (in the Centre)

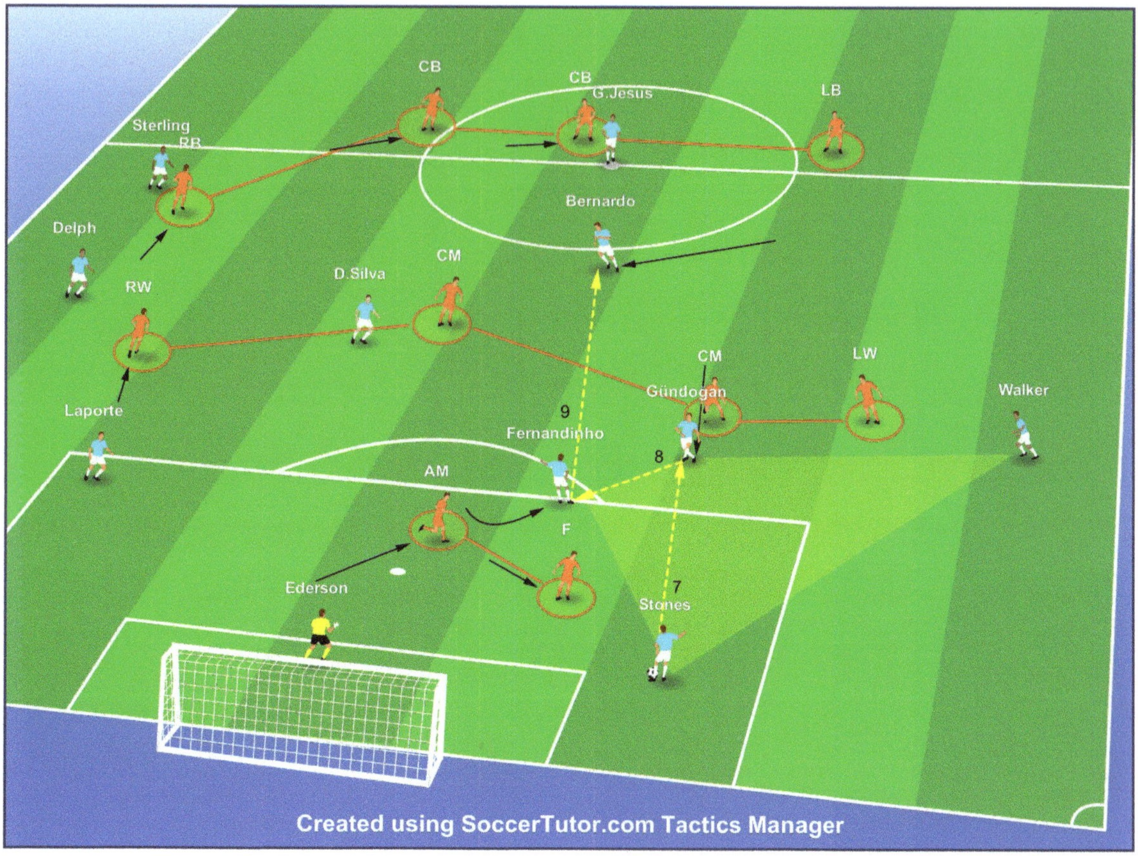

This continues on from the previous page and the right centre back (**Stones**) plays a forward pass to the attacking midfielder (**Gündoğan**), who has dropped back to receive and act as the link player to move the ball to the unmarked defensive midfielder (**Fernandinho**).

The Lyon attacking midfielder (AM) was unable to close down **Fernandinho** in time, so he is able to play a forward pass to break through Lyon's midfield line and takes 6 Lyon players (first 2 pressing lines) out of the game.

The attacking midfielder (**Bernardo**) took advantage of Lyon's defensive line shifting to the other side of the pitch and is able to receive unmarked in a dangerous central position where he has the space to launch a dangerous attack.

Key Point: In this situation, Manchester City's attacking midfielders had the ability to turn and drive forward with the ball at their feet or play a pass into space for a teammate who was in a better position or had more speed.

The same phase continues on the next page.

Build Up Play to Break Lines Against High Pressing

7/7. Attacking Midfielder's Pass Wide for Advancing Full Back (Attack)

This continues on from the previous page after the attacking midfielder (**Bernardo**) receives a forward pass from the defensive midfielder (**Fernandinho**).

Bernardo quickly identified space on the right side and delivered a well-timed pass for the oncoming run of Manchester City's speedy right back (**Walker**).

Walker received and surged forward with the ball, exploiting the space in between Lyon's midfield and defensive lines.

As the attack progressed, Manchester City were able to create a clear goal scoring opportunity which forced a vital save from the Lyon goalkeeper.

Key Point: This example highlights how Manchester City used precise passing and movement to bypass the opposition's pressing structure, creating a clear opportunity to transition from build up play in defensive areas into a fast attack.

SESSION BASED ON THE TACTICS OF PEP GUARDIOLA

Build Up Play to Break Lines Against High Pressing

Session for PEP GUARDIOLA Tactics - **Build Up Play to Break Lines Against High Pressing**

SESSION FOR THIS TACTICAL SITUATION (3 PRACTICES)

1. Build Up Play to Break Lines Through the Defensive Midfielder Functional Passing Circuit

1a. Attacking Midfielder's Dribble + Pass to GK to Complete Sequence

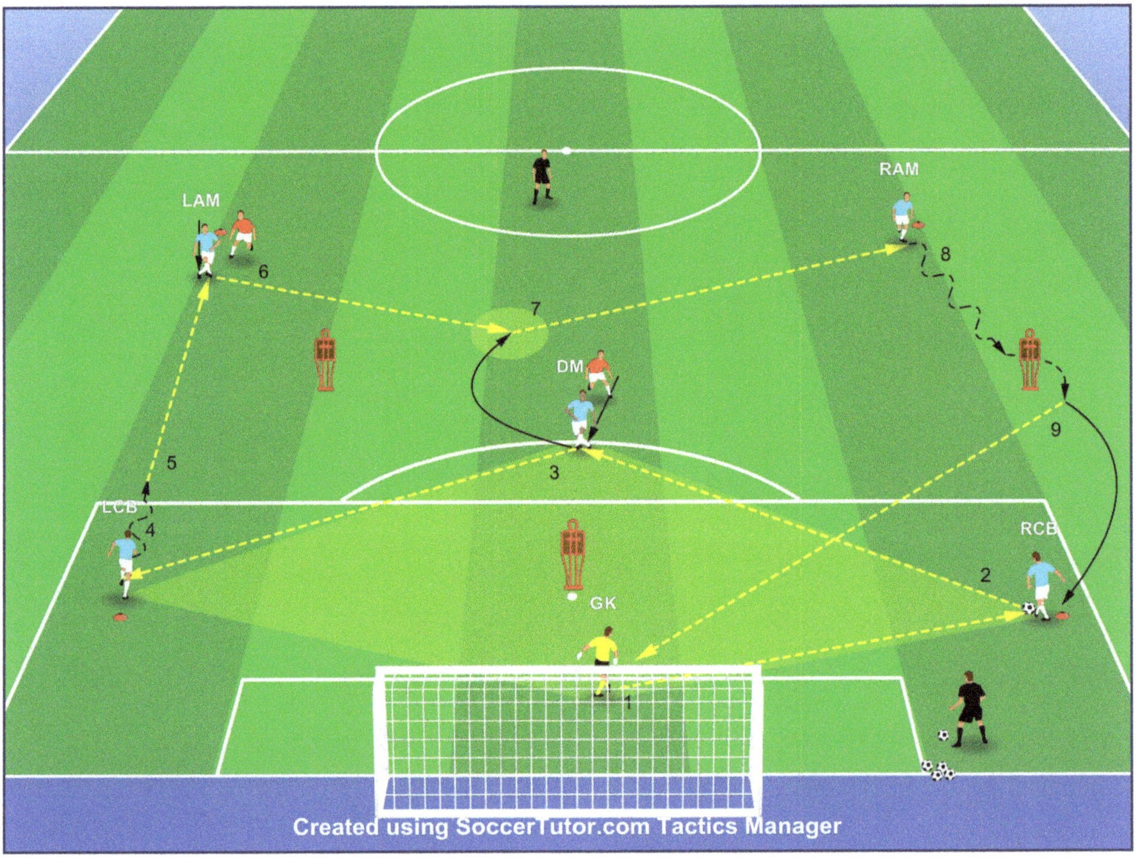

Practice Description (Variation 1a)

- The 4 cones mark out positions for 2 blue centre backs (**LCB** & **RCB**) and 2 attacking midfielders (**LAM** & **RAM**). The defensive midfielder (**DM**) operates in the centre. There are 3 mannequins (opponents) and 2 active red players who mark and press the **DM** and **LAM**.

- The **GK** starts with a pass to the right centre back (**RCB**). **RCB** passes to **DM**, who is pressed, so passes back to the left centre back (**LCB**). **LCB** drives forward and uses the left attacking midfielder (**LAM**) as a link player to move the ball back to **DM**.

- **DM** passes across to **RAM**, who dribbles past the mannequin and passes to **GK**.

- All players rotate their positions: **RCB** → **DM** → **LCB** → **LAM** → **RAM** → **RCB**.

- The sequence is repeated in the opposite direction (first pass **GK** to **LCB**).

Session for PEP GUARDIOLA Tactics - Build Up Play to Break Lines Against High Pressing

1b. Attacking Midfielder's Long Pass to GK to Complete Sequence

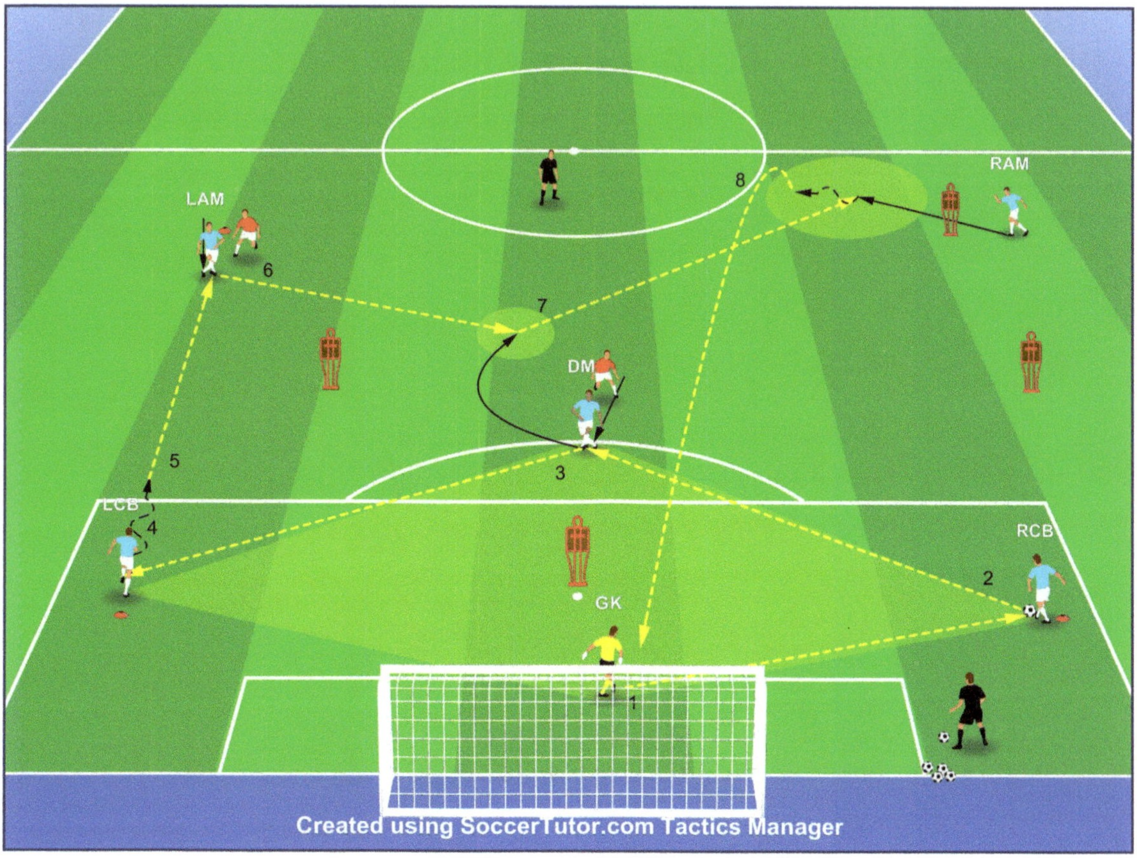

Practice Description (Variation 1b)

- In this variation, the right attacking midfielder (**RAM**) moves into a higher position and moves inside to receive.
- **RAM** takes a touch and delivers a long aerial pass back to the goalkeeper (**GK**).
- All players rotate their positions:
  RCB → DM → LCB → LAM → RAM → RCB.
- The sequence is repeated in the opposite direction (first pass **GK** to **LCB**).

Coaching Points

1. Precision and accuracy in passing.
2. Maintain effective coordination between the player in possession, the link player, and the receiver.
3. Controlled dribbling with the ball staying close to feet.

Session for PEP GUARDIOLA Tactics - Build Up Play to Break Lines Against High Pressing

PROGRESSION

2. Build Up Play to Break Lines with Double Rhombus Structure Functional Target Player Game

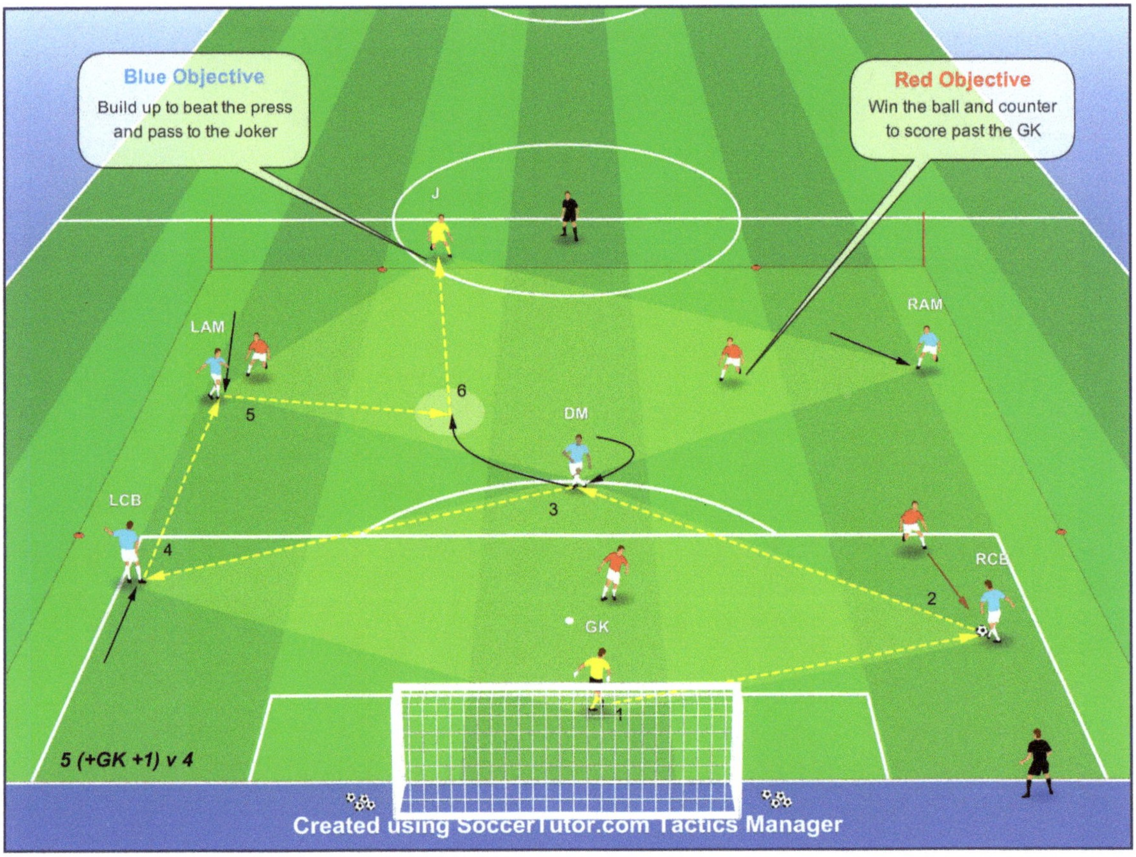

Practice Description

- The blues have 2 centre backs (**LCB** & **RCB**), 1 defensive midfielder (**DM**), and 2 attacking midfielders (**LAM** & **RAM**) from Manchester City's 4-3-3. The reds defend and press in a 2-2 shape.

- **Blue Objective:** Play through or bypass the press and deliver a low pass to the **Joker (J)**, who moves freely outside the playing area, and acts as the target man.

- **Red Objective:** Win the ball and then counter attack (4 v 5 +GK) to score.

- When the reds press a blue centre back and block passes to **DM**, the attacking midfielders (**LAM** in diagram) can link play to bypass the press effectively.

- **When the Joker Receives:** Play either restarts from **GK** or the **Joker (J)** joins the reds for a 5 v 5 (+GK) attack, which the blues must defend.

- **Key Point:** This practice coaches ball circulation in the 2 highlighted rhombus structures, focusing on link player connections.

Session for PEP GUARDIOLA Tactics - Build Up Play to Break Lines Against High Pressing

PROGRESSION

3. Build Up Play to Break Lines Against High Pressing Teams Target Player Game

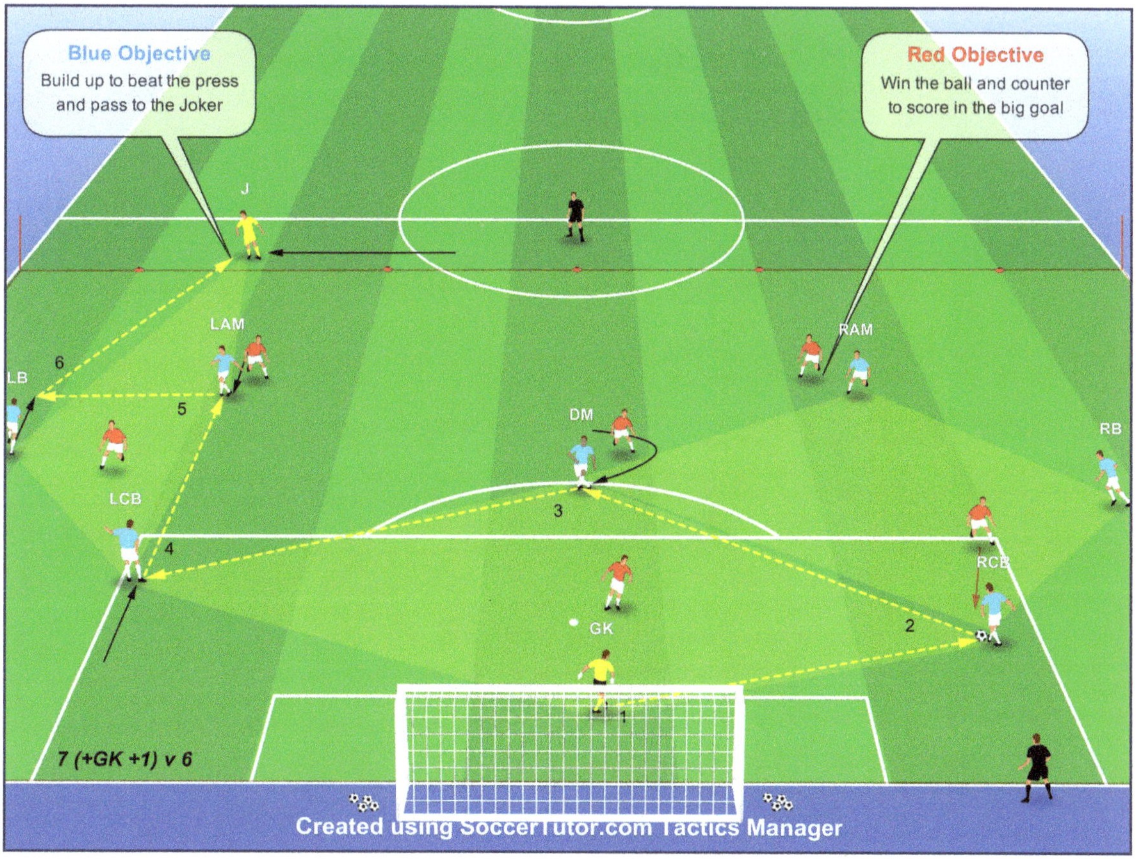

Blue Objective: Build up to beat the press and pass to the Joker

Red Objective: Win the ball and counter to score in the big goal

7 (+GK +1) v 6

Practice Description

- In this progression of the previous practice, we add 2 full backs so the blues are in a 4-3 shape from Manchester City's 4-3-3. There are 2 reds added too so they now press in a 4-2 shape.
- **Team Objectives:** Remain the same for both the blue and red teams.
- The increase in player numbers increases the range of link-up opportunities and potential actions based on the defending team's movements - one example is shown in the diagram.

- **When the Joker Receives:** Play either restarts from **GK** or the **Joker** (**J**) joins the reds for a 7 v 7 (+GK) attack, which the blues must defend.

Coaching Points

1. Maintain effective spacing with staggered positioning across the pitch.
2. Precision and quality in every pass.
3. Choose passes intelligently based on the type of pressing applied by the opponents.

Patient Build Up and Possession Against High Pressing

Tactical Solutions for Patient Build Up and Possession Against High Pressing

In the previous sections, we examined Manchester City's use of forward play to bypass their opponents' pressing. Now, we turn our attention to tactics for advancing through ball circulation and switching play, which is an effective method for maintaining compactness while playing out from the back against high pressing.

The key aspect lies in how Pep Guardiola's players occupy the pitch to **circulate the ball and force the opposition out of their pressing structure**. A striking example of this approach being successful comes from Manchester City's 4-1 Premier League victory against Manchester United (6th March 2022). Rather than pushing the ball forward at every opportunity, **City shifted the focus to horizontal movement of the ball**, aiming to isolate United's defensive block and **create a 9v6 numerical advantage across the width of the pitch**. The intent was not just to bypass the immediate pressure but to gradually **unbalance the defensive shape**, **opening up more reliable passing options and spaces to exploit**.

In this game, Pep Guardiola's adjustment was most evident in the role of the forward. Instead of the more direct approach used previously with Gabriel Jesus, **Phil Foden was used as a "false nine."** This offered **increased positional fluidity**, as Foden's ability to drift to the centre left helped destabilise United's defensive structure. Additionally, the attacking midfielder **Bernardo** dropped deeper alongside defensive midfielder **Rodri**, forming a **double pivot that provided a stable base for controlled horizontal passing** and supported the gradual expansion of the attacking shape.

Key Point: The combination of patient ball circulation, compact positioning, and adaptable player roles allowed Pep Guardiola's Manchester City team to pull their opponents out of their shape. By doing so, the team not only bypassed high pressing situations, but also created opportunities to progress with greater control and precision.

Patient Build Up and Possession Against High Pressing

1/19. Short Goal Kick to Right Centre Back

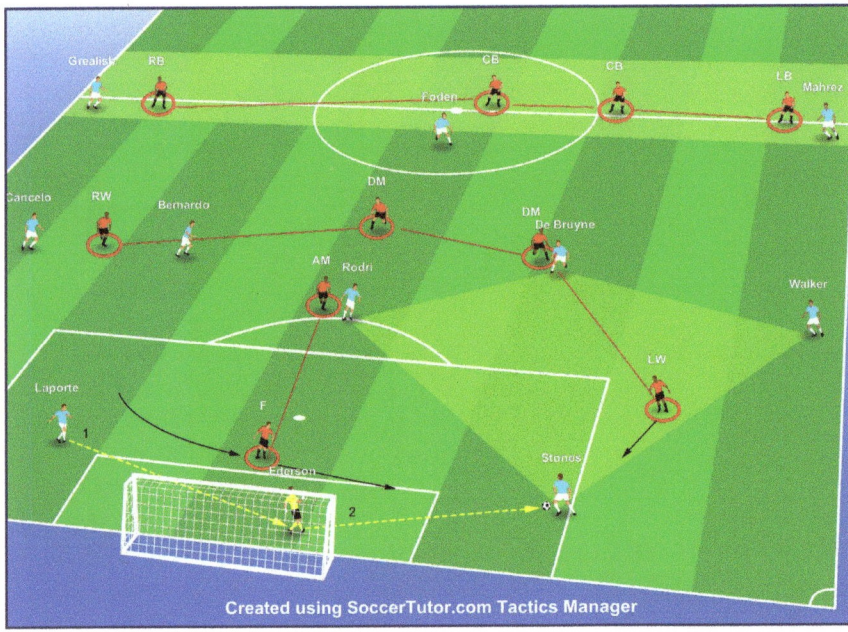

Manchester City were in their usual 4-3-3 and Manchester United used a 4-2-3-1, with the attacking midfielder (AM) tasked with marking the City DM (**Rodri**).

Left centre back (**Laporte**) passed the ball to the GK (**Ederson**), who, under pressure from the forward (F), quickly passed to the right centre back (**Stones**).

2/19. Centre Back's Forward Pass to Def. Midfielder (Link Player)

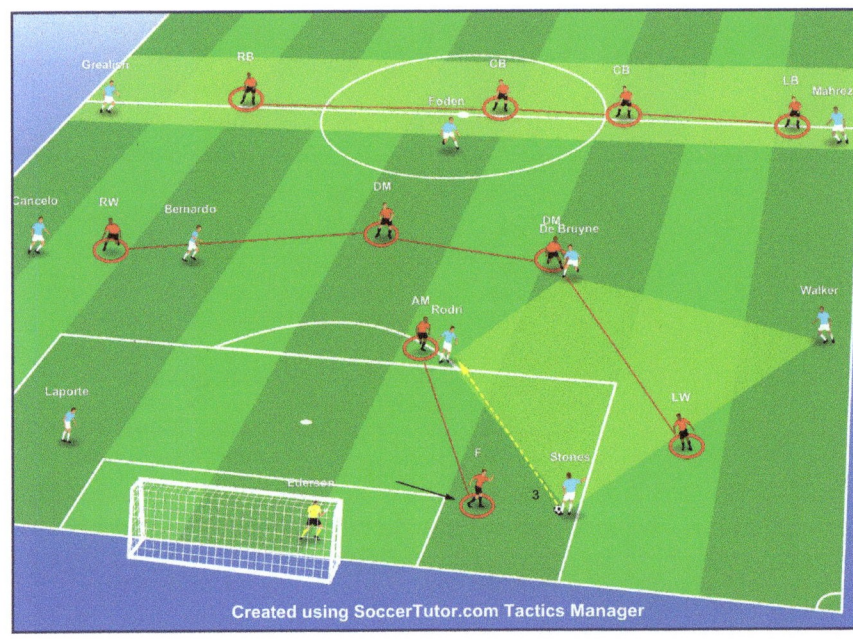

The Manchester United forward (F) carries on his movement to put **Stones** under pressure.

The aim from this point is to move the ball to the right back (**Walker**), who is free and available in space behind the United left winger (LW).

Stones makes a good decision to use the defensive midfielder (**Rodri**) as a link player, so passes to him.

Patient Build Up and Possession Against High Pressing

3/19. Defensive Midfielder's Pass Wide to Unmarked Right Back

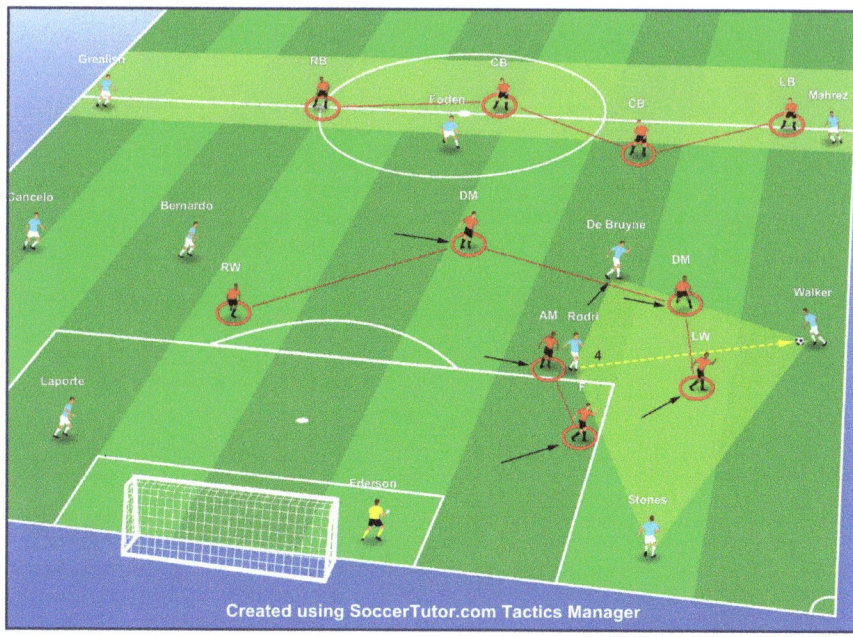

This follows on from the previous diagram which shows **Stones** using **Rodri** as a link player to move the ball to **Walker**, who is unmarked.

As **Walker** receives, United's defensive midfielder (DM) shifts across and the left winger (LW) moves to back and across to close him down.

4/19. Right Back's Pass Back to Centre Back (Forward Pass Too Risky)

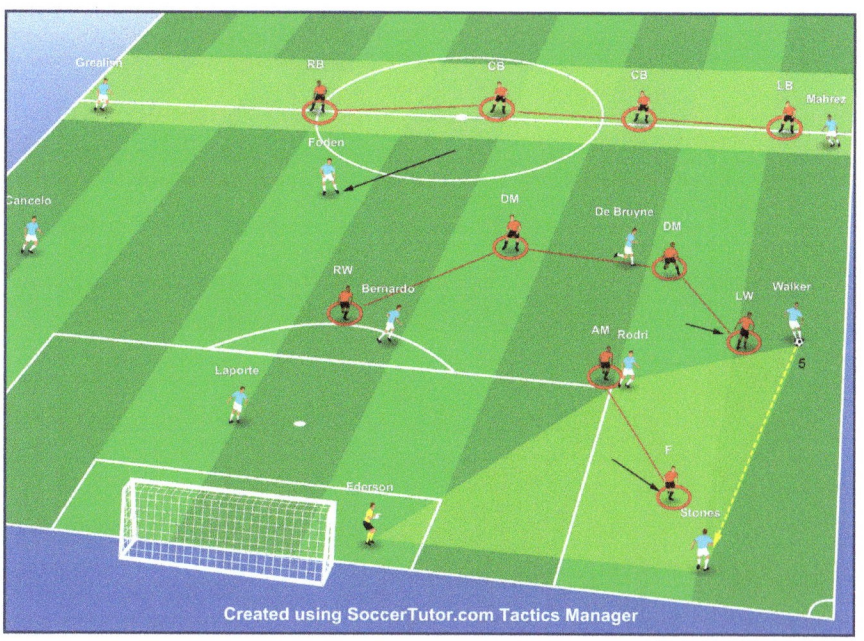

Although attacking midfielder **De Bruyne** runs off the back of United's DM, **Walker** notices the good defensive movements of the opposition and decides not to force the play towards him with a risky pass.

He instead passes back to **Stones**, who can then play back to the GK (**Ederson**) to start a switch of play.

Patient Build Up and Possession Against High Pressing

5/19. Manchester City's Two Rhombuses Tied Together by the GK

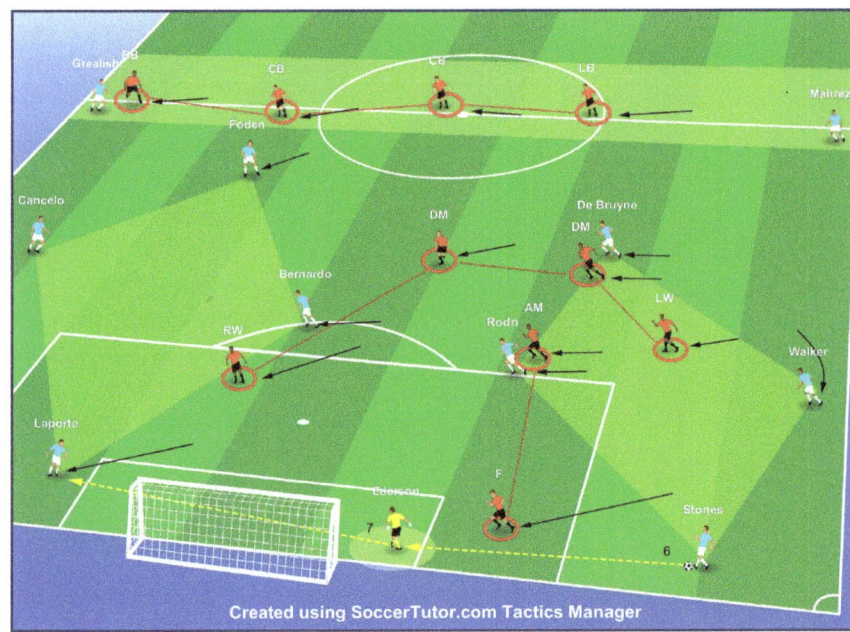

Stones passes to **Ederson**, who is the only player to tie the two rhombuses together, key for Manchester City's structure to play out from the back.

The forward (**Foden**) drops back and the attacking midfielder (**Bernardo**) moves across.

Ederson passes to the centre back on the other side (**Laporte**).

6/19. Centre Back's Pass Wide to Unmarked Left Back

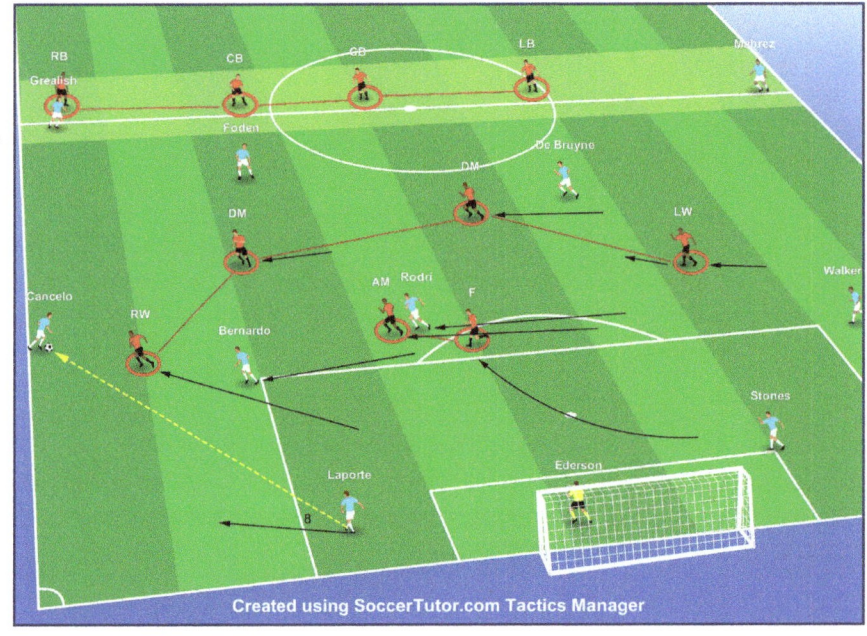

Laporte saw an opportunity to break the first line of pressure with a good pass to the left back (**Cancelo**).

If the pass was accurate, **Cancelo** would have received behind the right winger (RW) and could immediately develop the play forward.

However, the pass is not strong and **Cancelo** decides to simply maintain possession instead.

Patient Build Up and Possession Against High Pressing

7/19. Playing Back to Reset After Failed Line Breaking Pass

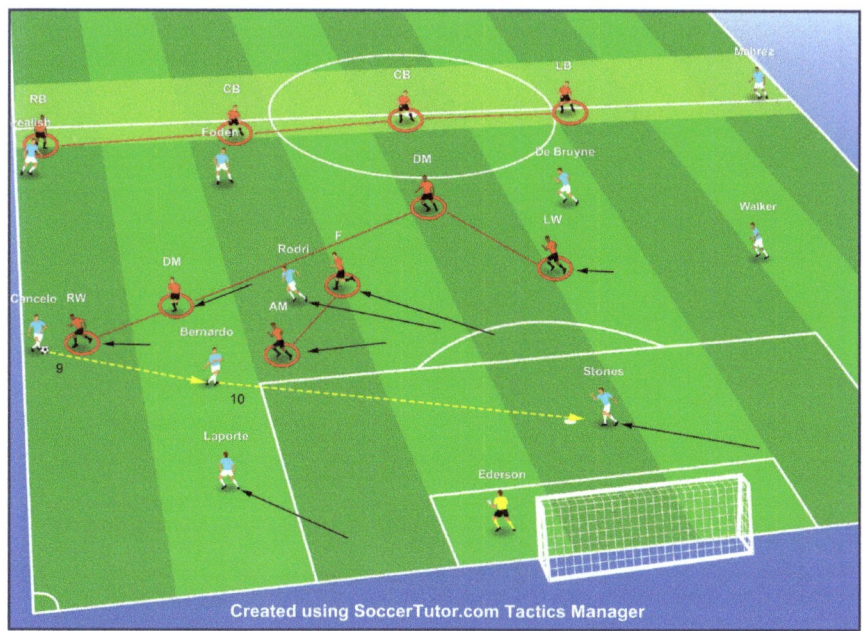

Cancelo passes inside to attacking midfielder (**Bernardo**, who is then put under pressure by Manchester United's attacking midfielder (AM).

Bernardo passes back to the right centre back (**Stones**), who was free in the centre of the box.

8/19. Centre Back Carries Ball into Space to Push the Team Forward

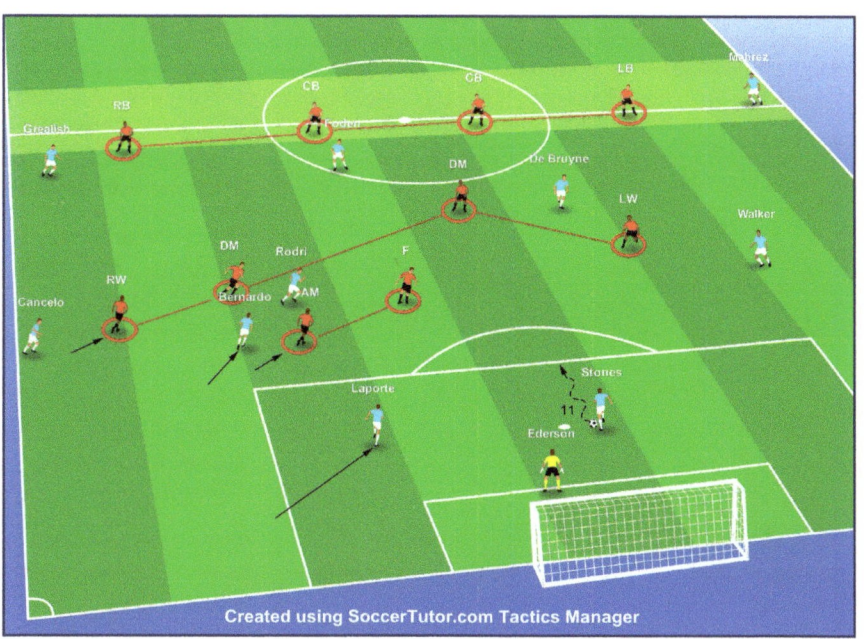

The quick movement of the ball forced Manchester United to move their defensive block deeper.

Stones moves forward with the ball as Manchester City now aim to initiate their build up play higher up the pitch.

Patient Build Up and Possession Against High Pressing

9/19. Creating a 2v1 Numerical Advantage vs Opposing Forward

Manchester United are now deeper and more compact.

The left centre back (**Laporte**) moved back into the centre as the right centre back (**Stones**) moved forward with the ball.

City have a 2v1 advantage against the United forward (F) in the centre of the pitch, which they aim to exploit.

10/19. Centre Back Moving to the Side to Receive in Space

Laporte shifts across to the left away from the ball.

Stones passes to him so he can receive with time on the ball.

Patient Build Up and Possession Against High Pressing

11/19. Centre Back's Pass to Left Back (Numerical Equality Around Ball)

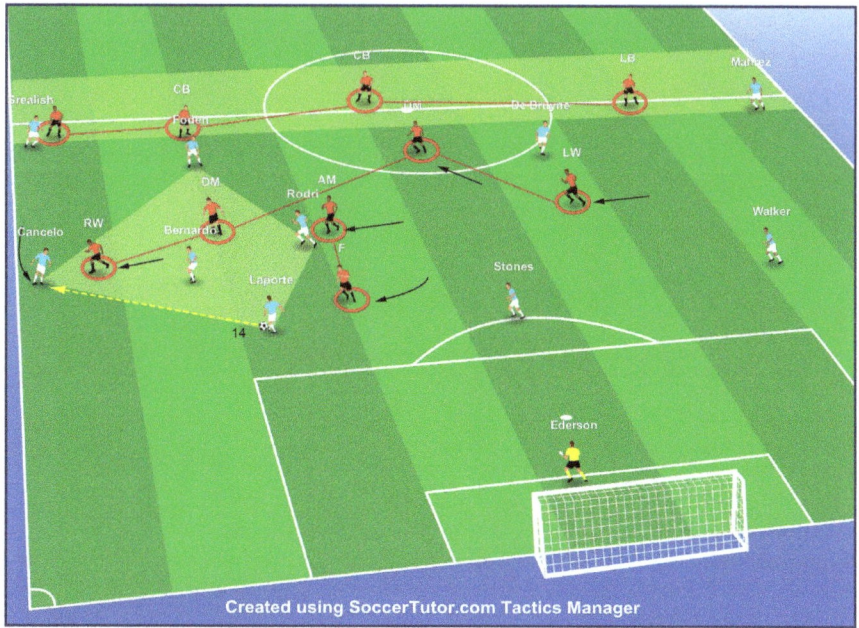

Laporte passes to the left back (**Cancelo**) but there is a numerical equality on that side with each player marked.

This situation is much more effective for dribbling than for trying to play in behind United's pressure lines, but **Cancelo** decides to take the easiest option and retain possession (next diagram).

12/19. Left Back's Pass Back to Centre Back (No Forward Options)

Cancelo can see teammates on the inside but they are all marked.

Cancelo therefore decides to play back to the centre back (**Laporte**).

Manchester City can again reset the play and circulate the ball to the other side of the pitch to disrupt United's defensive structure.

Patient Build Up and Possession Against High Pressing

13/19. Left Centre Back's Pass Back to the Goalkeeper (Reset)

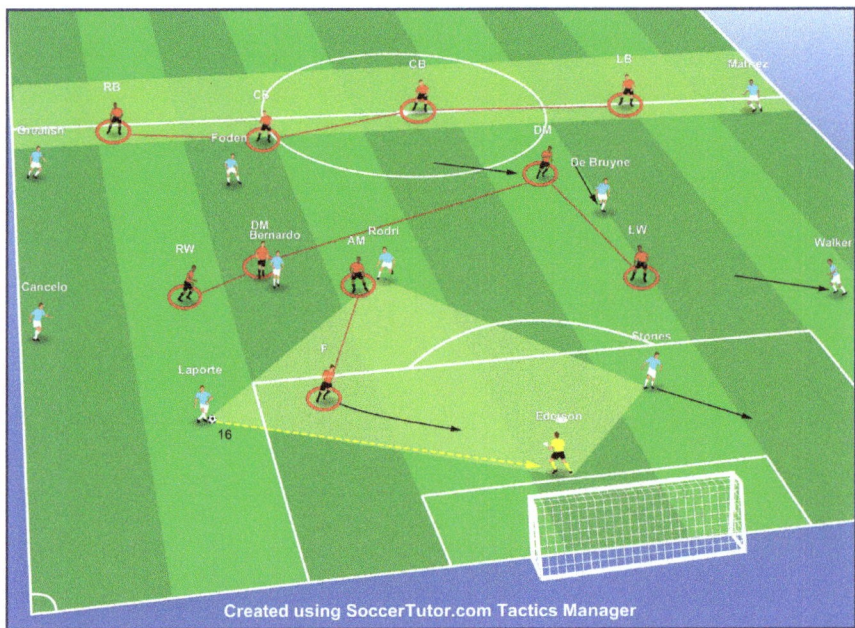

Laporte passes back to the GK (**Ederson**). United's defensive shape changes as they move forward, with the forward (F) leading the press (on the GK).

The right centre back (**Stones**) and right back (**Walker**) shift wide to provide passing options. **De Bruyne** (attacking midfielder) drops back to provide support.

14/19. GK's Pass to Right Centre Back (Build Up on Right Side)

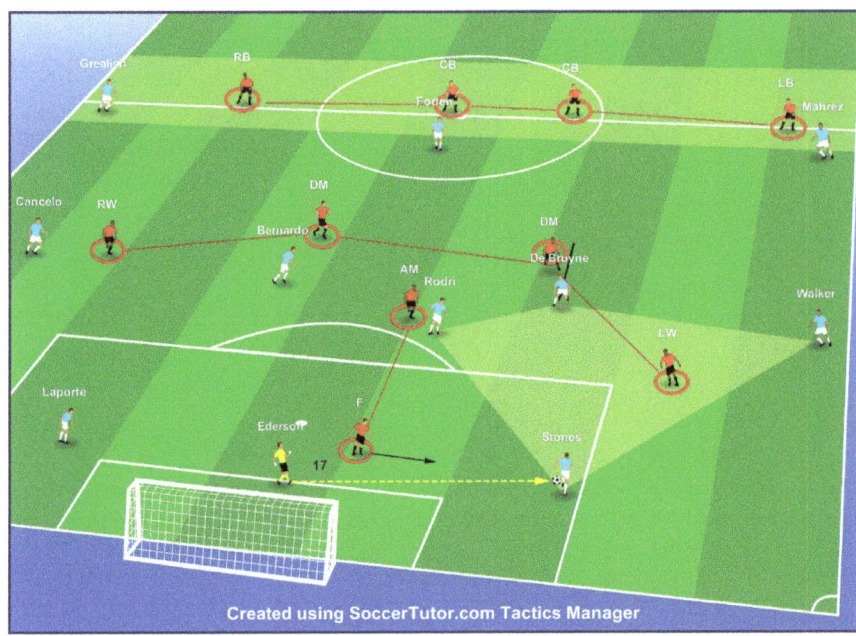

With the forward's (F), **Ederson** passes to **Stones**, who had quickly positioned himself well to the right side of the goalkeeper.

Stones, taking advantage of **De Bruyne's** movement, attracts the attention of the left winger (LW), and has the aim of moving the ball to the right back (**Walker**), who is unmarked in space.

Patient Build Up and Possession Against High Pressing

15/19. Centre Back to Right Back via the Att. Midfielder (Link Player)

The aim from this point is to move the ball to the right back (**Walker**), who is free and available in space behind United's left winger (LW).

Stones makes a good decision to use the attacking midfielder (**De Bruyne**) as a link player. He passes to him, and he passes wide to the unmarked **Walker** behind the line of pressure.

16/19. Opposition Recover Well and Block Passing Options

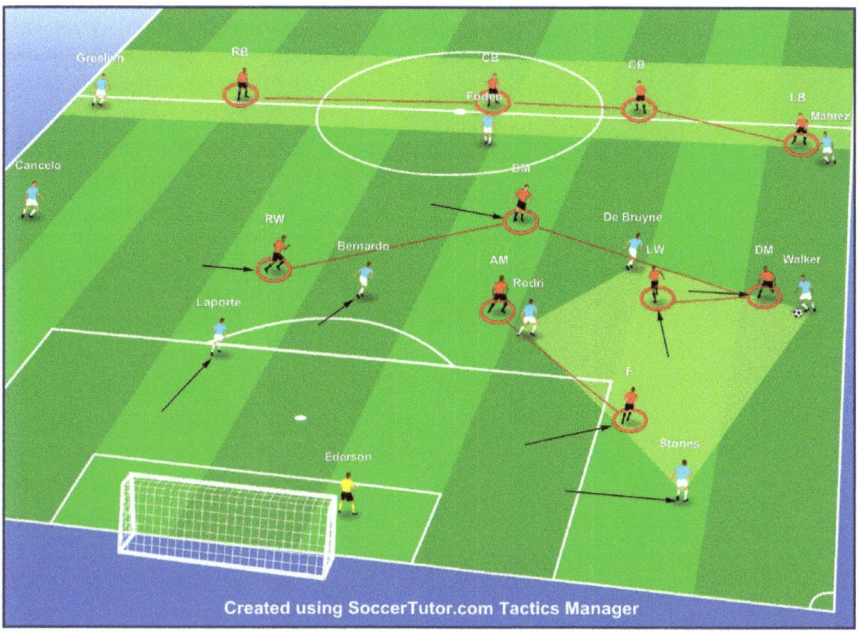

Manchester United defended this situation well. The defensive midfielder (DM) closed down **Walker** quickly and the left winger (LW) tracked the run of **De Bruyne**.

Again, like previously, **Walker** preferred not to force the play. However, this time he did not have the support of **Stones**, who is marked by the forward (F).

Patient Build Up and Possession Against High Pressing

17/19. Drive Inside and Pass into Centre to Start Switch of Play

The right back (**Walker**) used his speed and strength to evade his opponent and carry the ball inside, before passing in between 2 opponents to the left centre back (**Laporte**).

By doing this, **Walker** created a new rhombus shape with himself, the 2 centre backs, and the goalkeeper.

18/19. Centre Back's Pass to Left Back to Bypass 2 Lines of Pressure

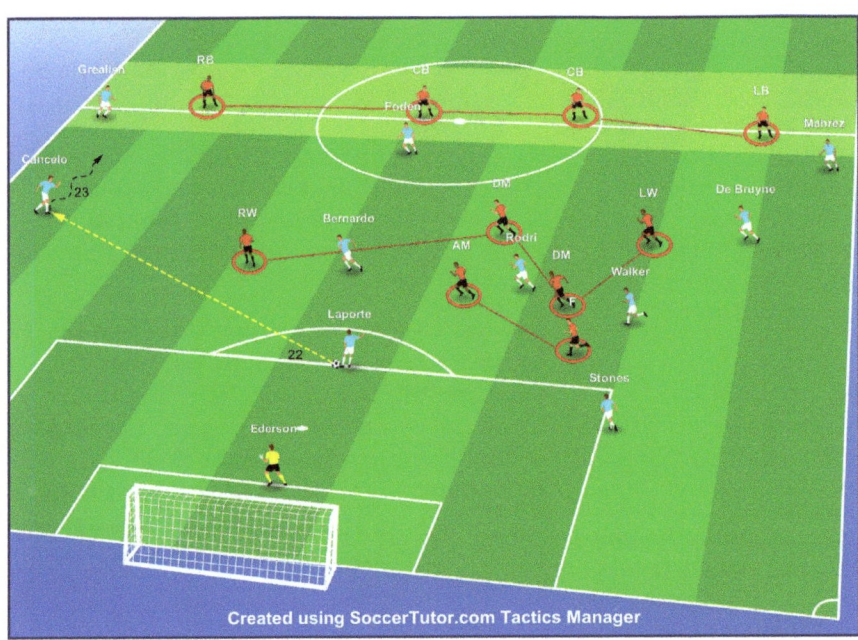

Laporte receives on the edge of the box and quickly plays a firm accurate pass out to the left back (**Cancelo**), who was in an advanced wide position beyond the opposition's midfield line.

Cancelo was able to drive forward with the ball.

Patient Build Up and Possession Against High Pressing

19/19. Long Switch of Play to Winger After Opposition Reorganise

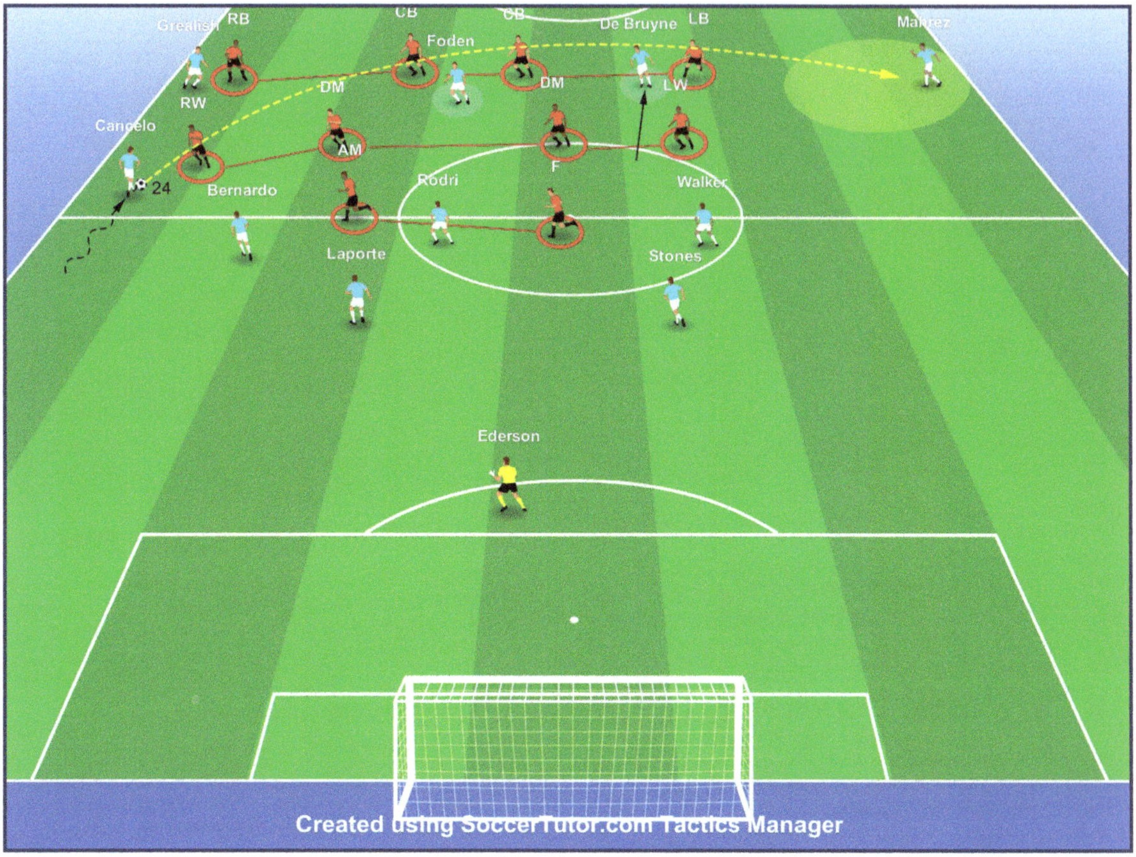

In this situation, Manchester United were quick to organise themselves into a structured 4-4-2 defensive shape. However, they had been **forced back deep into their own half**, which presents opportunities for Manchester City.

With the ball on the left side, the forward (**Foden**) and the attacking midfielder (**De Bruyne**) positioned alongside him, the United left back is forced to be positioned towards the centre.

From this point, the **aim is to move the ball to the right winger (Mahrez), who is free in space** on the right flank and has great dribbling, crossing, and finishing ability to finish the attack.

As shown in the diagram, in this example, the left back (**Cancelo**) plays an accurate long switch of play pass, and **Mahrez** is able to receive and enter the final stage of attack.

Key Point: This shows just one example of how effective this tactic has been for Manchester City under Pep Guardiola. Their patient passing, tight positioning, and adaptable roles disrupt their opponents' defensive shape, bypassing high pressing and enabling precise ball progression to attack with success.

Patient Build Up and Possession Against High Pressing

Passing Options for the Full Back in Possession

1. Effective Ball Circulation Options for the Full Back in Possession

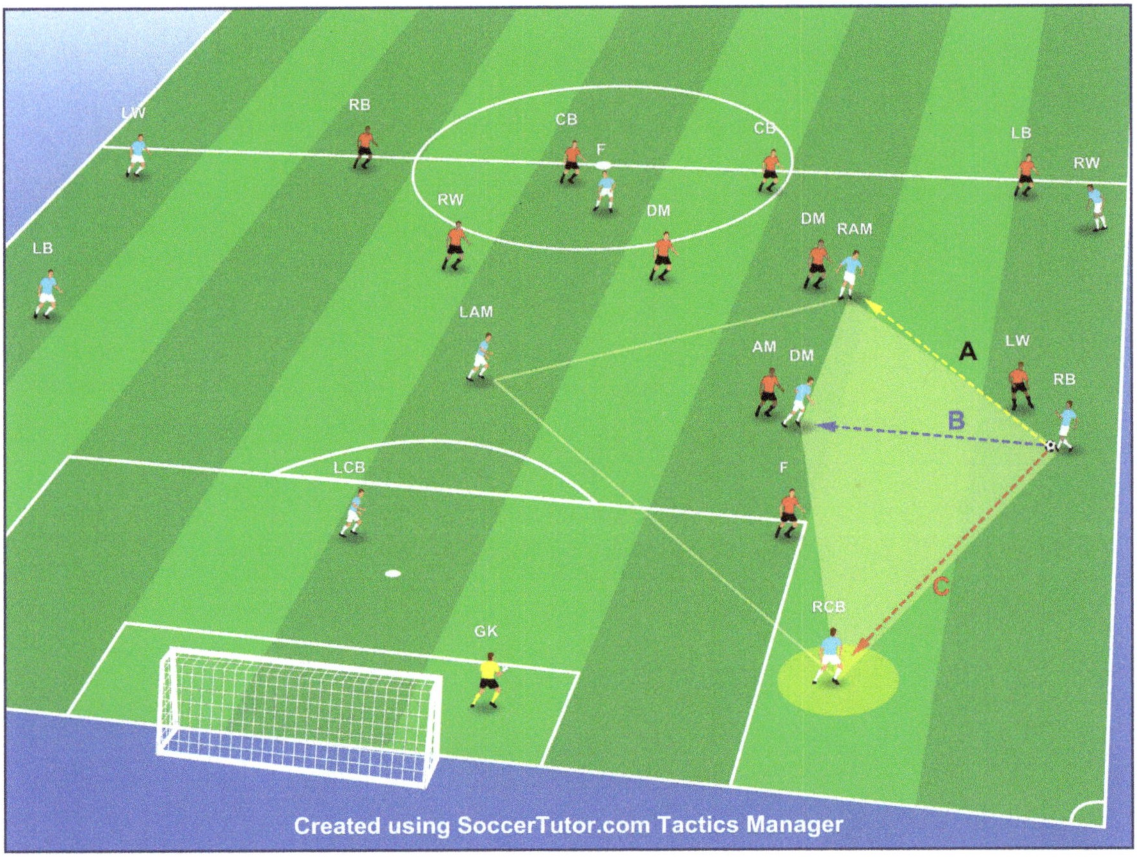

To maintain possession and circulate the ball across the pitch, it is vital to occupy space effectively and use intelligent decision making.

In this example from Manchester City's 4-1 Premier League win against Manchester United (6th March 2022), it is evident that the full back must have at least 3 passing options.

As shown, the ball carrier (**RB**) is aiming to switch play to the opposite side and has 3 alternatives at varying heights of the pitch:

Option A: Attacking Midfielder (**RAM**).

Option B: Defensive Midfielder (**DM**).

Option C: Centre Back (**RCB**).

If the defending players are positioned as shown, with the opposing forward (F) near the edge of the box, the **most effective pass to bypass pressure and develop play towards the weak side is to RCB.**

Patient Build Up and Possession Against High Pressing

2. Full Back Evades Pressing Winger Before Passing

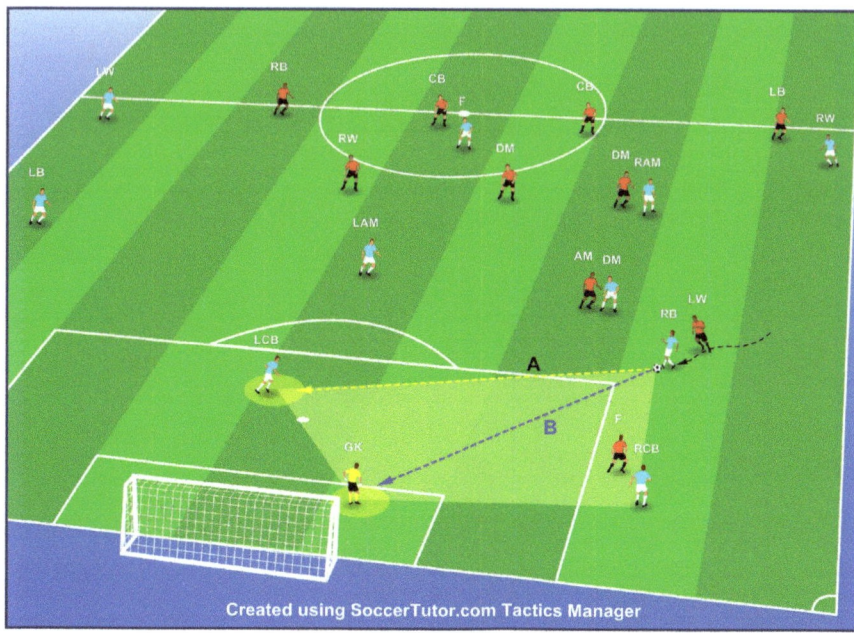

In this variation of the previous example, the opposing left winger (LW) pressed the Manchester City right back (**RB**) and closed off all passing options.

RB recognises the situation and adjusts by driving inside before passing back to **LCB** (**Option A**) or the **GK** (**Option B**).

3. Full Back Plays Around Pressing Forward

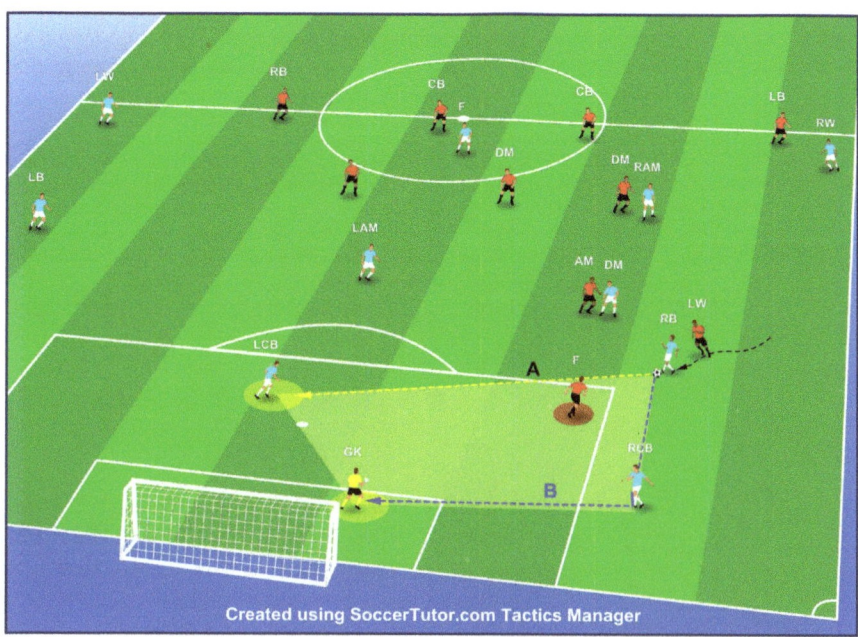

In another variation, if the opposing forward (**F**) applies pressure, the pass back to the **GK** is blocked, but **RB** can play around them.

Option A to **LCB** remains the same.

However, to move the ball to the **GK** (**Option B**), the right centre back (**RCB**) must be utilised as a link player.

Patient Build Up and Possession Against High Pressing

4. Navigating High Pressure Through Link Players

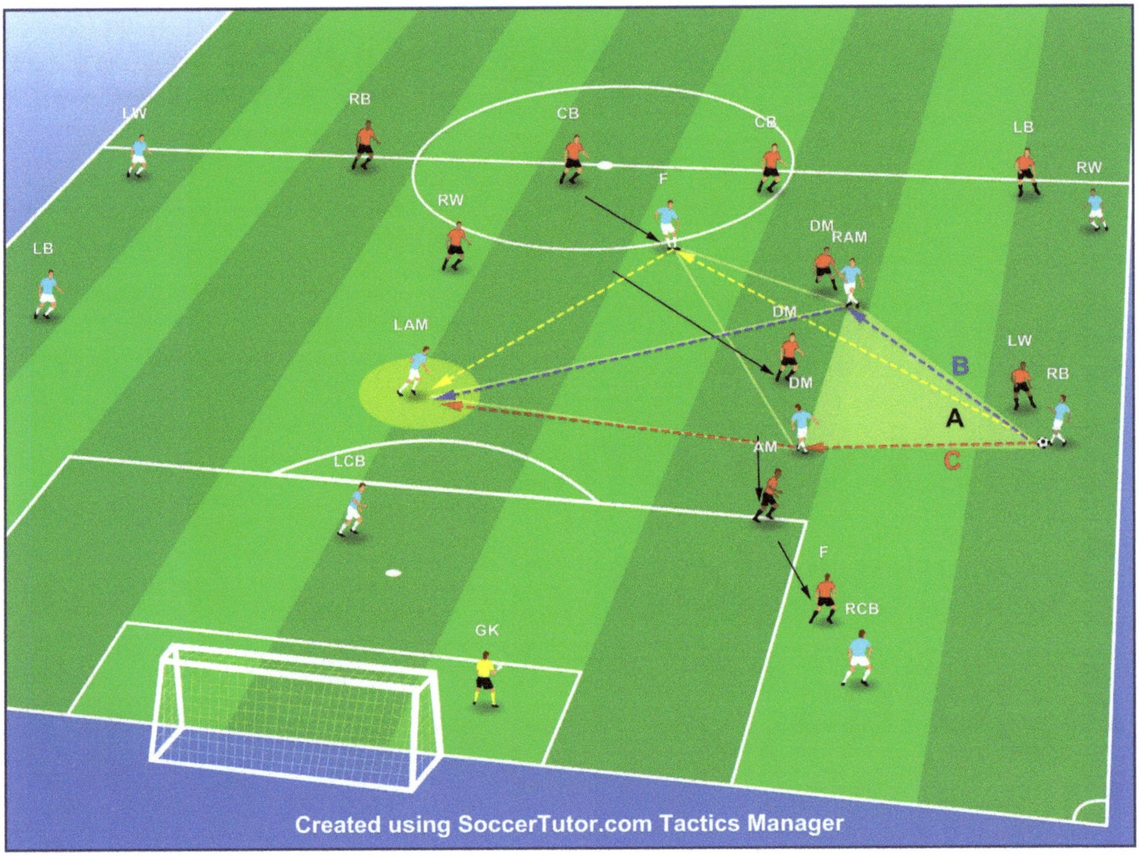

In the final variation, we show a less common reaction from the opposition, who push forward here with ultra-aggressive pressing. This cuts off passing options in the deeper areas of the pitch (as shown in the previous examples), so the full back in possession (right back - **RB**) must demonstrate awareness and composure.

To overcome this pressure, it is **essential to utilise a link player**.

By activating these players, **RB** can direct the ball to a teammate who is free in space (attacking midfielder - **LAM** in diagram example). This neutralises the immediate threat and creates opportunities to exploit spaces left by advancing opponents.

Option A shows a line breaking pass to the forward (**F**) between the lines, as he drops back to receive before passing to **LAM**, which opens up the other side of the pitch.

Option B shows a pass to the attacking midfielder (**RAM**), who acts as a link player to move the ball to **LAM**.

Option C shows the defensive midfielder (**DM**) acting as the link player to move the ball to **LAM**.

Key Point: Manchester City's approach requires precise execution, strong positional awareness, and effective coordination between teammates to maintain control and progress the play.

SESSION BASED ON THE TACTICS OF PEP GUARDIOLA

Patient Build Up and Possession Against High Pressing

Session for PEP GUARDIOLA Tactics - Patient Build Up and Possession Against High Pressing

SESSION FOR THIS TACTICAL SITUATION (2 PRACTICES)

1. Position Specific Patient Build Up and Possession Technical Passing Circuit

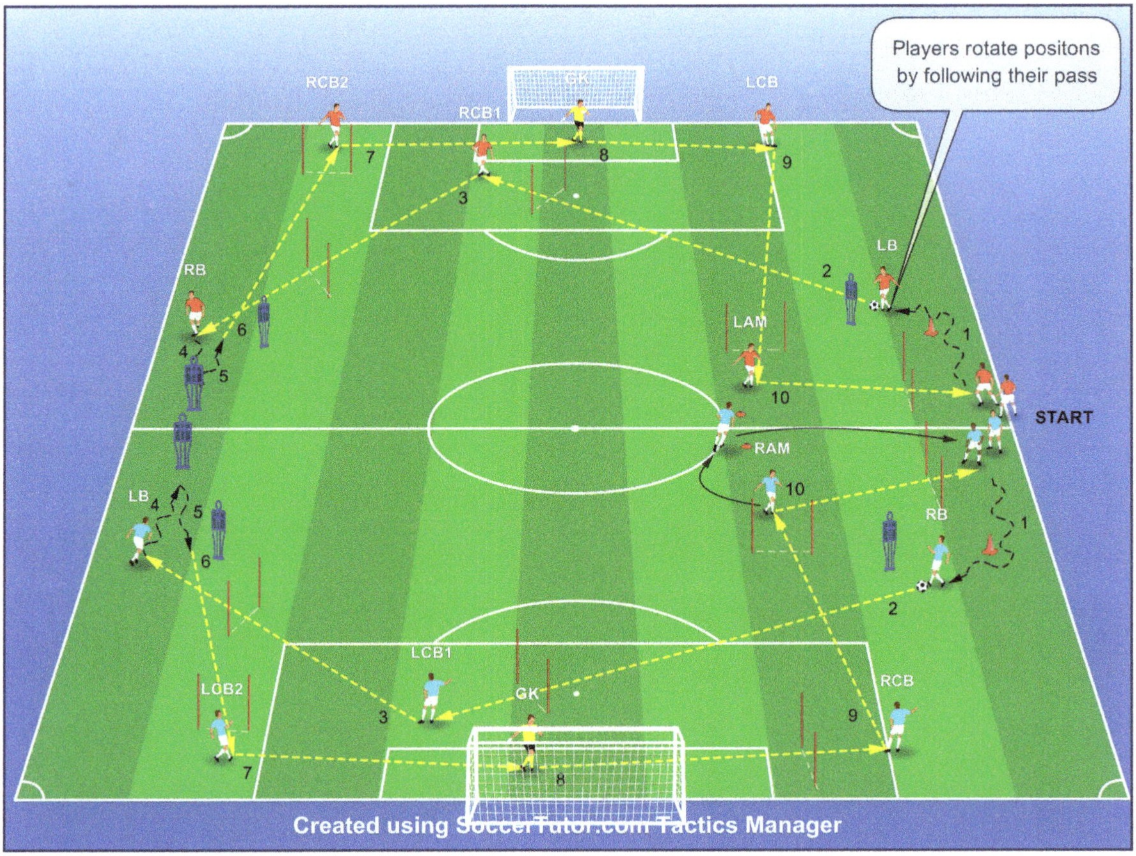

Practice Description

Players are split into groups and follow their pass to rotate positions (except **GK**). This description follows the blue players passing through pole gates.

1-2. The right back (**RB**) dribbles inside and passes to the left centre back (**LCB1**).

3-6. **LCB1** plays a diagonal pass to the left back (**LB**), who dribbles forward to the mannequin, turns back, and then passes to the other left centre back (**LCB2**).

7-8. **LCB2** passes to the **GK**, who passes to the right centre back (**RCB**).

9-10. **RCB** passes forward to the attacking midfielder (**RAM**), who passes to the start for the next player waiting.

Coaching Points

1. Sharp and quick passes to simulate match intensity.
2. Accurate first touches to best set up the next action.
3. Correct body shape and positioning to optimise movement and passing angles.
4. Controlled dribbling with ball close to the feet.

Session for PEP GUARDIOLA Tactics - Patient Build Up and Possession Against High Pressing

PROGRESSION
2. Patient Build Up and Possession Against High Press Positional Two Phase Game

Phase 1/2: Positional Possession Game Switching Side to Side

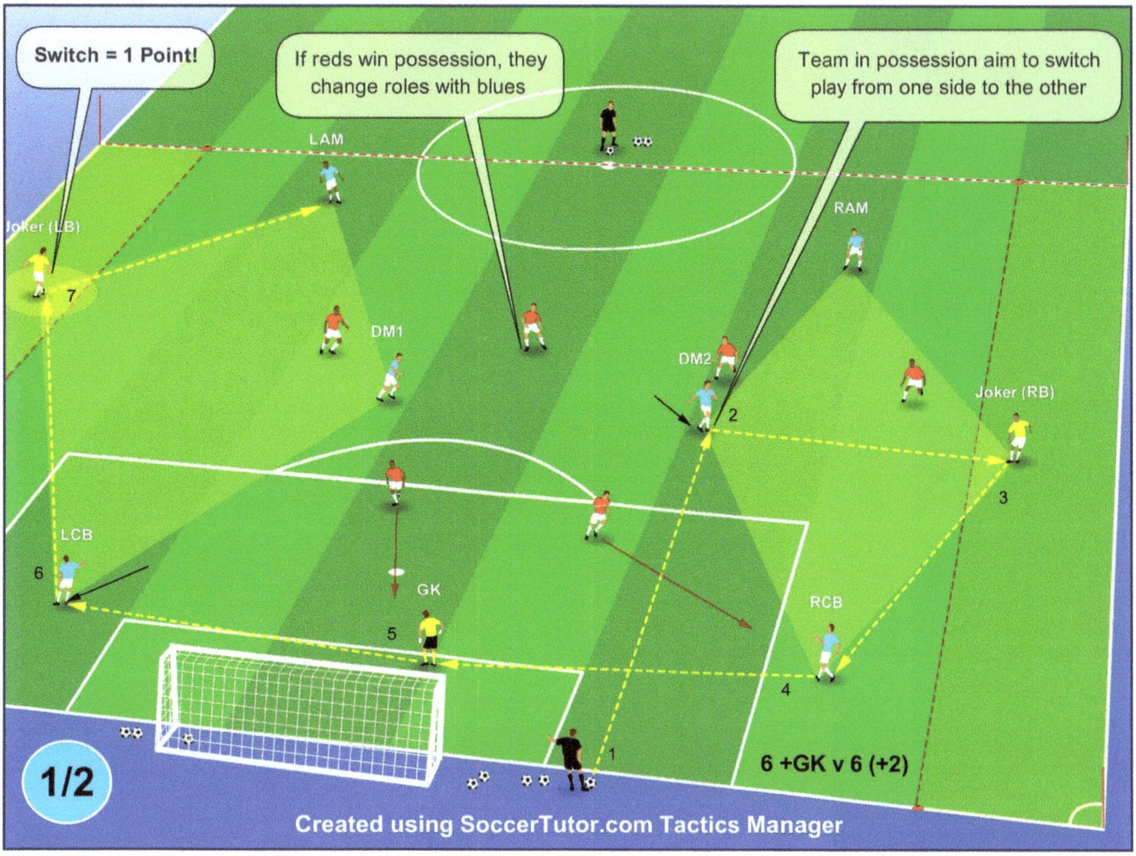

Switch = 1 Point!

If reds win possession, they change roles with blues

Team in possession aim to switch play from one side to the other

6 +GK v 6 (+2)

Note: There are 2 defensive midfielders (1 extra) for this practice.

Practice Description (Phase 1)

- The first phase is a 6 +GK v 6 (+2) positional game.
- The **possession team (blues) form 2 rhombuses**, 1 on each side, which are only connected by the goalkeeper (**GK**).
- The Jokers (**J**) act as full backs for the team in possession.

- **Blue Objective:** Circulate ball from one side of pitch to the other (1 Point).
- **Red Objective:** Win the ball and then maintain possession with the support of the Jokers + GK.
- On the coach's whistle, the practice moves into Phase 2 (see the next page).

Session for **PEP GUARDIOLA Tactics** - **Patient Build Up and Possession Against High Pressing**

Phase 2/2: Possession/Attack vs Defence/Counter Attack

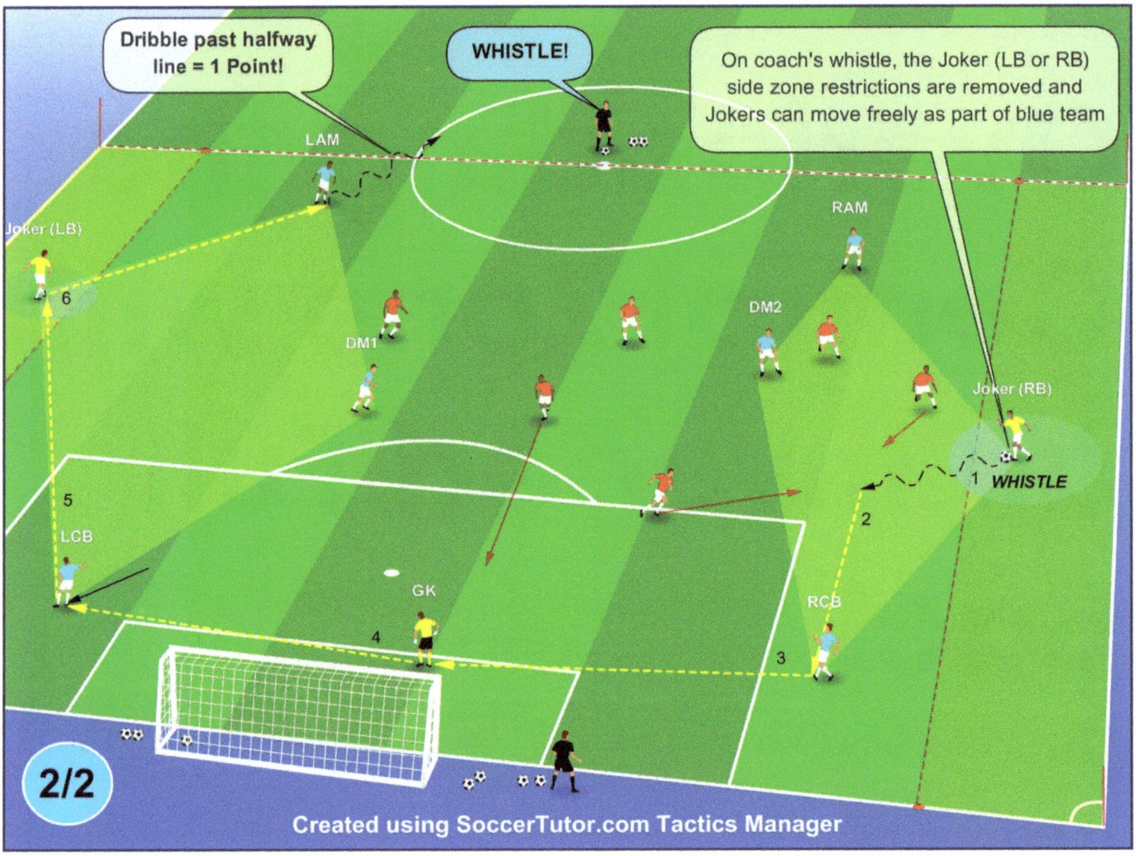

Diagram annotations:
- Dribble past halfway line = 1 Point!
- WHISTLE!
- On coach's whistle, the Joker (LB or RB) side zone restrictions are removed and Jokers can move freely as part of blue team

Note: There are 2 defensive midfielders (1 extra) for this practice.

Practice Description (Phase 2)

- On the coach's whistle, the positional game moves into Phase 2 and changes to an attack vs defence situation.

- The side zone restrictions are removed and the Jokers (both full backs) join the blue team to create an 8 +GK v 6 situation.

- **Blue Objective:** Circulate ball from one side of pitch to the other (1 Point). After a set amount of switches, an additional point can be scored by dribbling past the halfway line (as shown in diagram).

- **Red Objective:** The 6 defenders work together in a compact formation to win the ball, and then launch a quick counter attack to try and score. (6 v 8 +GK).

- On the coach's whistle, the practice reverts back to the Phase 1 rules and objectives *(see previous page)*.

Coaching Points

1. Quality in ball circulation (passing, receiving, body shape, and dribbling).
2. Make effective intelligent decisions under pressure.
3. Ensure proper positioning and spacing on the pitch.

Overloading the Central Zone with an Inverted Full Back

Overloading the Central Zone with an Inverted Full Back

Tactical Solutions for Possession Play Against a Mid-Block

In this section of the book, we now move into the **middle third of the pitch, a crucial area where tactical battles often dictate the flow of the game**. Pep Guardiola's Manchester City team demonstrate the ability to either:

1. Force the opposition to retreat through precise ball circulation.
2. Engage opposition who are strategically positioned across the middle of the pitch.

Regardless of how the tactical situation develops, this section examines the principles and strategies Manchester City use against a mid-block press.

One of the most fascinating aspects of Guardiola's approach is the **fluidity with which his players adapt their positioning in response to the opponent's setup**. This flexibility serves a critical purpose to **push the opposition further back into their defensive third, gaining more control and creating opportunities to exploit space**.

Central to achieving this goal is Manchester City's ability to manage the possession phase. Through precise ball control and passing, the team is able to **shift between systems seamlessly, surround the opposition**, and **neutralise any counter-pressing attempts**. This patient, controlled approach forms the backbone of their tactics in this area of the pitch.

However, Guardiola's strategy is not limited to circulating the ball around the perimeter. **When gaps appear in their opponents' defensive organisation, Manchester City quickly exploit them by launching attacks directly from the middle third**.

These attacks can take shape through the middle using quick passing combinations, or more commonly through the flanks, where **Manchester City excel at creating overloads and breaking through the defensive block**.

In the pages to follow, we will explore these approaches in detail, uncovering how City's adaptability and precision consistently unsettle their opponents and help them to gain complete control of their matches.

Overloading the Central Zone with an Inverted Full Back

Overloading the Central Zone by Changing the Team Shape

1. Outnumbered (6v8) on Side of Pitch with 4-3-3 Shape

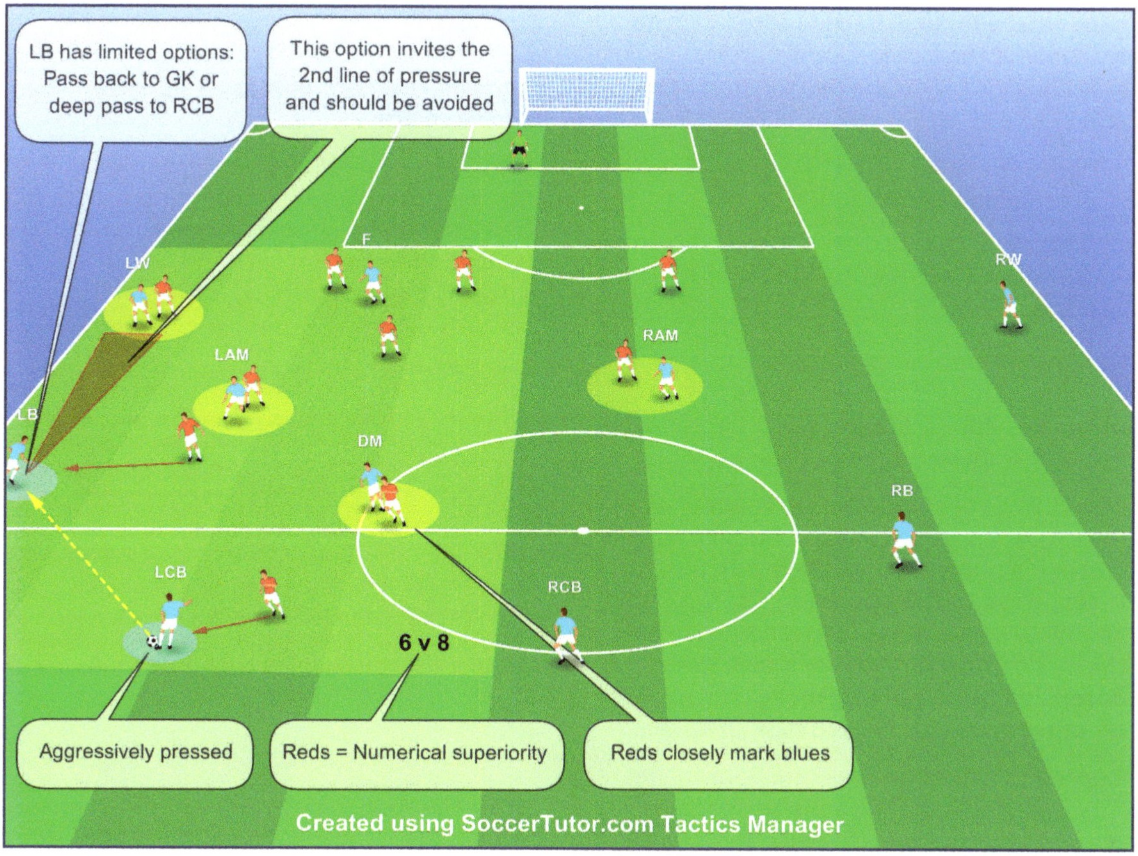

Manchester City's 4-3-3 formation can favour the opponent's pressing, as shown in the diagram.

In this example, we show the 4-3-3 against a 4-4-1-1 press (red opposing team).

The opposing forward presses the left centre back (**LCB**), which forces a pass out wide to the left back (**LB**). This triggers tight marking of Manchester City's players on that side and the opposition have a numerical advantage (6v8).

As the opponents have established a numerical superiority in the highlighted area, ball retention is difficult.

With the pass to the forward (**F**) blocked, Manchester City have 2 Options:

1. **Long pass back to the goalkeeper**.
2. **Switch of play pass to right back (RB)**.

Key Point: This example highlights the need for dynamic positioning to create passing options and bypass pressing lines.

Overloading the Central Zone with an Inverted Full Back

2. Positional Adjustments from 4-3-3 to 3-2-4-1 (Create Overloads)

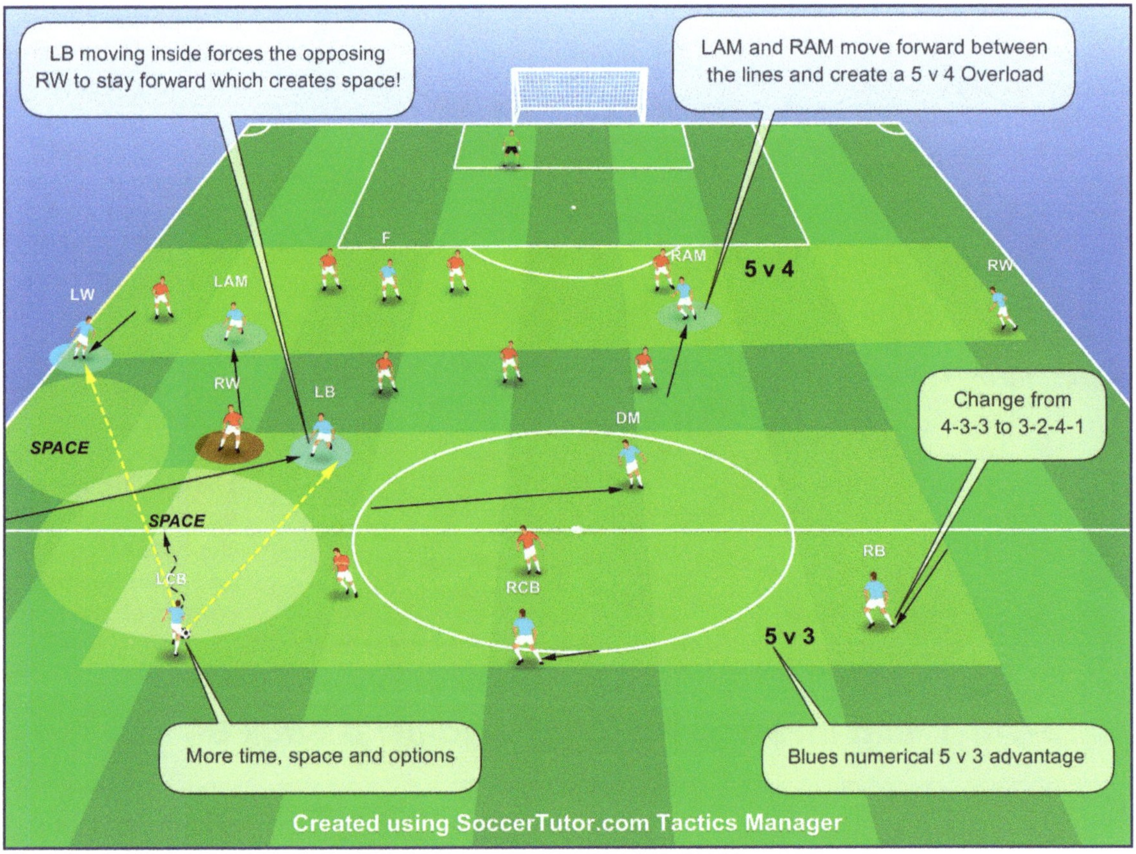

Passing to a wide player positioned deeper than the opposition's second line of pressure often invites pressing and should generally be avoided, unless done to shift the opposition to one side and exploit space on the opposite side.

Manchester City shift from 4-3-3 to 3-2-4-1 by inverting the left back (LB) into midfield and pushing the attacking midfielders (LAM and RAM) in between the lines. This creates a 5v3 advantage in the central zone and 5v4 in the high zone, **preventing the opposition's midfield and defensive lines from pushing up to apply pressure**.

This structure provides **numerical superiority** and helps **maintain control**, enabling **smooth ball circulation** and **progress into open areas**.

The opposing winger (RW) stays high to cover **LB**, opening up space for the Manchester City winger (**LW**) to receive.

LAM and **RAM's** advanced positions cause problems for the opposition's defensive line. If the red full back moves to cover **LW**, **LAM** can exploit the space in behind, while the red centre back has to be aware of both **LAM** and the forward (**F**).

Key Point: Adjusting from 4-3-3 to 3-2-4-1 creates central and high zone overloads that prevent opposition pressure and open spaces for attacking progress.

Overloading the Central Zone with an Inverted Full Back

3a. 3-2-4-1 with Inverted Full Back Against a Back 4

Passing options in a 3-2-4-1 shape

The centre back (**LCB**) in possession is supported by 3 teammates: The left winger (**LW**) between the lines, the inverted left back (**LB**), and the other centre back (**RCB**).

This forces the red back 4 into difficult defensive decisions and City's **positioning creates openings to bypass the defensive line and maintain control of the ball**.

3b. 3-2-4-1 with Inverted Full Back Against a Back 5

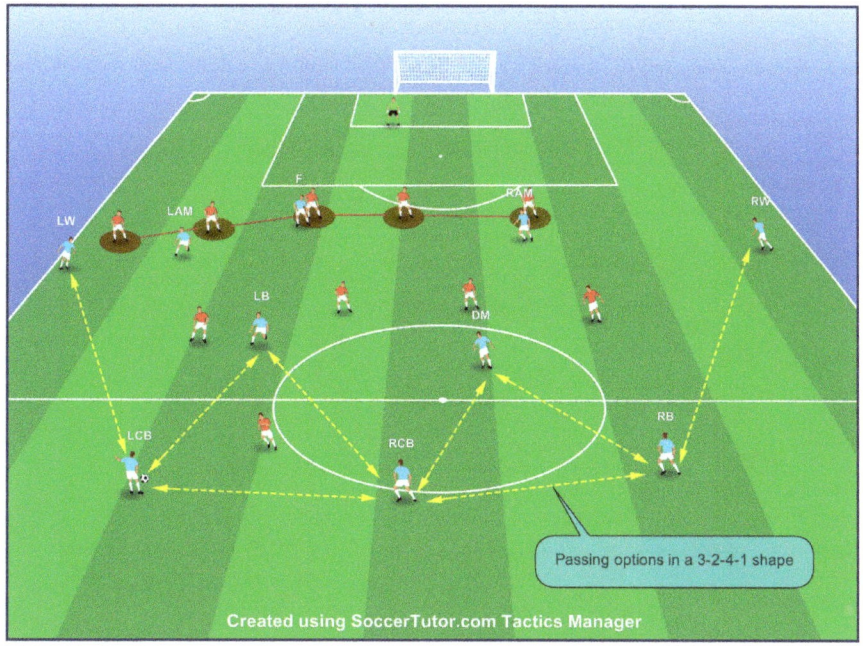

Passing options in a 3-2-4-1 shape

With 5 players on the perimeter (**LW, LCB, RCB, RB, RW**), 2 central midfielders (**LB & DM**), and 3 positioned between the lines (**LAM, RAM, F**), City can move the ball efficiently against a back 5.

Numerical and positional superiority is secured, allowing them to exploit gaps and circulate the ball effectively.

SESSION BASED ON THE TACTICS OF PEP GUARDIOLA

Overloading the Central Zone with an Inverted Full Back

Session for PEP GUARDIOLA Tactics - Overloading the Central Zone with an Inverted Full Back

SESSION FOR THIS TACTICAL SITUATION (4 PRACTICES)

1. Position Specific Technical Passing in the Central Zone with an Inverted Full Back

Quality is key! Focus on weight of pass, speed, body shape, control, and timing of movement!

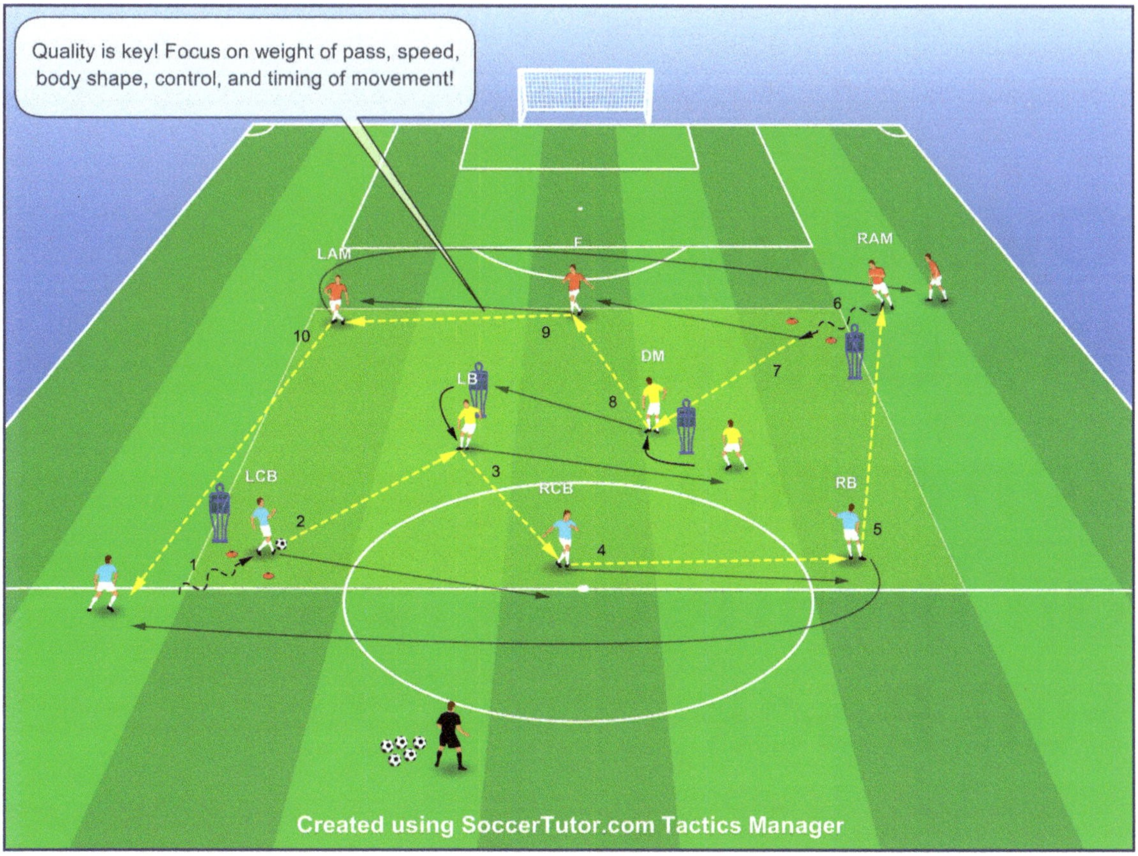

Practice Description

- We have 4 blue players, 3 yellows, and 4 reds in a 3-2-2-1 shape from Manchester City's 3-2-4-1 possession phase shape (wingers not included).
- The passing sequence for the blues and reds is mirrored, both combining with the yellow players in the centre.
- All players rotate within their groups.
- Practice in both directions and once the players are comfortable, play with 2 balls simultaneously from **LCB** and **RAM**.

Passing Sequence

1-2. The left centre back (**LCB**) dribbles through the cone gate and passes to the inverted left back (**LB**) in a central midfield position.

3-4. **LB** passes back to the other centre back (**RCB**), who passes across to the right back (**RB**).

5. **RB** passes forward to the right attacking midfielder (**RAM**).

6-10. **RAM** → **DM** → **F** → **LAM** → **LCB**.

PEP GUARDIOLA - COACHING FLUID POSITIONAL ROTATIONS

Session for **PEP GUARDIOLA Tactics** - Overloading the Central Zone with an Inverted Full Back

PROGRESSION

2. **Positional Possession in the Central Zone Combined Two Phase Practice**

Phase 1/2: Technical Passing Sequence

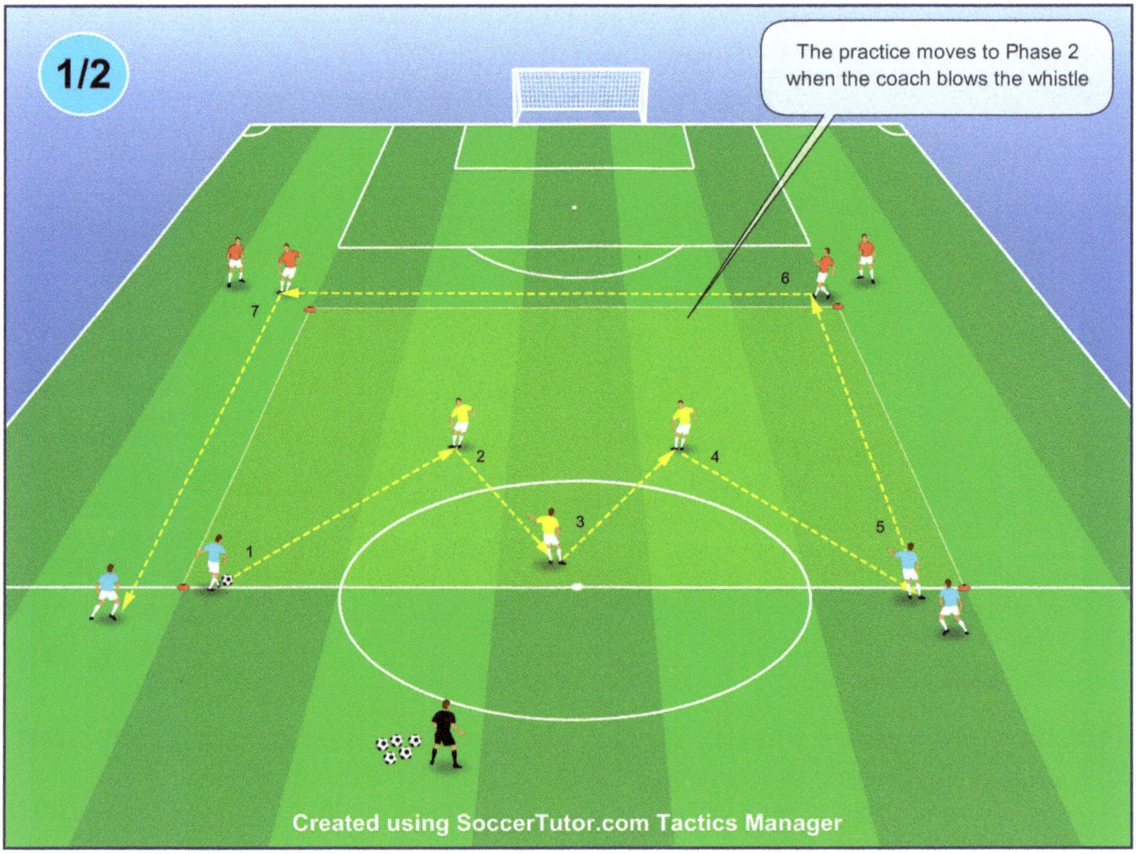

The practice moves to Phase 2 when the coach blows the whistle

Practice Description (Phase 1)

- Combined practices integrate a specific technical-tactical phase with a positional game situation phase which trains key decision making under pressure.

- We play in the same size area with the same number of players as the previous practice in the session. **The sequence of passes is shown in the diagram** (**1-7**). The blue and red players take turns in each corner and **do not follow their passes**.

- On the coach's whistle, the practice progresses into a positional game with the players quickly repositioning themselves (see Phase 2 diagram and description on the next page).

Coaching Points

1. Maintain high ball speed throughout.
2. Focus on the correct body shape and receiving technique.

Session for PEP GUARDIOLA Tactics - Overloading the Central Zone with an Inverted Full Back

Phase 2/2: Positional Possession Game

Coach's Whistle
Blues quickly change to 3-2-2 shape (from 3-2-4-1) vs 4 red defenders

4 (+3) v 4

WHISTLE!

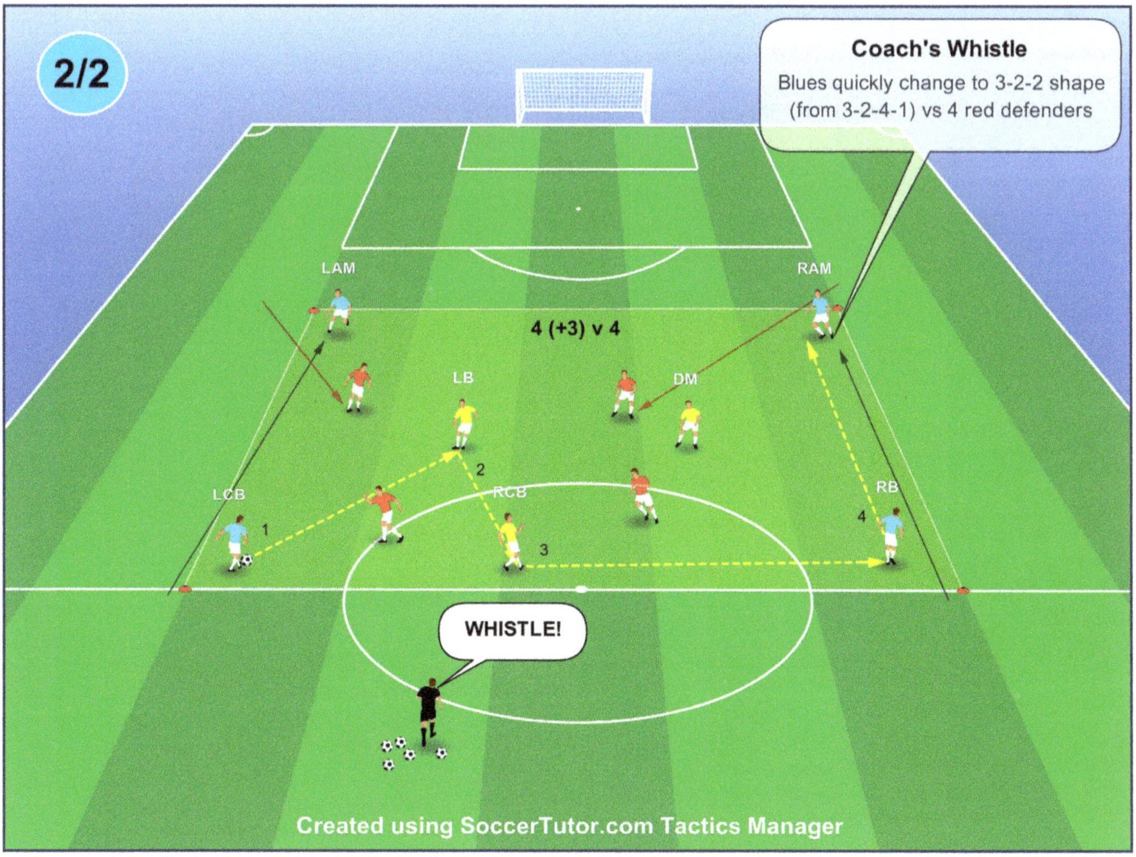

Practice Description (Phase 2)

- We follow on from Phase 1 (previous page) into Phase 2 with a 4 (+3) v 4 positional possession game
- On the coach's whistle, the blue and yellow players move into 3-2-2 from Manchester City's 3-2-4-1 possession phase shape (no wingers or forward). The reds form a 2-2 defensive shape.
- **Blue Objective:** Maintain possession with the 3 yellow Jokers and **complete a set amount of passes = 1 Point**. With a 7v4 numerical advantage, the possession team can consistently find passing options based on the defensive movements of their opponents.
- **Red Objective:** Win the ball and switch roles with the blue team.

Coaching Points

1. Ensure high quality ball circulation.
2. Occupy spaces effectively to create passing lanes, even by using subtle movements.
3. Effective decisions under pressure.
4. Execute key technical actions (passing, receiving, body shape, intercepting, and challenging) with precision.
5. Focus on developing technical-tactical relationships within the central structure, crucial for managing possession.

Session for **PEP GUARDIOLA Tactics** - Overloading the Central Zone with an Inverted Full Back

PROGRESSION

3. Switching Play with Inverted Full Back 6 (+3) v 6 Positional Possession Game

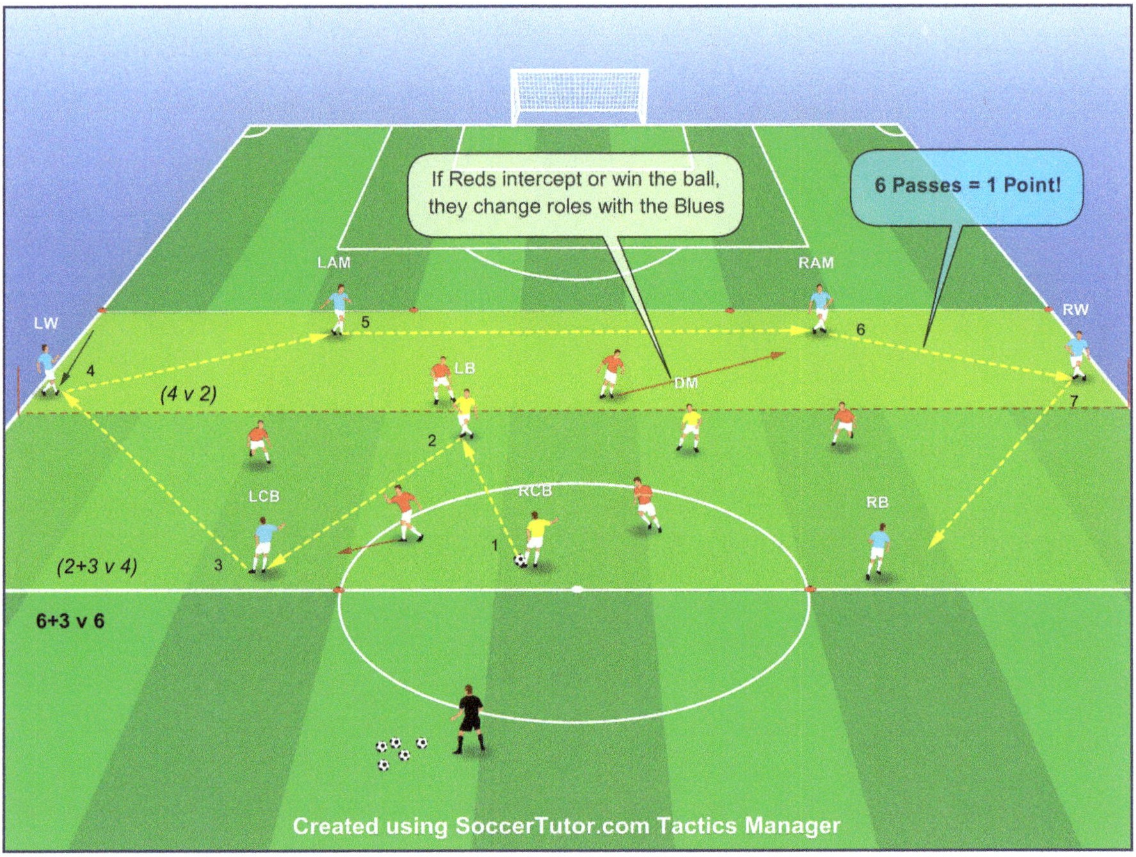

![Diagram showing the 6+3 v 6 positional possession setup with blue team in 3-2-4 shape (LCB, RCB, LB, DM, LAM, RAM, LW, RW) and red players, with notes: "If Reds intercept or win the ball, they change roles with the Blues" and "6 Passes = 1 Point!" — zones marked (4 v 2) and (2+3 v 4).]

Practice Description

- In this progression, 2 wingers/wide players are added for both teams.
- We have 6 blue players and 3 yellows using a 3-2-4 shape from Manchester City's 3-2-4-1 possession phase shape.
- The blue defence and midfield lines (3-2) are in the white zone with 4 red players. The 4 blue attacking players are in the smaller yellow zone with 2 red players.
- **Blue Objective:** Complete 6 consecutive passes = <u>1 Point</u>.
- **Red Objective:** Win the ball and change roles with the blue team.

Coaching Points

1. Maintain high quality ball circulation.
2. Occupy spaces effectively to create passing lanes with subtle movements.
3. Make intelligent and effective decisions under pressure.
4. Execute key technical actions (passing, receiving, body shape, intercepting, and challenging) with precision.

PROGRESSION

4. Positional Rotations in Possession Phase Against a Back 5 in a 9v5 Conditioned Game

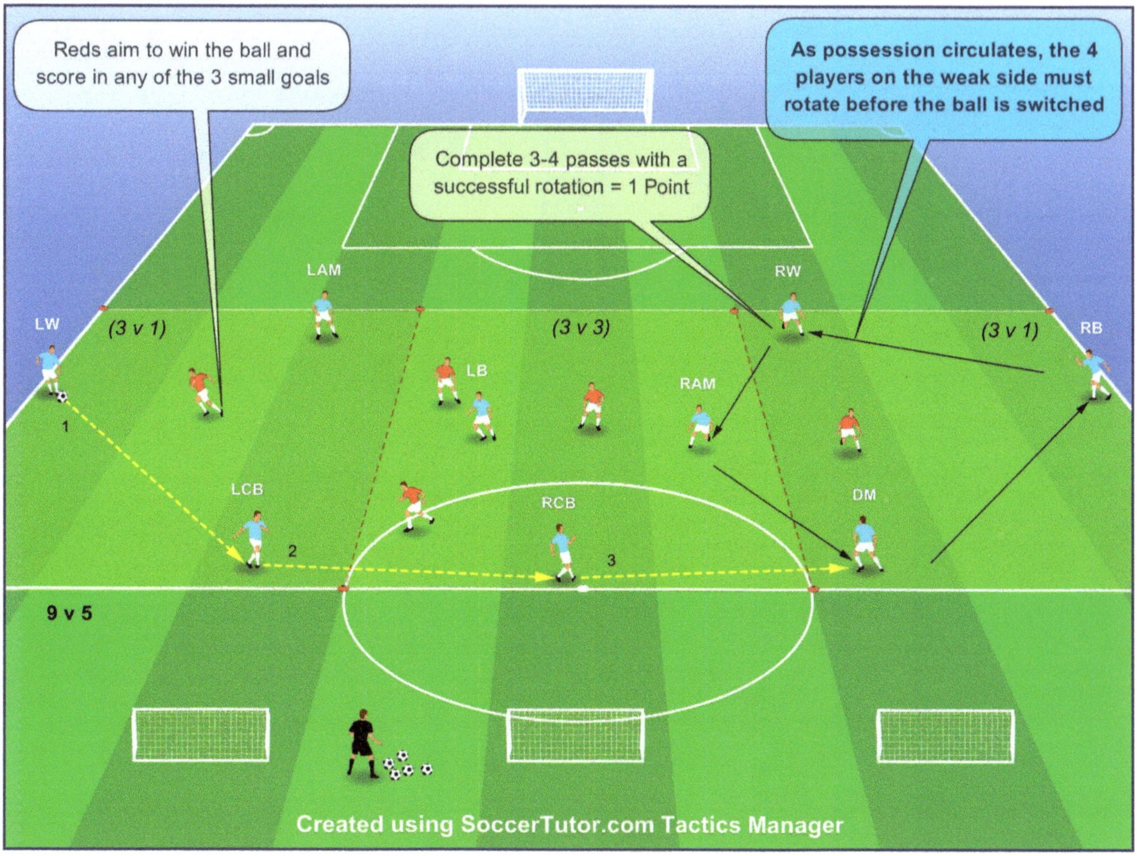

Reds aim to win the ball and score in any of the 3 small goals

Complete 3-4 passes with a successful rotation = 1 Point

As possession circulates, the 4 players on the weak side must rotate before the ball is switched

Practice Description

- This practice trains for situations when the opposition play with a back 5. They therefore only have 5 players left to contest possession in the middle third.

- **Key Point (vs Back 5):** Ball circulation is easier at the back, but finding spaces between the lines, in wide areas, or behind the defensive line becomes more challenging. The possession team must focus on positional rotations to avoid providing fixed reference points, particularly between the lines.

- **Blue Objective:** Complete 3-4 passes while the 4 players on the weak side make at least one full rotation, as shown.

- **Red Objective:** Win the ball and score in one of the 3 small goals (outside of playing area).

Coaching Points

1. Time off-the-ball movements (rotations) to provide support effectively.
2. Make strategic and effective game decisions.

Through Passes in Behind from the Middle Third

Through Passes in Behind from the Middle Third

For Pep Guardiola's team, progressing the ball all the way to the opposition's penalty box is not always a tactical necessity. When facing certain systems of play/formations, it is often more effective to attack the space in behind earlier rather than searching for tight spaces near the penalty area. This approach allows Manchester City to **exploit open spaces behind the defensive block before the opposition can fully organise their shape**, **creating opportunities for direct and decisive attacking actions**.

Manchester City's ability to adapt to different defensive formations, such as the 5-4-1, 5-3-2, 3-4-2-1, 4-4-1-1, and 4-3-3, highlights their tactical flexibility. These setups typically see opponents stationed deep in their defensive third, requiring Pep Guardiola's team to **bypass multiple lines of pressure with precision and speed**. Instead of engaging in prolonged build up play around the box, **City utilise early, targeted movements to catch the defence off guard**.

In such situations, the team relies heavily on the wingers, attacking midfielders, and the forward to penetrate defensive lines. The pace and explosiveness of players like **Gabriel Jesus** before and now **Haaland** are pivotal in **exploiting gaps and spaces left by the opposition**.

Additionally, the well timed runs of attacking midfielders like **De Bruyne** and **Gündoğan**, known for their sharp instincts and impeccable timing, add a dynamic edge to Manchester City's attack. These movements not only **stretch the defensive line** but also **create opportunities for overloads and quick interchanges in dangerous areas**.

The examples to follow in this section of the book show how Manchester City execute through passes in behind from the middle third of the pitch against various defensive setups.

Key Point: By combining tactical discipline with individual brilliance, Manchester City showcase their ability to adapt their strategy to the opposition's defensive structure while maintaining attacking fluidity and efficiency. This method remains a key element of Pep Guardiola's philosophy, enabling his team to consistently unlock defences and maintain their dominance in the final third.

Through Passes in Behind from the Middle Third

Through Passes for the Winger's Run in Behind

1. Centre Back's Through Pass for Winger's Run in Behind

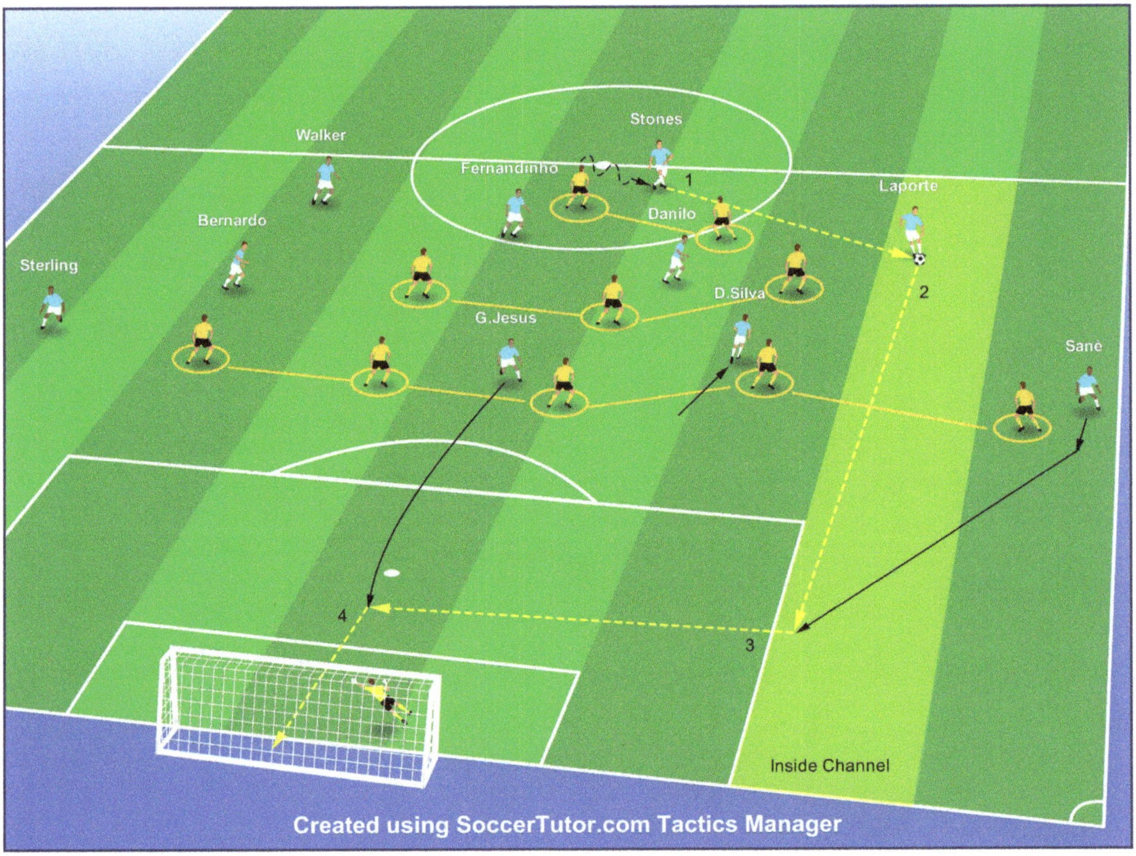

The example is from a 3-0 Premier League win against Wolverhampton Wanderers (14th January 2019). As Wolves used the 5-3-2, **City's 3-2-4-1 possession phase shape created a numerical advantage in the central zone**, so they looked to play in behind from the middle third.

The left back (**Danilo**) is inverted in a central midfield position to create a double pivot with the defensive midfielder (**Fernandinho**) and a 3+2 build up shape.

Right centre back (**Stones**) evades his direct opponent to play to the free left centre back (**Laporte**) in the inside channel.

The left attacking midfielder (**D. Silva**) dropped back to draw the attention of the Wolves right centre back, which created an opportunity for **Laporte** to play a deep precise pass for the run of right winger (**Sané**) from outside to in, to receive in behind. **Sané** passes the ball across the box for the forward (**G. Jesus**) to score.

Through Passes in Behind from the Middle Third

2. Full Back's Through Pass for Winger's Run in Behind (into Box)

The example is from a 5-0 Premier League win against Norwich City (21st August 2021). Norwich used a 5-4-1 formation and Pep Guardiola's team exploited space through a **quick calculated switch of play**.

Initially, Manchester City moved the ball from the left flank with left back (**Cancelo**), left winger (**Grealish**), and left attacking midfielder (**Palmer**) drawing Norwich's defensive focus. The ball was then quickly switched to the right via centre back (**Laporte**) and defensive midfielder (**Rodri**) to the right back (**Walker**).

When **Walker** received, the right attacking midfielder (**Bernardo**) moved closer, drawing the Norwich centre back with him.

This movement created space for **G. Jesus**, who was playing as a right winger in this match, to exploit behind.

Walker played an accurate through pass inside the Norwich left wing back, which was well-timed for the run of **G. Jesus** to receive in behind and inside the box.

G. Jesus passes the ball across the box for **Sterling** to score.

Note: *A similar goal was scored earlier in the match by* **Grealish**. *Pep Guardiola and Manchester City are experts in exploiting defensive imbalances through structured movement and incisive passing.*

Through Passes in Behind from the Middle Third

Through Passes for the Attacking Midfielder's Run in Behind

1. Winger Cuts Inside + Through Pass for Attacking Midfielder's Run

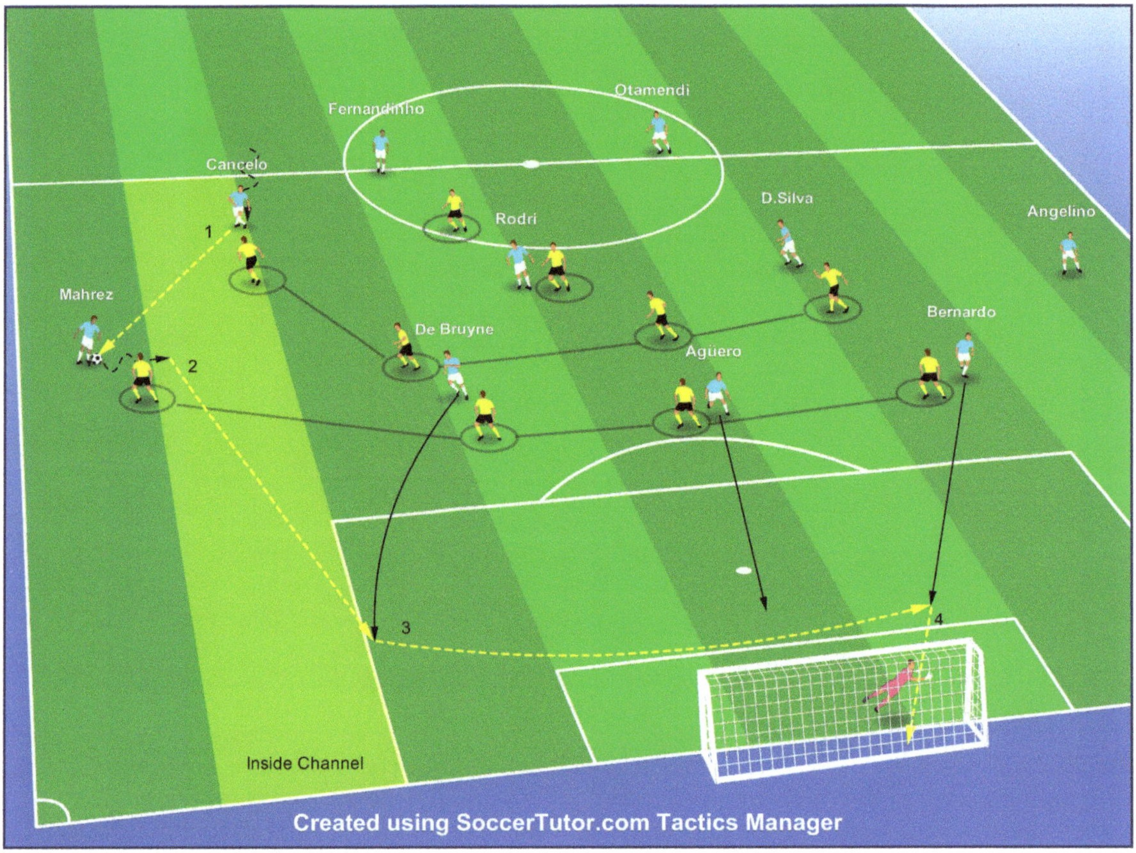

Manchester City often use attacking midfielders to make runs in behind, with their wingers generating space to play a penetrating through pass.

A great example of this came in an 8-0 Premier League win against Watford (21st September 2019), who used a 4-4-1-1. City used a 2-3-4-1 possession phase shape.

The right back (**Cancelo**), positioned centrally, drew in pressure and then passed wide to the right winger (**Mahrez**).

The right attacking midfielder (**De Bruyne**) made a run in behind while the left attacking midfielder (**Bernardo**) and the forward (**Agüero**) made runs into the box.

De Bruyne's perfectly timed run and low cross bypassed the defence, allowing **Bernardo** to score at the far post.

2. Full Back's Through Pass for Attacking Midfielder's Run in Behind

The second example of an attacking midfielder making a run in behind for a through pass from the middle third is from Manchester City's 4-0 Premier League win against Brighton (31st August 2019), who used a 3-4-2-1 formation.

Pep Guardiola's team used dynamic positioning to create goal scoring opportunities.

With the left winger (**Sterling**) in a central position, **Brighton's entire defensive organisation is within the width of the box, which leaves space wide**. This creates space for the left back's (**Zinchenko**) pass outside of Brighton's shape for the run of the left attacking midfielder (**D. Silva**).

After a quick ball circulation, the left centre back (**Laporte**) passed to **Zinchenko** in the inside channel, drawing pressure from the Brighton midfield. **Sterling** moved toward the ball, creating space behind him, while **D. Silva's** run exploited the situation.

D. Silva received the ball inside the box and cut it back for the right attacking midfielder (**De Bruyne**) to score.

Key Point: These examples show 2 of the many times Pep Guardiola's Manchester City team have shown their ability to exploit defensive structures with precise movements and coordination in this game situation (attacking midfielder in behind).

Through Passes in Behind from the Middle Third

Through Passes for the Forward's Run in Behind

Another effective method Manchester City used was to attack the space typically occupied by the forward.

This approach has been more effective since the arrival of **Haaland** in 2022. He has exceptional pace and intelligent movement, which allows him to **exploit the space in behind the defensive line**.

This example is from Manchester City's 3-1 Premier League win against Leeds United (28th December 2022), who used a 4-3-3. City used a 3-2-4-1 possession phase shape with **Haaland as the focal point**.

The left centre back (**Aké**) receives from his partner (**Akanji**) under minimal pressure, so is able to play forward. The left attacking midfielder (**Gündoğan**) pulled the opposing right centre back forward, which created space for **Haaland's** curved run in behind.

Haaland met **Aké's** precise pass on the edge of the box and attempted a first time finish. Though it didn't result in a goal (the goalkeeper saved), this perfectly highlights City's ability to exploit defensive gaps with precise passing and **Haaland's movement being a key tactic in Guardiola's system**.

SESSION BASED ON THE TACTICS OF PEP GUARDIOLA

Through Passes in Behind from the Middle Third

Session for PEP GUARDIOLA Tactics - Through Passes in Behind from the Middle Third

SESSION FOR THIS TACTICAL SITUATION (6 PRACTICES)

1. Through Passes for the Winger's Run in Behind Combination Play

Practice Description

- This practice has 2 groups of 10 players with 4 positional roles: 1 Full back (**RB**), 2 centre backs (**LCB** and **RCB**), 1 attacking midfielder (**LAM**) and 1 winger (**LW**).

- The sequences start simultaneously with **RB** receiving from the coach and passing back to **RCB**, who passes across to **LCB**.

- As **LCB** receives, **LAM** moves back and towards him, as if to draw an opponent away. At the same time, **LW** makes a run into the space in behind this movement (see page 122 for analysis).

- **LCB** plays a through pass in between the 2 mannequins. **LW** receives, dribbles forward, and moves to the start.

- Halfway through, adapt the practice to run the same sequence on the right side of the pitch (**LB**, **LCB**, **RCB**, **RAM**, & **RW**).

Coaching Points

1. Quick ball movement by defenders.
2. Synchronised movements of the attacking midfielder and winger.
3. Focus on the accuracy and timing of the through passes.

PEP GUARDIOLA - COACHING FLUID POSITIONAL ROTATIONS

Session for PEP GUARDIOLA Tactics - Through Passes in Behind from the Middle Third

PROGRESSION

2. Through Passes for the Winger's Run in Behind Combination Play and Finishing

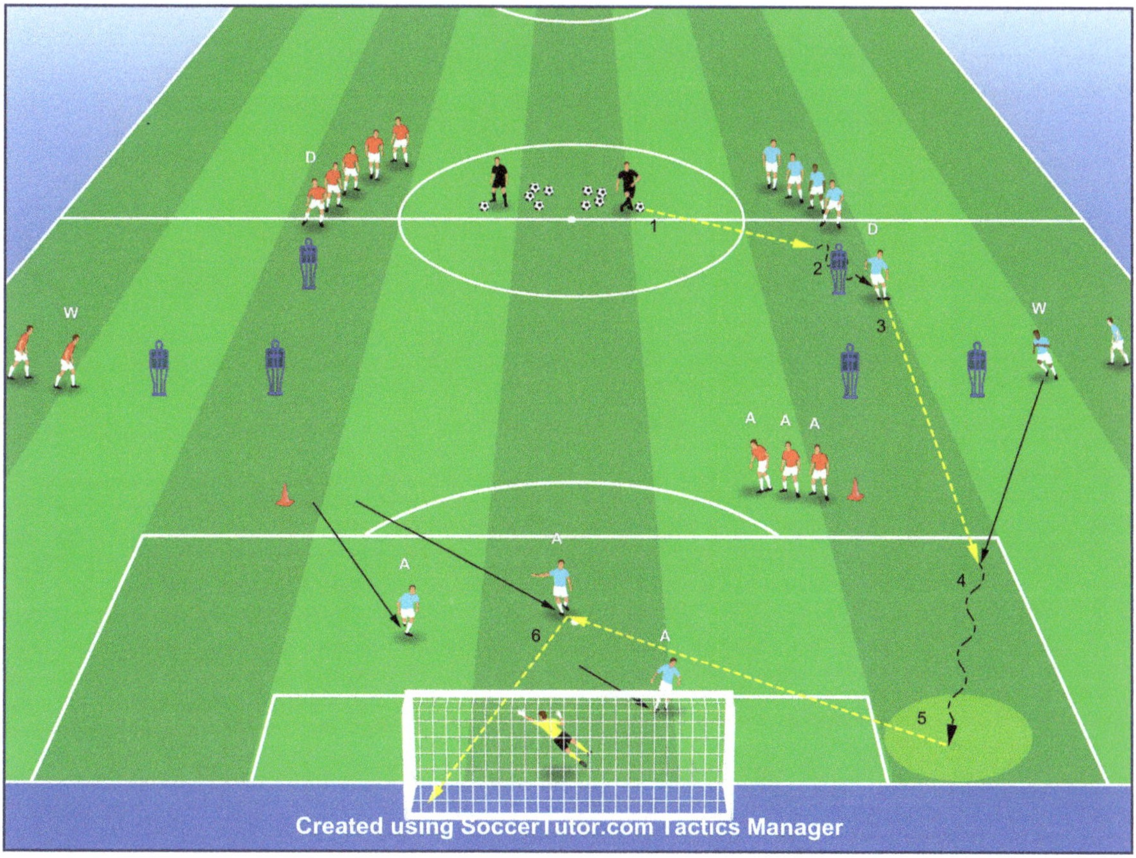

Practice Description

- This practice has 2 groups of 10 players on either side and they play alternately. There are 4 positional roles: 1 defender (**D**), 1 winger (**W**), and 3 attackers (**A**).

- The sequence starts with **D** receiving from the coach and dribbling past the mannequin. **W** makes a run in behind and **D** plays a well-timed through pass in between the 2 mannequins.

- **W** receives in behind, dribbles forward and crosses the ball (cut back in diagram) for one of the 3 attackers (**A**) to score.

- The 3 attackers coordinate to attack the near post, back post, and centre of the box. Once the attack is complete, the other group start the same sequence.

- Halfway through, the teams switch sides so the players practice on both flanks.

Coaching Points

1. Execute technical actions (through pass, cross, and finish) with precision.
2. Ensure correct and coordinated timing of movements to be most effective.

Session for PEP GUARDIOLA Tactics - Through Passes in Behind from the Middle Third

PROGRESSION

3. Through Passes for the Attacking Midfielder's Run in Behind Combination + Conditioned Game

Phase 1/2: Functional Passing Combination

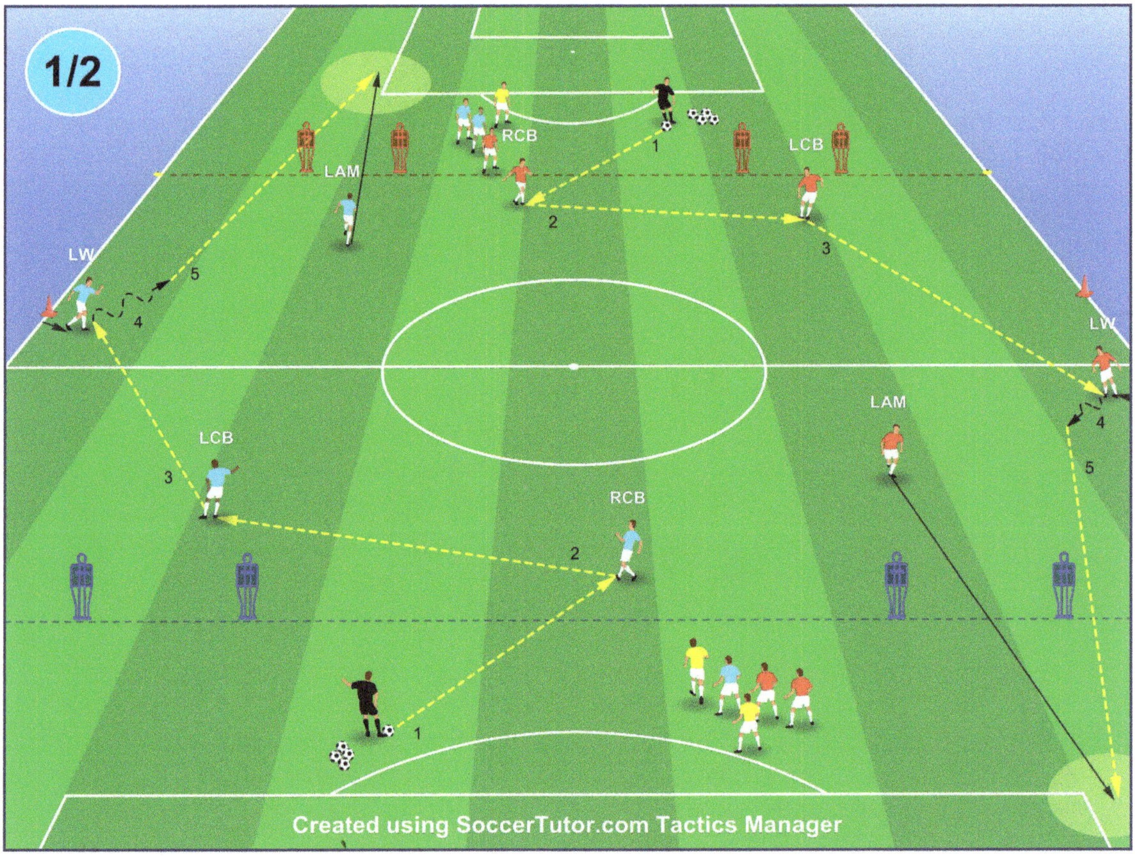

Practice Description (Phase 1)

- We have 7 blue players, 7 red players, and 3 yellow players, but during Phase 1 all players act the same.

- The coaches start by passing 2 balls into play simultaneously. The right centre backs (**RCB**) receives and passes across to the left centre back (**LCB**).

- **LCB** passes to the winger (**LW**), who receives, moves inside with the ball, and then plays a through pass outside the 2 mannequins for the run of the attacking midfielder (**LAM**) in behind.

- The players rotate by following their passes and **LAM** moves to the opposite side in this continuous practice.

- Halfway through, adapt the practice to run the same sequence on the right side of the pitch (**LCB**, **RCB**, **RW** & **RAM**).

Variation: Through pass in between the 2 mannequins to encourage varied and adaptive passing angles.

Session for PEP GUARDIOLA Tactics - **Through Passes in Behind from the Middle Third**

Phase 2/2: Tactical Conditioned Game (Combined Practice)

Practice Description (Phase 2)

- Following on from Phase 1, on the coach's whistle, the practice changes to a conditioned **7v7 (+3) game**.
- The **possession team (blues) are set up in a 3-2-4-1 shape** with the Jokers (**J**) taking up the roles of the defensive midfielder (**DM**) and 2 wingers (**LW** and **RW**).

Possession Team Objective:

- Complete 8 consecutive passes within playing area = 1 Point.
- Execute a through pass for the run of an attacking midfielder to receive in behind = 3 Points. See analysis on page 124.

Coaching Points

1. Maintain high quality ball circulation (receiving, passing, and body shape).
2. Effective and intelligent tactical decision making in play.
3. Precise timing of the attacking midfielder's run in behind.
4. Deliver accurate and well-timed through passes.
5. Support ball circulation with timely movements e.g. Drop deep to create space.
6. Execute coordinated movements between players in advanced positions.

Session for PEP GUARDIOLA Tactics - Through Passes in Behind from the Middle Third

PROGRESSION

4. Through Passes for Winger's Run in Behind Combination + Conditioned Game

Phase 1/2: Functional Combination with Passive Defending

Practice Description (Phase 1)

- In the first phase, 2 teams of 10 perform the same sequence in opposite halves of the pitch. 4 defending players are passive and 1 (deepest) is active.

- The centre back (**CB**) receives from the coach, shifts the ball away from pressure, and passes across to the full back (**LB**).

- As **LB** receives, the attacking midfielder (**LAM**) drops back to draw an opponent out. At the same time, the winger (**LW**) makes a run into the space in behind (see **pages 122-123** for analysis).

- **LB** plays a through pass in between the 2 opponents. **LW** receives, dribbles forward, and crosses for the forward (**F**) to score, who is in an active 1v1 duel against a defender.

- **Each goal scored counts toward the red and blue teams' totals** and is carried forward into Phase 2 (see next page).

Session for PEP GUARDIOLA Tactics - Through Passes in Behind from the Middle Third

Phase 2/2: Tactical Conditioned Game (Combined Practice)

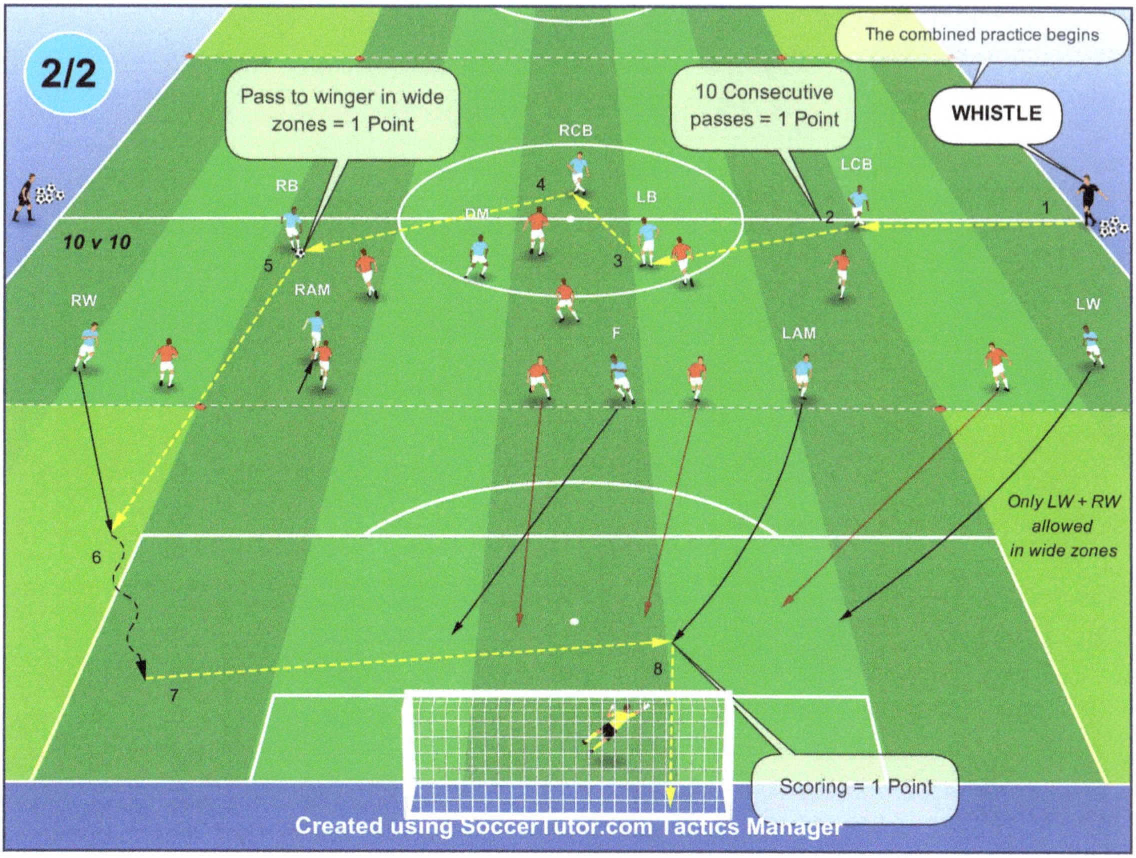

(Diagram: 10 v 10. Pass to winger in wide zones = 1 Point. 10 Consecutive passes = 1 Point. WHISTLE — The combined practice begins. Only LW + RW allowed in wide zones. Scoring = 1 Point.)

Practice Description (Phase 2)

- Following on from Phase 1, on the coach's whistle, the practice changes to a conditioned game. **The team that is losing after Phase 1 (blues) start with the ball and can score 1 Point if they**:

    a) Complete 10 consecutive passes within the middle third of the pitch.

    b) Play a through pass for a winger (**LW** or **RW**) into a yellow wide zone.

    c) Score from the winger's cross.

- The defending team's players (reds) are not allowed to enter the wide zones, so the blue wingers (**RW** in diagram) can deliver their crosses uncontested.

- The forward (**F**), the opposite side attacking midfielder (**LAM**), and winger (**LW**) attack the cross and try to score. The 3 red defenders try to stop them.

- The practice then resets and the blues must attack on the left side. **If a goal is not scored or the reds win the ball, the team roles are reversed**. Points from Phase 2 are added to the goals scored in Phase 1, and the team with the highest total are the winners.

Coaching Points: Effective game decisions (alternate dribbling and passing), precise timing and synchronisation between players. Focus on execution of through pass, cross, finish, and duels.

PEP GUARDIOLA - COACHING FLUID POSITIONAL ROTATIONS

Session for PEP GUARDIOLA Tactics - Through Passes in Behind from the Middle Third

5. Possession in the Centre + Through Passes for the Forward's Run in Behind

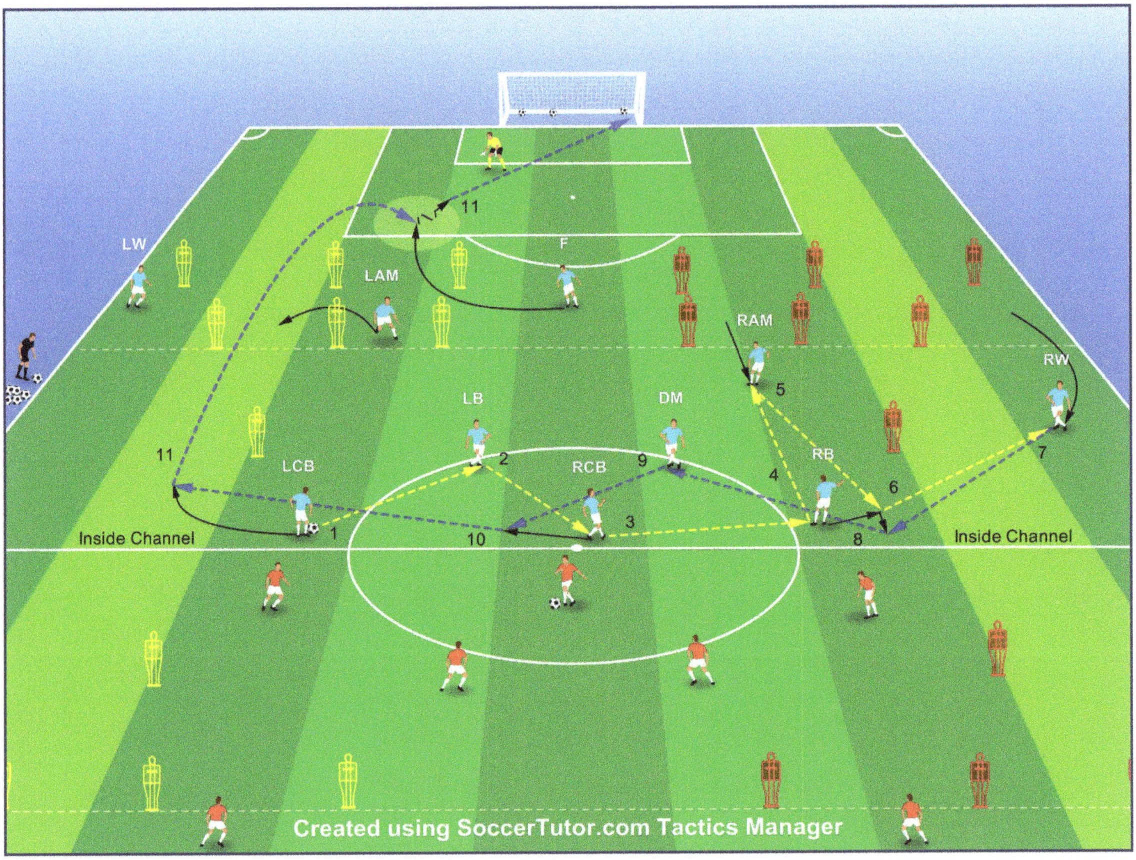

Practice Description

- This practice is performed by both teams (reds and blues) simultaneously in each half of the pitch.
- The players are organised in a 3-2-4-1 shape (see page 126 for full analysis).
- The objective is to execute at least 2 full switches of play before playing in behind for the forward (**F**) to score.
- **Phase 1:** The attacking midfielders (**LAM** & **RAM**) and wingers (**LW** & **RW**) drop below the mannequins which represent opposing midfielders, and help with the switching of play, as shown.

- **Phase 2:** When the left centre back (**LCB**) or right back (**RB**) receives in the inside channel, they attempt to play a pass in behind for the run of the forward (**F**), who receives and tries to score.

Coaching Points

1. High quality ball circulation when switching play.
2. Synchronised movements between attacking midfielders and forward to finish attacks. In the diagram example, **LAM** moves into the inside channel as if to draw a defender out and help create space for **F** to receive in behind.

Session for PEP GUARDIOLA Tactics - Through Passes in Behind from the Middle Third

PROGRESSION

6. Through Passes in Behind from the Middle Third 10v6 (+GK) Tactical Game

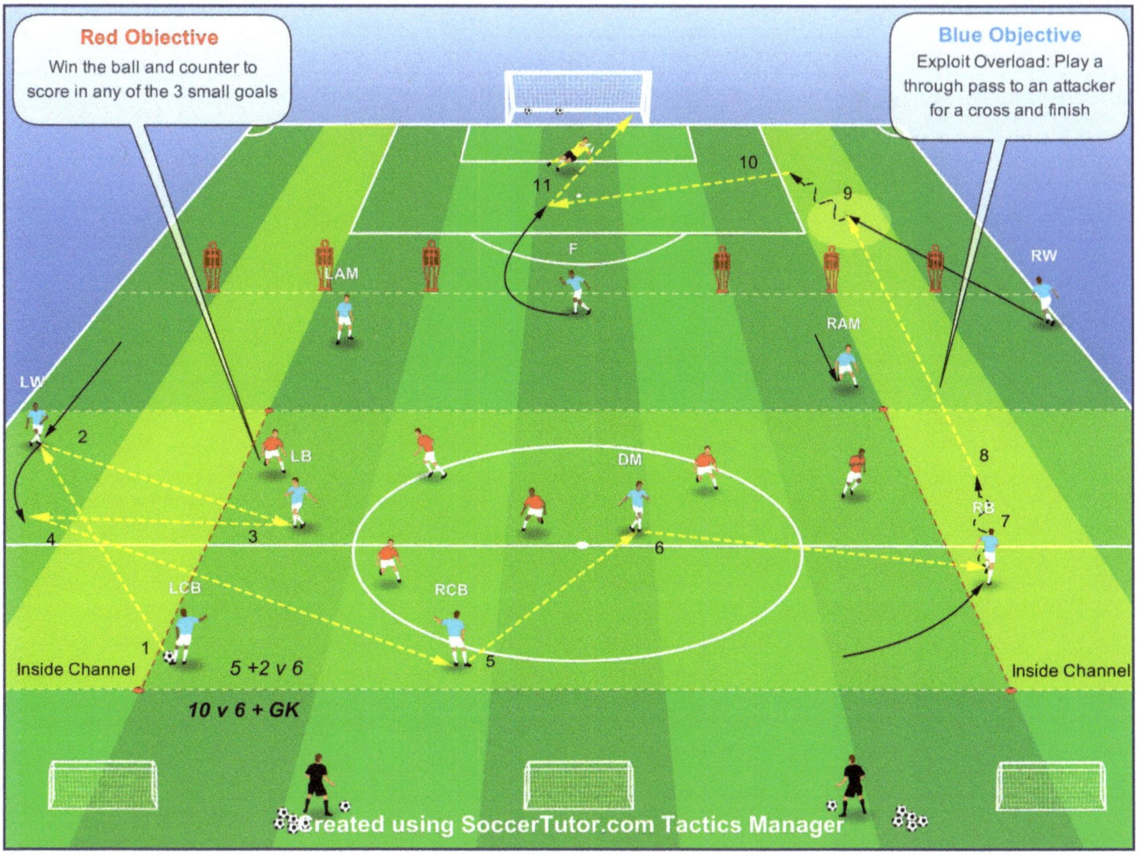

Red Objective
Win the ball and counter to score in any of the 3 small goals

Blue Objective
Exploit Overload: Play a through pass to an attacker for a cross and finish

Practice Description

- The blue team are in Manchester City's 3-2-4-1 possession phase shape.

- **Blue Objective:** Exploit the 5 (+2) v 6 numerical advantage in the central white zone to create time and space to attack. The attacking midfielders (**LAM** & **RAM**) and wingers (**LW** & **RW**) drop back to help with ball circulation and help determine the optimal time to play in behind for the run of **LW**, **RW**, **LAM**, **RAM** or the forward (**F**) - See full analysis of all options on pages 121-126.

- The through passes are played by the left centre back (**LCB**) or right back (**RB**) from the inside channel. The pass used depends on the coordinated movements of the attackers on that side.

- In this example, **RB** receives and drives forward, **RAM** drops as if to draw a defender out, and **RB** plays a through pass for **RW**, who crosses for **F** to score.

- **Red Objective:** Win the ball and counter to score in the 3 small goals. The 6 red players use a 4-1-1, 4-2, 5-1, 1-4-1, or 3-2-1 shape at the coach's discretion.

Attacking in the Final Third with Positional Rotations

Tactical Solutions for Attacking in the Final Third

This chapter analyses the primary tactics Pep Guardiola uses in the final (attacking) third of the pitch, where **precision and tactical intelligence are essential**.

In this critical area of the pitch, Manchester City demonstrate remarkable adaptability, changing between these formations:

- 3-2-4-1
- 2-3-5
- 3-1-6

These **formation changes are used to counter Manchester City's opponents who focus on defensive compactness**, often retreating deep into their box. In the final third, the structure is carefully organised to maintain effective positioning and efficient use of space. This setup enables the team to **identify and exploit any small gaps in the opposition's defensive line**, ensuring opportunities are maximised.

The team positions itself to encircle the opponent's defensive block, establishing a shape that allows players to evaluate the tactical context. Depending on the spaces available, the team can decide to:

1. Play through the middle.
2. Attack down the flanks.
3. Continue to circulate the ball along the perimeter to stretch the opposition's defence and provoke mistakes.

Key Point: A key feature of Guardiola's approach is the connectivity between players. Each individual occupies a specific position relative to their teammates, forming a cohesive structure that supports fluid ball movement and quick transitions.

This dynamic approach allows the team to **run a variety of coordinated and adaptable sequences of play**, designed to exploit the spaces their opponents occupy and the gaps they inevitably leave.

In the final sections of this book, we will study how Pep Guardiola's team **utilise the half spaces** and explore their different attacking tactics which include the following:

- Penetrating passes through the centre of the pitch.
- Attacking in wide areas.
- Attacking on the flanks near the byline.
- Attacking around the edge of the box.

Each tactic reflects the thoughtful preparation and adaptability that define Manchester City's approach in the final third.

Attacking in the Final Third with Positional Rotations

Changing Shape from 3-2-4-1 to 2-3-5 in the Final (Attacking) Third

1. 4-1-4-1 or 4-2-2 Formation in the Defensive Third (Build Up Phase)

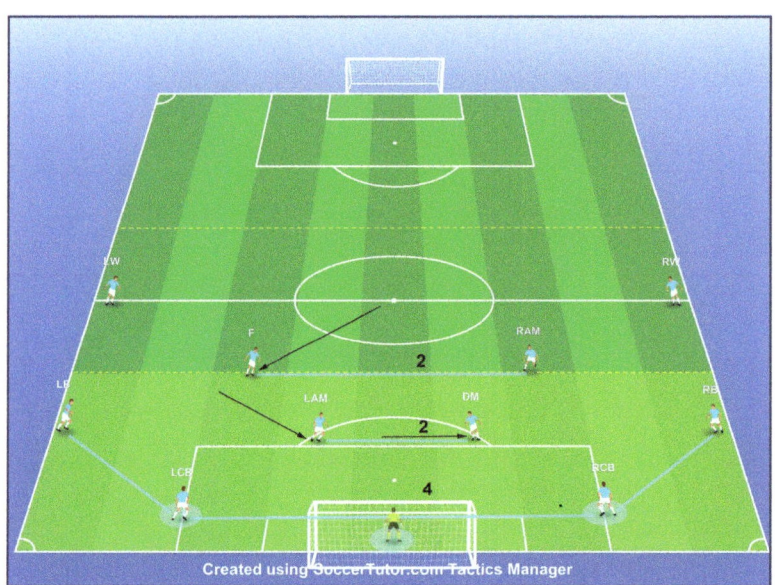

In the final third, Pep Guardiola adjusts his setup to exploit space and dictate play.

Here we show how Manchester City start with a 4-1-4-1 or 4-2-2 (diagram example) in the defensive third, before progressing the ball further up the pitch.

For the 4-2-2, an attacking midfielder (**LAM**) drops back to create a double pivot with the defensive midfielder (**DM**), and the forward (**F**) drops back to fill in his position.

2. 3-2-4-1 Formation in the Middle Third (Possession Phase)

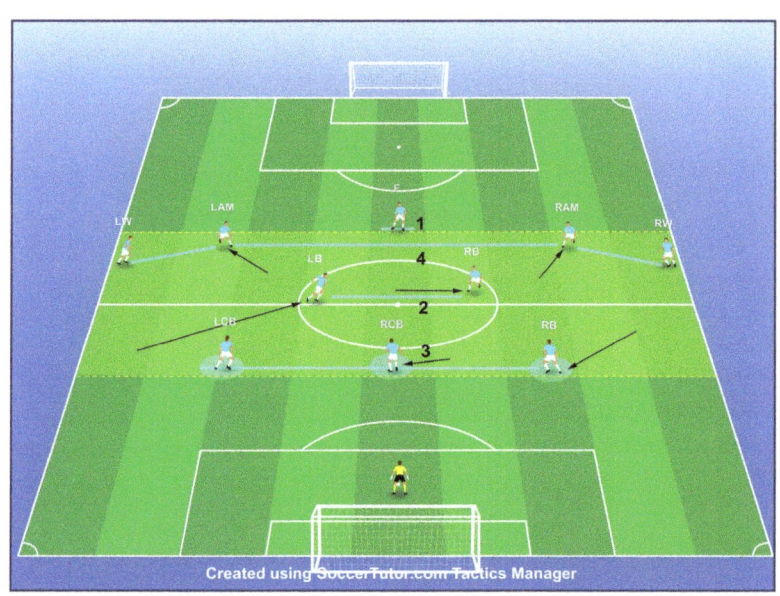

Manchester City shift to a 3-2-4-1 shape in the middle third and a more advanced structure for attacking.

The left back (**LB**) inverts into midfield to create a double pivot with the defensive midfielder (**DM**) and the right back (**RB**) shifts inside to create a back 3.

By pushing both attacking midfielders (**LAM** & **RAM**) into high positions, City have 5 players near to the opposition's defensive line, allowing for effective perimeter ball circulation and attacking opportunities.

3. 2-3-5 Formation in the Final Third (Attacking Phase)

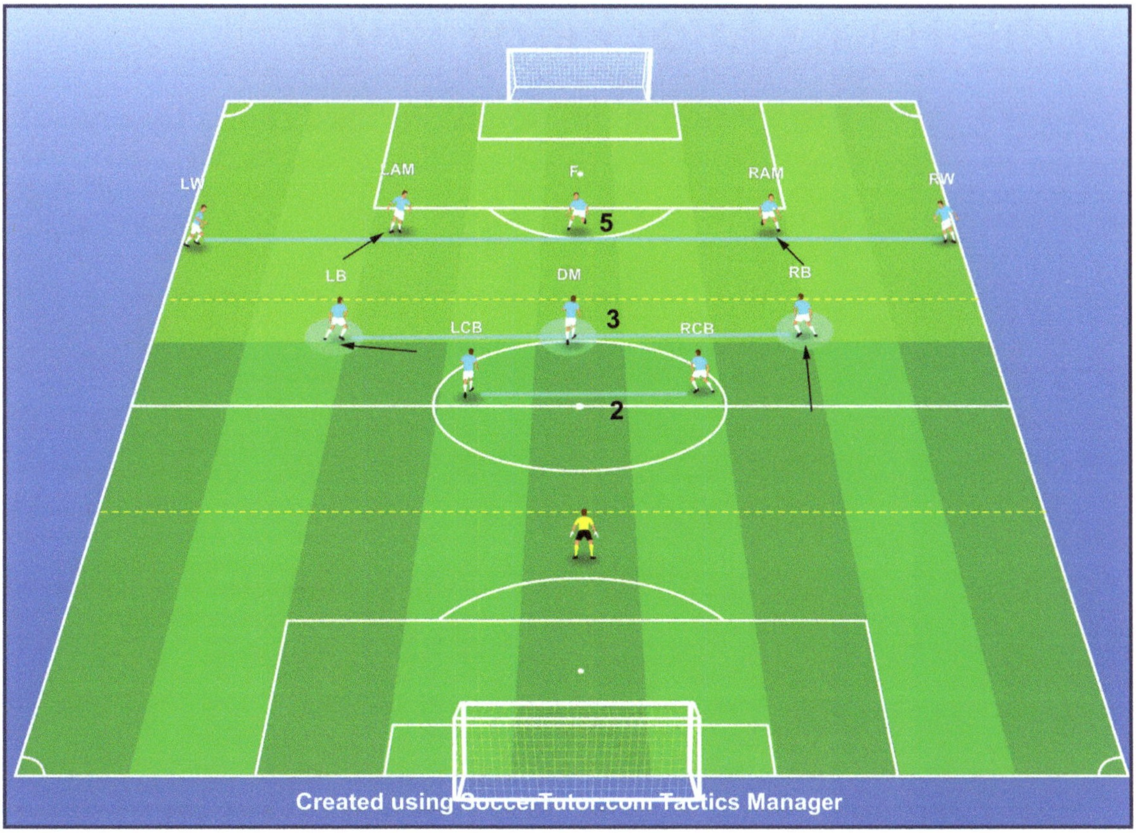

Pep Guardiola's adaptable structure ensures control across all thirds of the pitch. In the final third, Manchester City often form a **2-3-5 shape**. The right back (**RB**) pushes forward into midfield and both attacking midfielders (**LAM** and **RAM**) push high either side of the forward (**F**).

This structure **stretches the opposition both horizontally and vertically, creating positional superiority**. With 2 centre backs providing stability, 3 midfielders maintaining control, and 5 attackers, City exert **constant pressure on the defensive block**.

LAM and **RAM** overload the central spaces and **F** exploits spaces in behind, disrupting the opposition's organisation.

This precise positioning **generated gaps**, allowing Manchester City to **produce high quality chances** throughout the match with **well-executed overloads**.

Key Point: The 2-3-5 attacking phase shape exemplifies Pep Guardiola's commitment to positional play, offering Manchester City control, the ability to manipulate the opposition's defensive shape, and provide a variety of effective attacking options.

Providing Two Outside and Two Inside Options for Player in Possession

In Manchester City's tactical structure, the 3 attacking central players (forward and 2 attacking midfielders) are the team's foundation for directing play. This setup gives the player in possession the flexibility to adjust to the spaces created by teammates or left open by the opposition.

Whether positioned centrally or on one of the flanks, the ball carrier faces a decision:

1. Pass into central areas.
2. Pass into wide spaces.

This framework helps Manchester City maintain a fluid and controlled attacking approach.

As the diagrams to follow on the next 2 pages show, the player in possession generally has **4 Main Passing Options**:

1. Pass wide to the winger.
2. Pass to the attacking midfielder in the half space.
3. Pass to the other attacking midfielder in a central position.
4. Pass to the forward in the centre.

Key Point: This **"two outside and two inside options" decision making process ensures that no matter where the ball carrier is on the pitch, there are always clear choices available.**

The **5 attacking players create space and provide constant movement**, enabling the player in possession to maintain control and build attacking momentum with plenty of passing options. The **final decision is influenced by the tactical context and the defensive setup of the opposition**.

By selecting the most appropriate passing option within this framework, Manchester City can **sustain attacking fluidity, break down compact defensive blocks**, and **maintain dominance in the final third**.

Attacking in the Final Third with Positional Rotations

1. Pass Wide to the Winger (2-3-5)

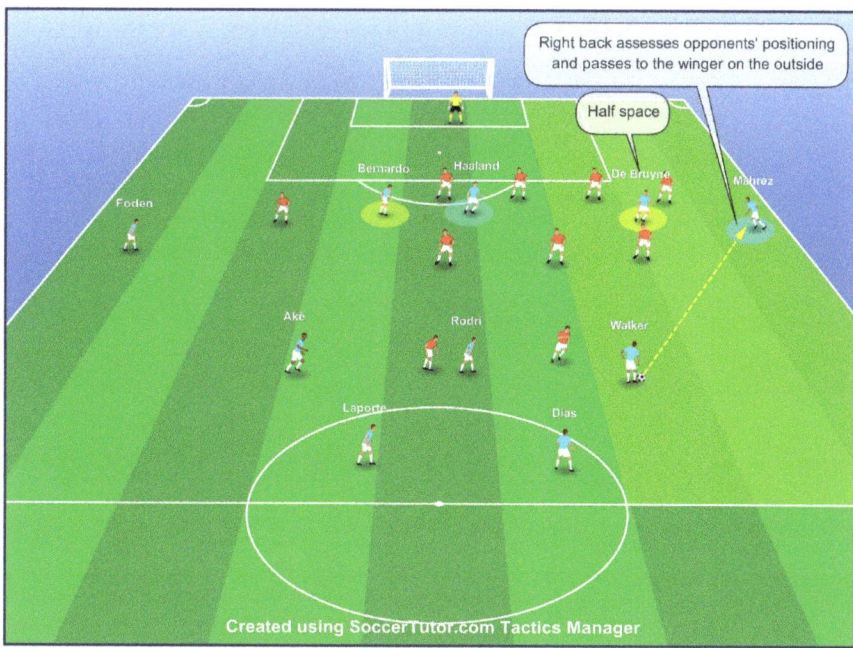

The right back (**Walker**) evaluates the positioning of the opponents and sees that the pass to the attacking midfielder (**De Bruyne**) is blocked and there is space out wide.

Therefore, he passes to the right winger (**Mahrez**), who is positioned on the outside.

2. Pass to the Attacking Midfielder in the Half Space (2-3-5)

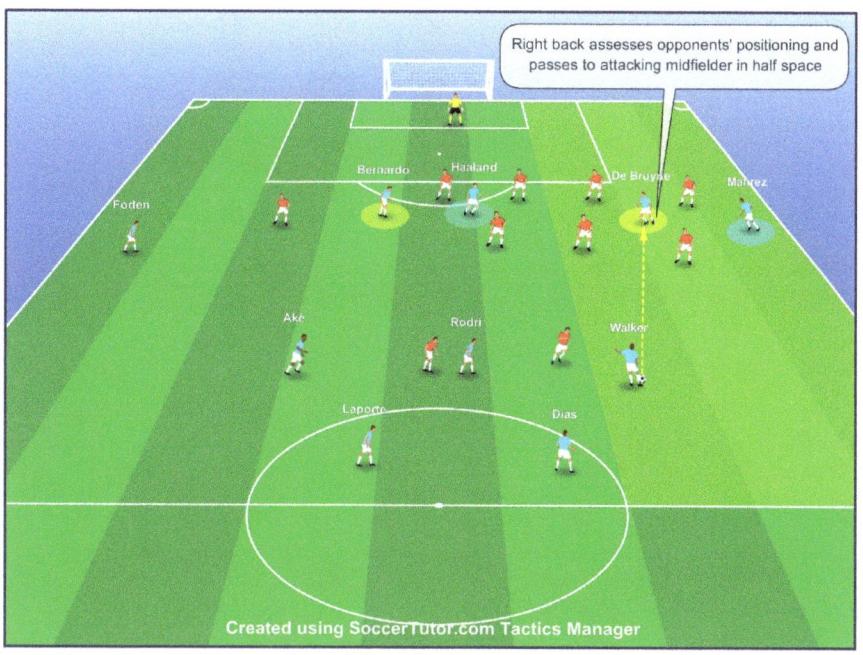

In this variation, the positioning of the opposition's defensive block is wider.

Walker quickly assesses the situation and is able to play between 2 opponents in between the lines to **De Bruyne** in the half space.

Attacking in the Final Third with Positional Rotations

3. Pass to the Attacking Midfielder in a Central Position (2-3-5)

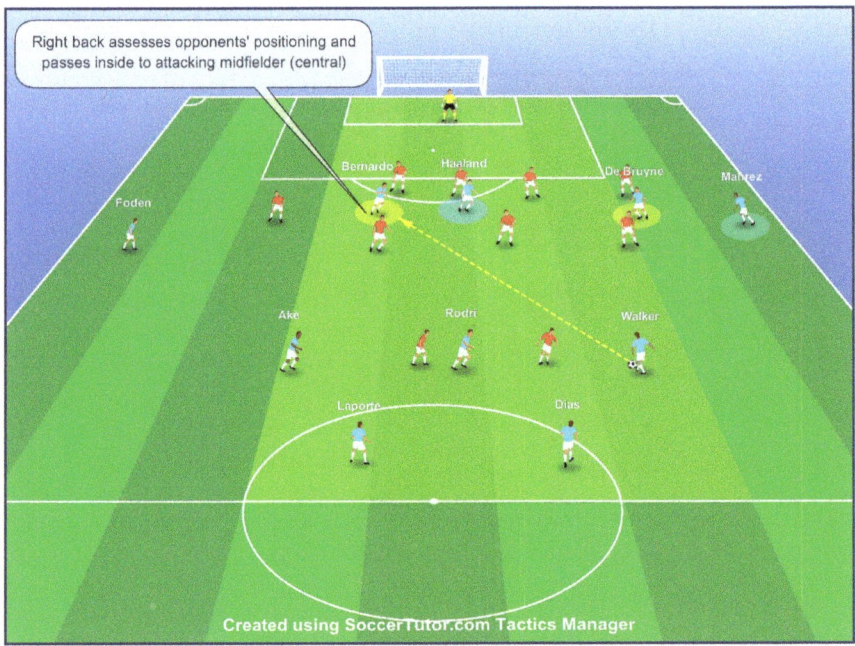

In this variation, the opposition's midfield line is less compact and more spread out across the pitch, which means there are potential gaps to exploit.

Walker recognises the situation and breaks through the midfield line with a pass to the other attacking midfielder (**Bernardo**), who is positioned centrally.

4. Pass to the Forward in the Centre (2-3-5)

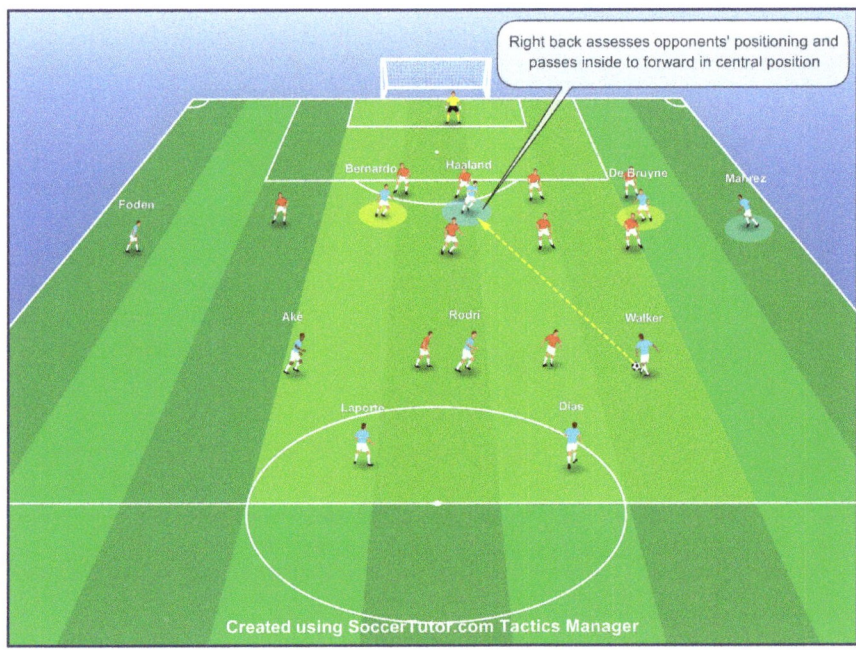

In this variation, there is a clear 2v2 situation in the wide right area, so **Walker** avoids passing there.

With the opposing right midfielder in a wide position to cover the left winger (**Foden**), **Walker** decides to breaks through the midfield line with a pass to the forward (**Haaland**) in the centre.

Attacking in the Final Third with Positional Rotations

Coordinated Development of Play and Positional Rotations

1. Patient Ball Circulation (Waiting for Opening)

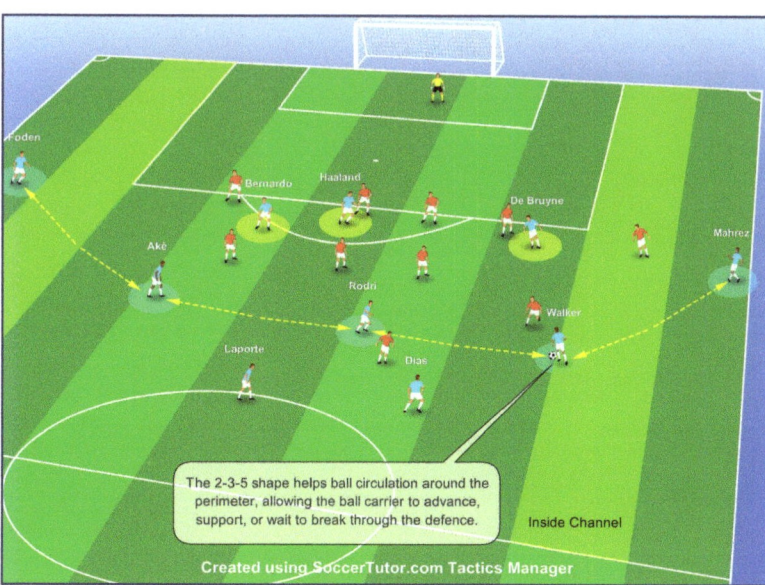

The 2-3-5 shape helps ball circulation around the perimeter, allowing the ball carrier to advance, support, or wait to break through the defence.

Inside Channel

The 2-3-5 shape offers key advantages when circulating the ball around the opponent's defensive block. The player in possession can either pass forward or maintain control. This patient approach helps **Manchester City wait for the ideal moment to progress forward**. Pep Guardiola's structure ensures possession dominance and continually probes the opponent's defence for openings.

2. Positional Fluidity to Become Unpredictable in the Final Third

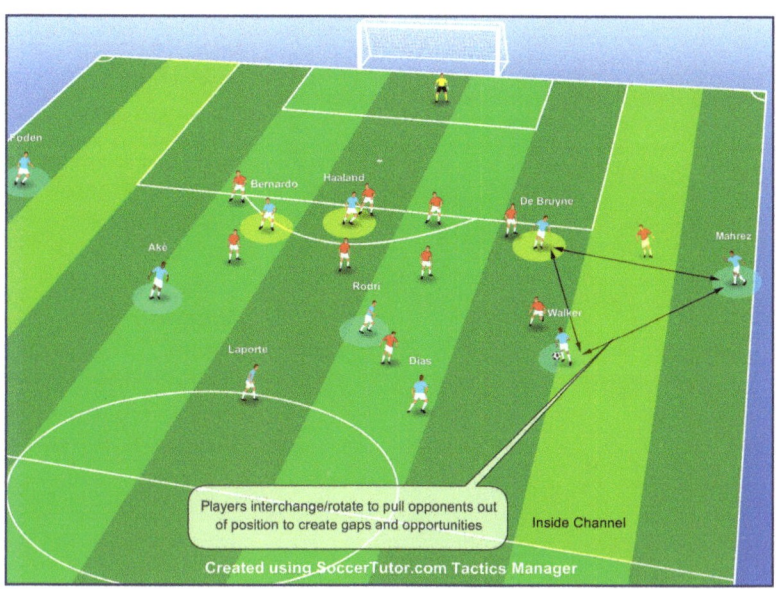

Players interchange/rotate to pull opponents out of position to create gaps and opportunities.

Inside Channel

Here we show the dynamic roles of the players on the right side of the pitch. This group's ability to **rotate and interchange positions keeps the opposition guessing**. By removing fixed reference points, they disrupt the defensive organisation, forcing constant adjustments. Such **fluid positioning occurs naturally within the game's flow**, presenting opportunities to exploit openings and progress the attack.

Attacking in the Final Third with Positional Rotations

Full Back's Options for Ball Circulation or Line Breaking Passes

Perimeter players in Guardiola's attacking structure are crucial for progressing from ball circulation to incisive attacks. Positioning players around the opposition's defensive block, **Manchester City can trigger teammates near the box or recycle possession**, **waiting for the right moment to play incisive passes**. They also engage supporting defenders to gain control and exploit gaps with quick switches of play.

The following **diagrams highlight tactical fluidity, showing how the ball carrier's options (to side, central, or diagonal) shift depending on the opposition's positioning**. This ensures seamless transitions from ball circulation to attack, sustaining pressure, and creating opportunities.

Key roles are the full back, winger, and attacking midfielder, who adapt to defensive tactics such as tight central marking or wide area pressure:

1. **Full back may shift inside to offer support.**
2. **Winger maintains width to stretch the defence.**
3. **Attacking midfielder can break forward to get in behind the defensive line.**

Key Point: This adaptability, rooted in positional play and awareness, allows Manchester City to take the initiative in exploiting defences, maintain control, and create opportunities to advance attacks.

1. Passing Options on the Perimeter Against a Central Block

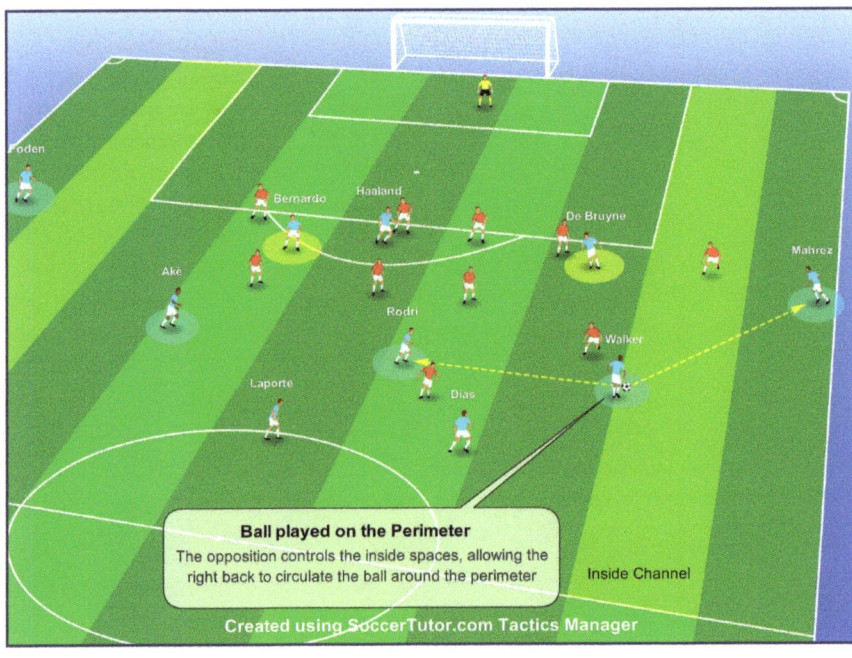

Ball played on the Perimeter
The opposition controls the inside spaces, allowing the right back to circulate the ball around the perimeter

Inside Channel

The **opposition's defensive setup is focused on blocking central spaces**. This allows the player in possession (right back - **Walker**) to circulate the ball along the perimeter, **maintain control and probe for openings**. This option enables him to use the width, creating time and space to initiate the next phase of play.

Attacking in the Final Third with Positional Rotations

2. Solutions to Pass Forward when Perimeter Options are Closed

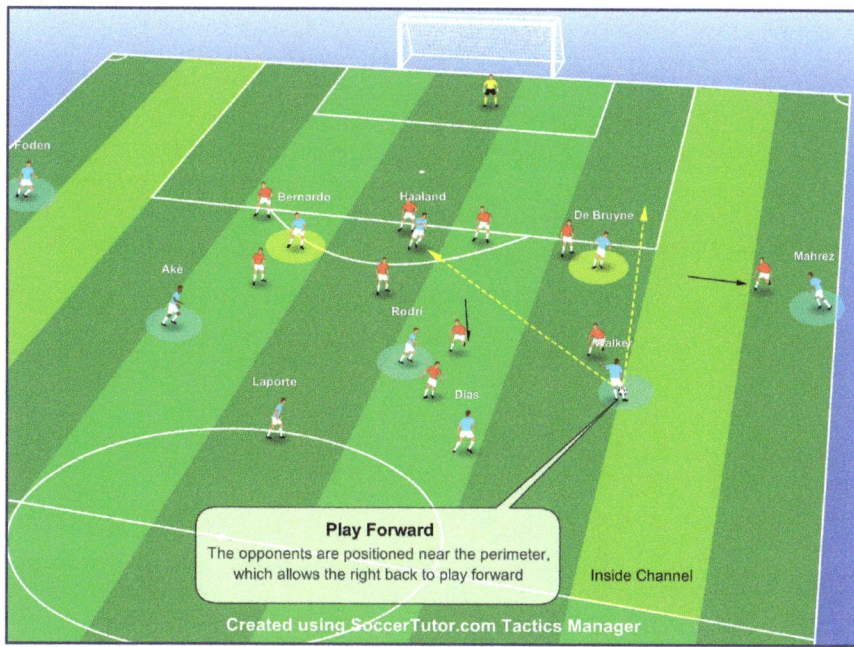

Play Forward
The opponents are positioned near the perimeter, which allows the right back to play forward

When the **opposition focus on closing off perimeter options**, the player in possession (right back - **Walker**) can play forward using through passes, either to feet or into space, as shown in the diagram example.

3. Options when Perimeter and Forward Passes are Closed

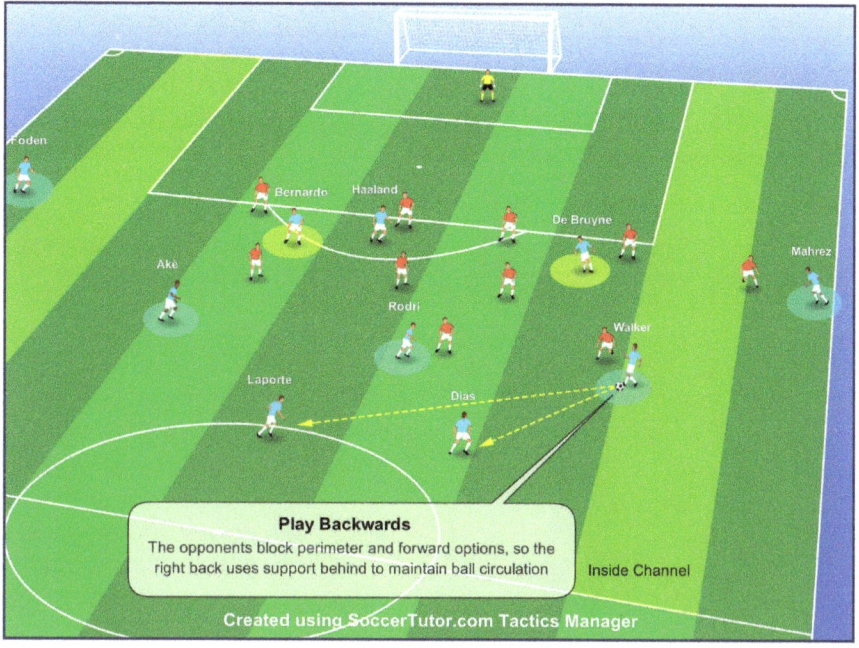

Play Backwards
The opponents block perimeter and forward options, so the right back uses support behind to maintain ball circulation

When the **opposition are able to close off the perimeter and forward options** by dropping all of their players behind the line of the ball, the player in possession (right back - **Walker**) can pass backwards to supporting players. These players help maintain possession and contribute to surrounding the opposition's defensive block.

Attacking in the Final Third with Positional Rotations

Winger's Options for Ball Circulation or Line Breaking Passes

1. Winger's Role in Stretching the Width of the Pitch

![Tactical diagram showing player positions: Foden, Bernardo, Haaland, De Bruyne, Mahrez, Ake, Rodri, Walker, Laporte, Dias. Labels: "Ball played from the Perimeter", "Inside Channel". Created using SoccerTutor.com Tactics Manager]

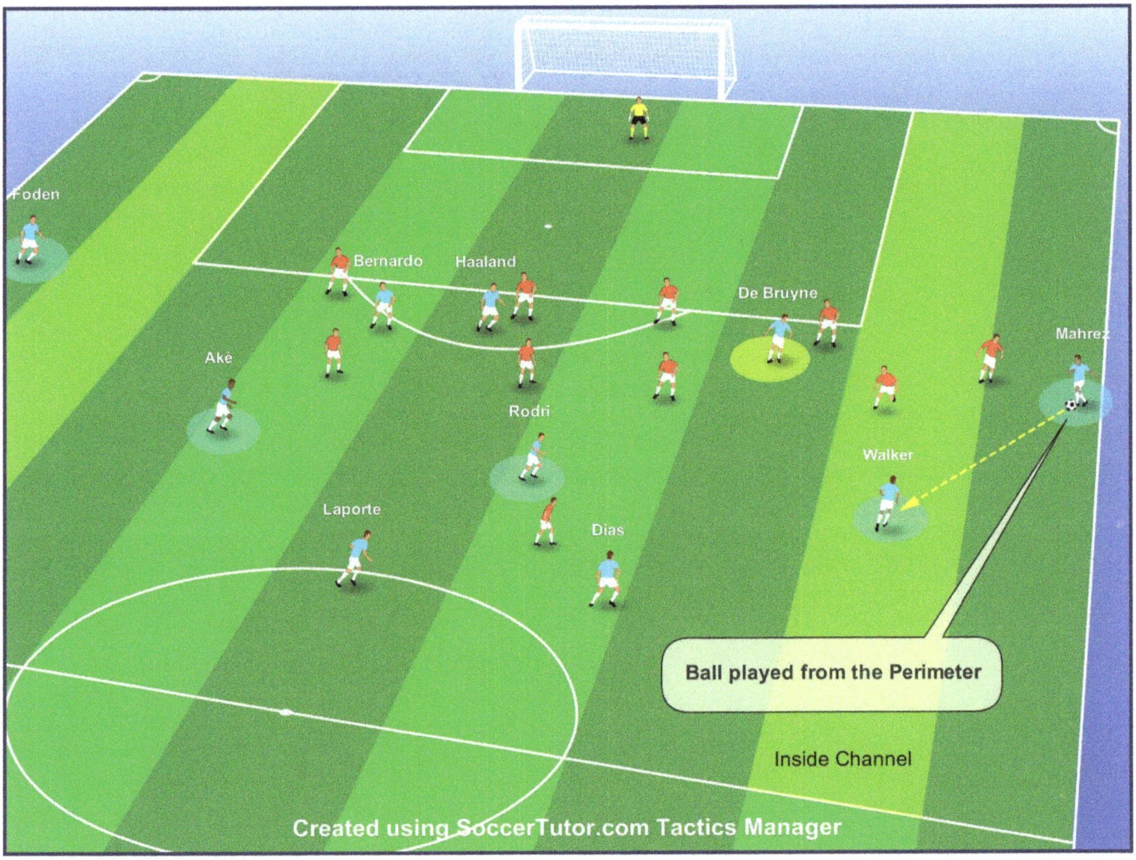

Key Point: When the opposition focus on blocking central spaces, the winger's role becomes crucial in stretching the width of the pitch.

By staying wide, the winger not only creates passing lanes but also forces the defensive line to shift horizontally. This movement **disrupts the compactness of the opposition's defensive block, opening gaps that teammates positioned between the lines can exploit**.

Additionally, the winger's positioning can provide an **outlet for quick switches of play**, allowing the team to **bypass crowded areas and access space on the opposite side of the pitch**. This tactical stretch also sets up opportunities for overlapping runs by the full back, creating numerical advantages on the flank.

Through this positioning, the winger ensures the team retains both width and fluidity in their attacking moves.

Attacking in the Final Third with Positional Rotations

2. Winger's Options to Break Through Defensive Lines

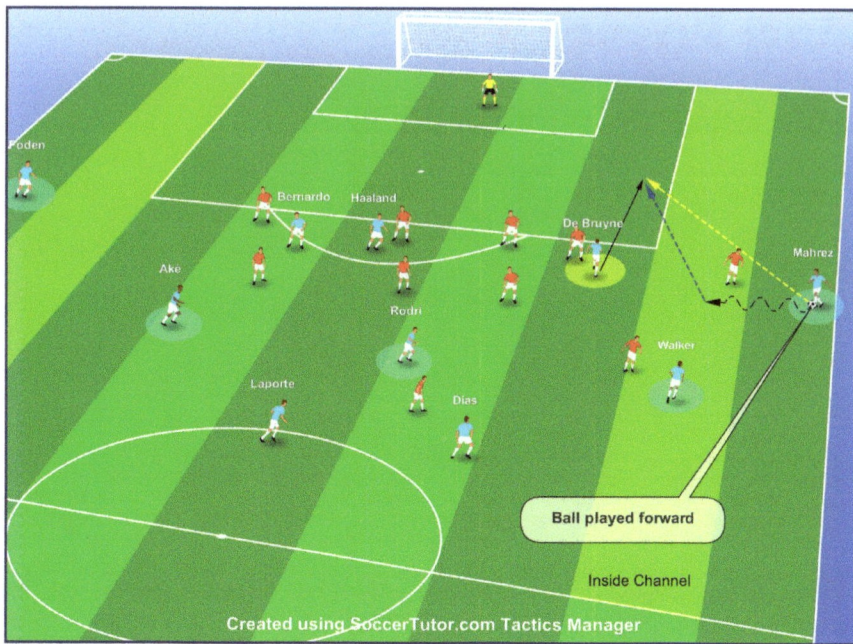

The winger (**Mahrez**) can combine with the full back (**Walker**) or the attacking midfielder to progress through the half space.

In this example, he delivers a decisive pass into the box for **De Bruyne's** run in behind.

Timing and coordination are key to breaking through the defensive lines.

3. Winger's Options to Play Backwards when Opponents Drop Back

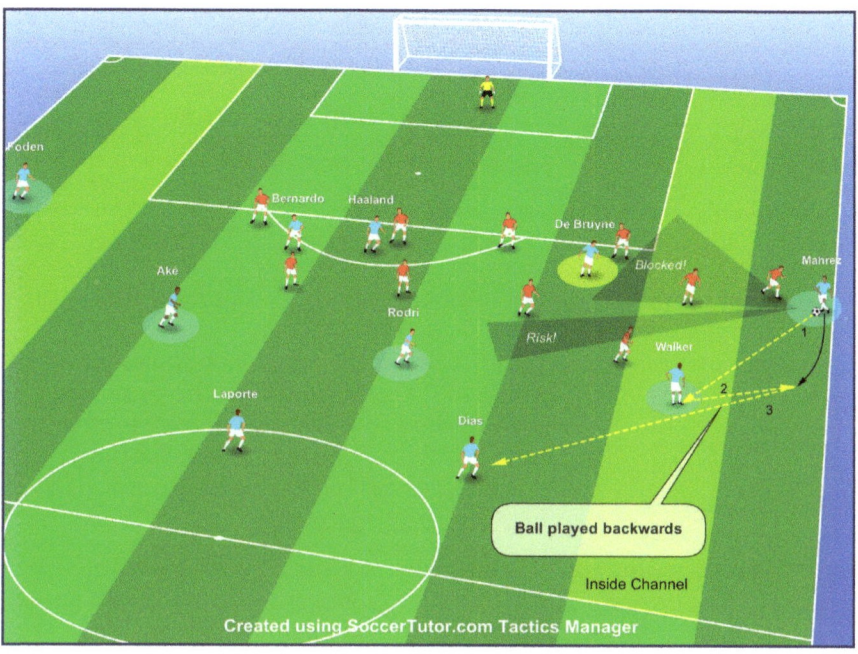

When the opposition's defensive block dropped back even deeper to cut off forward and inside passing options, the winger (**Mahrez**) would look to **recycle possession** to maintain control.

Key Point:
This resets the attacking phase while sustaining pressure on the defensive block.

PEP GUARDIOLA - COACHING FLUID POSITIONAL ROTATIONS

Attacking in the Final Third with Positional Rotations

Defensive Midfielder's Options for Ball Circulation or Line Breaking Passes

1. Passing Options on the Perimeter Against a Central Block

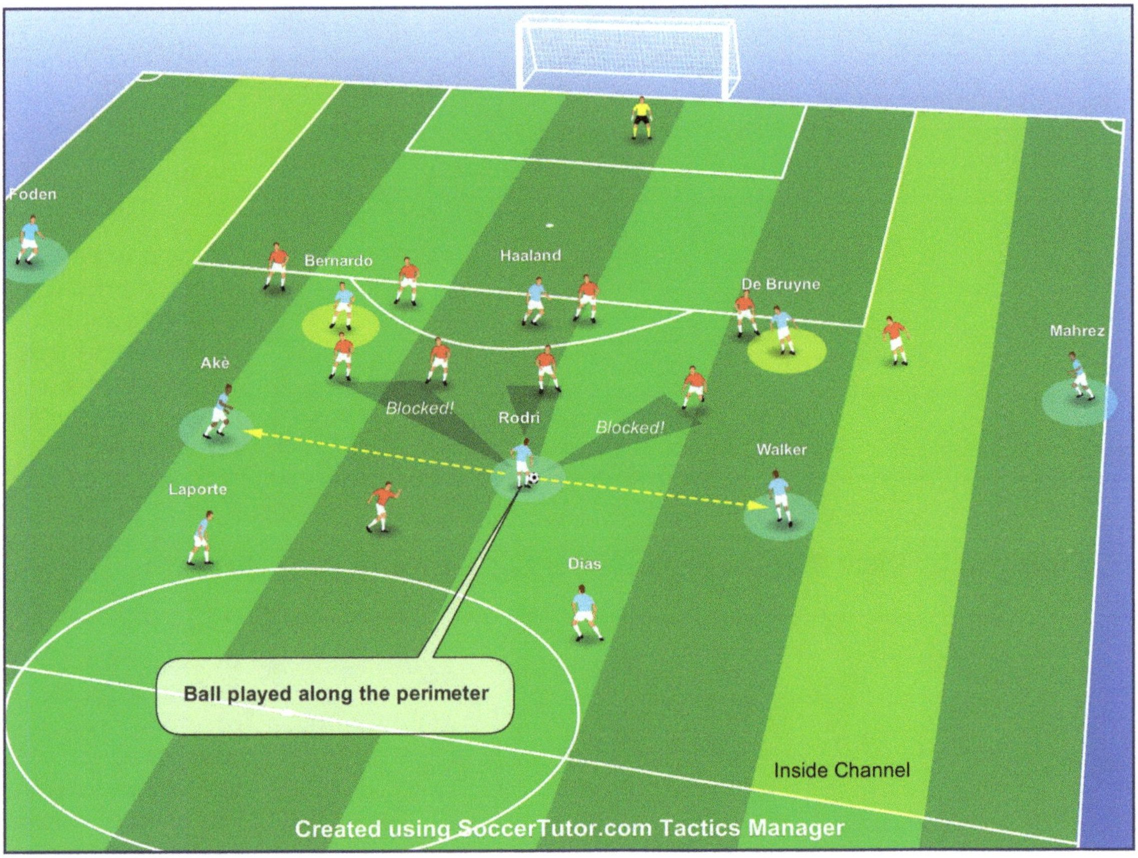

The **defensive midfielder (Rodri) plays a crucial role in Pep Guardiola's system, dictating the flow of play and exploiting spaces** based on the opposition's defensive positioning. When central spaces are available, **Rodri** can orchestrate the attack by finding teammates positioned between the lines, or by threading passes into the feet of the forward (**Haaland**). His vision and ability to scan the pitch is essential for **identifying gaps in the opposing defensive block**.

This **role requires Rodri to maintain positional flexibility**, moving horizontally to create passing angles, or dropping deeper to provide a safe outlet. His ability to attract pressure from opponents while remaining composed allows other teammates to exploit the free spaces.

Key Point: Rodri coordinates with the wingers or full backs to execute quick combination play, enabling City to bypass the midfield press and progress attacks.

Attacking in the Final Third with Positional Rotations

2. Defensive Midfielder's Solutions to Pass Forward in the Centre

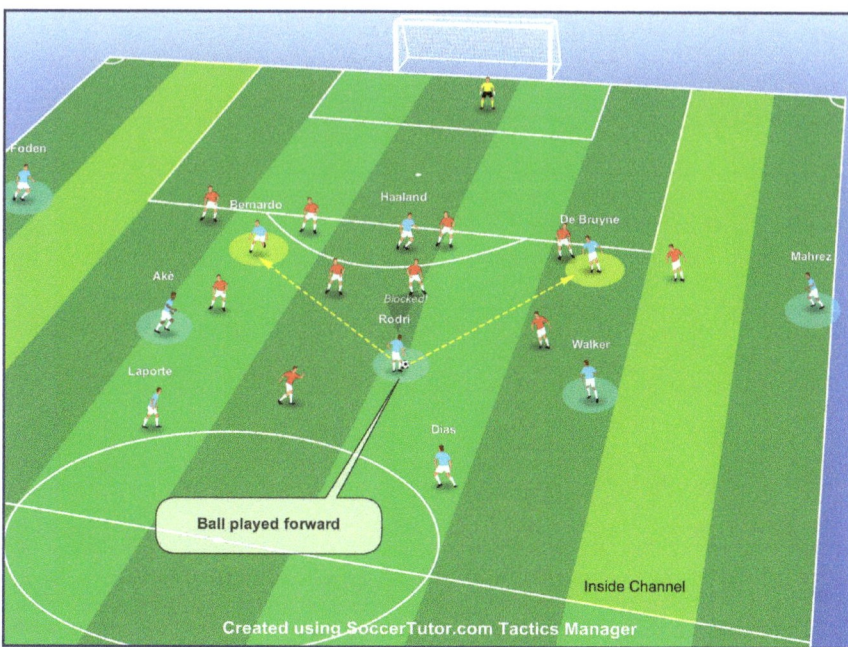

The defensive midfielder (**Rodri**) can utilise through passes into space for teammates in advanced positions, such as the attacking midfielders (**Bernardo** and **De Bruyne**) or the forward (**Haaland**).

These passes demand **precise timing to exploit movements** made to receive in small pockets of space (or in behind).

3. Options to Play Backwards when Opponents Drop Back

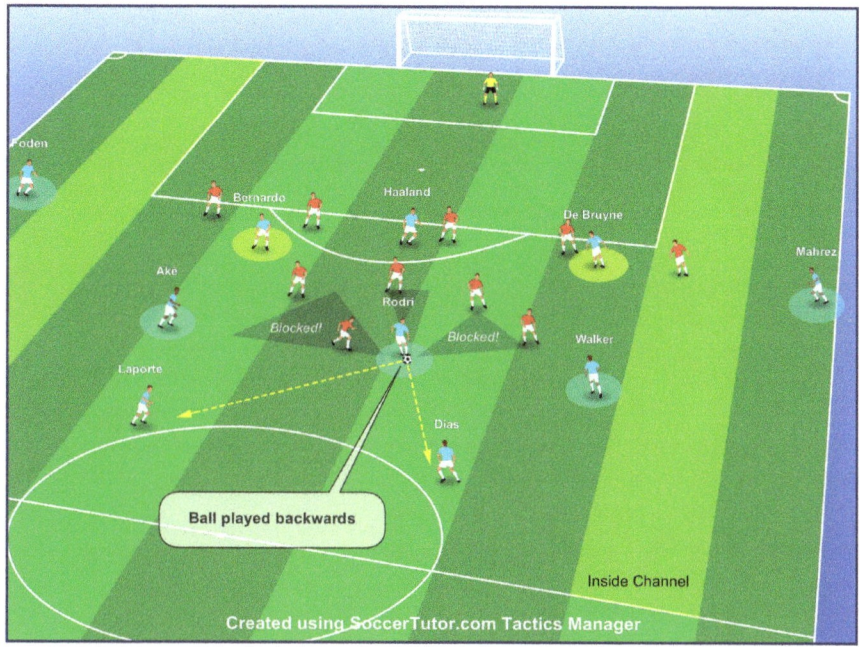

When the opposition's defensive block dropped back even deeper to shut down forward passing options, **Rodri would look to recycle possession** backwards to supporting defenders.

Key Point: This resets the attack, ensuring control and facilitating a switch of play to target weaker defensive areas.

Practice for PEP GUARDIOLA Tactics - Attacking in Final Third with Positional Rotations

PRACTICE FOR THIS TACTICAL SITUATION

Ball Circulation in the Final Third with Fluid Positional Rotations + Conditioned Attack

Phase 1/2: Ball Circulation to Switch Play with Rotations

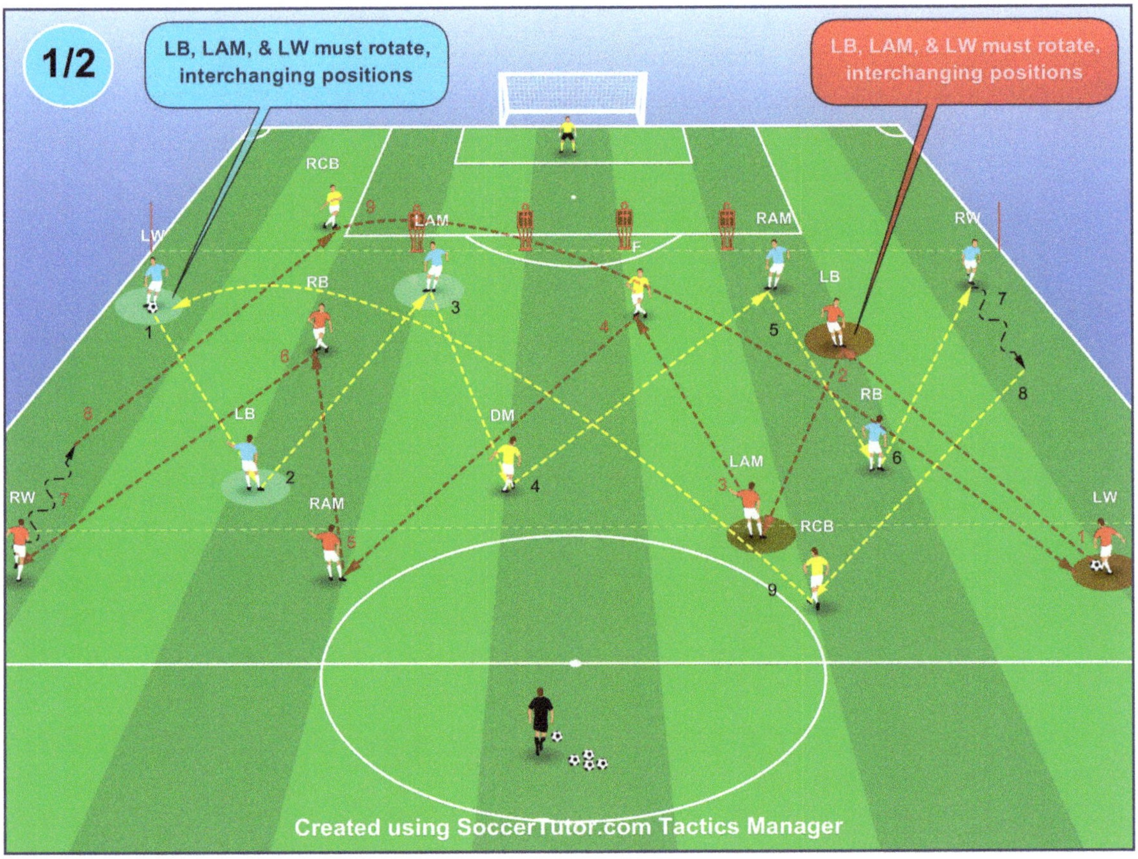

Practice Description (Phase 1)

- There are 2 teams with 6 players each (**LB, RB, LAM, RAM, LW,** and **RW**) + 3 Jokers (2 x **RCB, DM,** and **F**).
- The practice starts simultaneously from both left wingers (**LW**), with 2 balls.
- The shape is based on Manchester City's 2-3-5 attacking phase structure.
- **Objective:** Complete 3 switch of play sequences (1-9) as quickly as possible.
- The first 6 passes are simple diagonal ground passes. When the right winger (**RW**) receives, he dribbles forward before passing to **RCB**, who completes the sequence with an aerial switch of play pass back to the start (**LW**).
- **Rule:** The full back (**LB**), attacking midfielder (**LAM**), and winger (**LW**) rotate positions during the switch of play. This practices their awareness and timing for interchanges.

Practice for PEP GUARDIOLA Tactics - Attacking in Final Third with Positional Rotations

Phase 2/2: Positional 6v6 (+4) Possession Play Game

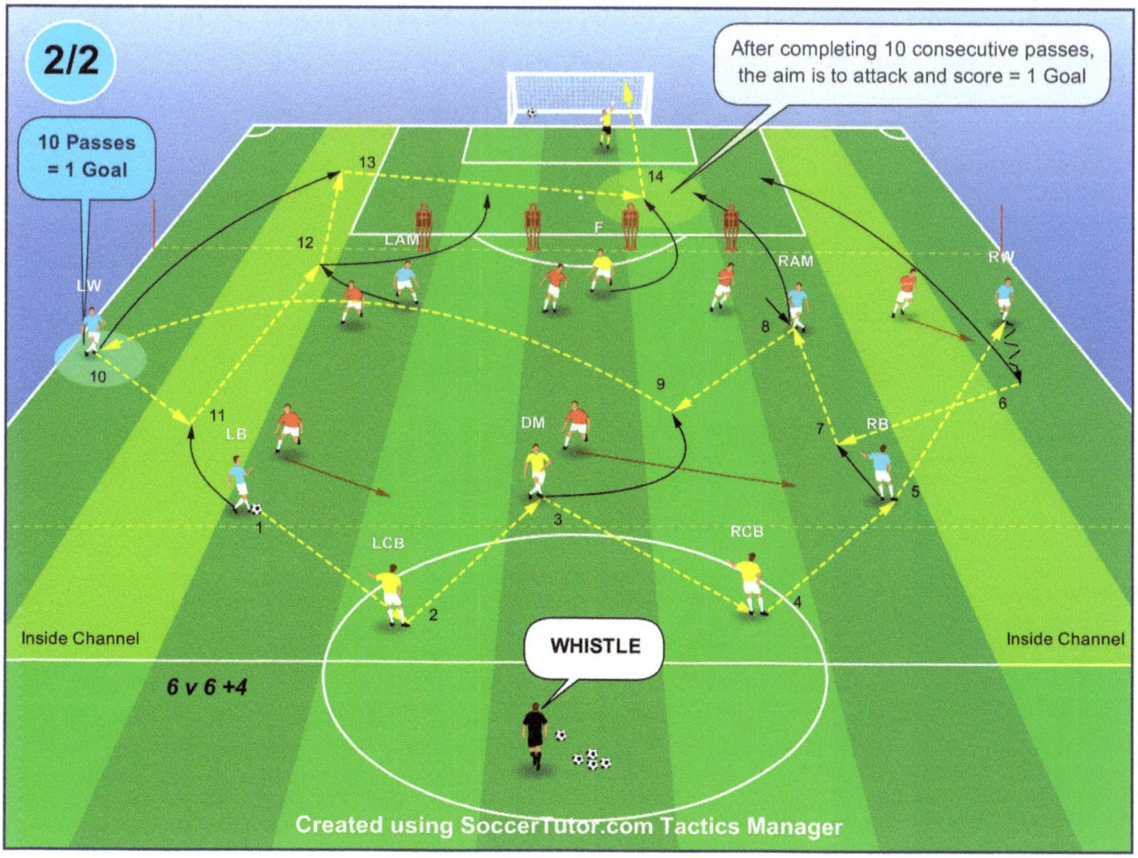

Practice Description (Phase 2)

- The practice changes to a positional game and the winners of Phase 1 start with the ball in a 2-3-5 attacking phase shape, supported by the 3 Jokers.

- **Blue Objective 1: Complete 10 passes** while maintaining good control of the ball and create opportunities to progress the play forward.

- **Blue Objective 2:** Once the 10 passes are completed, **advance forward to score**. The red defenders are not allowed to enter the box, which allows the attacking team to focus on exploiting space and executing their final movements with precision.

- **Blue Objective:** Win the ball and switch roles with the blues.

- On the coach's whistle, the practice resets to Phase 1 with the sequence performed in the opposite direction starting from the right wingers (**RW**).

Coaching Points

1. Precision in passing, receiving, and ball control.
2. Quick, intelligent decisions under pressure.
3. Occupy spaces to create/exploit passing lanes and rotate at the right moments to maintain fluidity and disrupt opponents.

Attacking Through Dynamic Half Spaces in the Centre

Attacking Through Dynamic Half Spaces in the Centre

Dynamic half spaces are the areas behind the opposition's midfield line, and between the opposing centre back and full back, which play a crucial role in central attacking developments.

Although Pep Guardiola and Manchester City often favour wide play, their ability to attack centrally when opportunities arise is just as important.

Key Point: It is important we clarify our definition of the half spaces, which may differ to other books or content you have read previously. For this book, corridors are considered to be static, predefined zones of the pitch often used as reference points for positional play. The **"Dynamic Half Spaces"** are considered to be fluid and vary depending on the compactness and positioning of the opposition's defensive block. The tighter and more compact the block is, the smaller the half spaces become.

These half spaces are key to **generating scoring chances, dismantling defensive structures**, and **breaking through the final line of defence**.

Occupation of these dynamic half spaces is a strategic priority for Pep Guardiola and Manchester City. By positioning themselves effectively, **players in dynamic half spaces force defenders to make decisions**, constantly presenting tactical challenges.

Centre backs are hesitant to step out and contest players in the dynamic half spaces, as it risks leaving the other centre back exposed (leaving them 1v1 with a forward) and can disrupt their team's defensive shape. Similarly, full backs are reluctant to shift too far inside, especially when City's wide players maintain their width and stretch the defensive line.

To counteract Manchester City's use of the dynamic half spaces, many teams adapt to use a back 5 to remain compact. However, this approach frequently cedes midfield control to Pep Guardiola's team, allowing them to dominate possession, manipulate central spaces, and dictate the tempo of the match.

Attacking Through Dynamic Half Spaces in the Centre

Utilising the Dynamic Half Spaces to Receive in Between the Lines

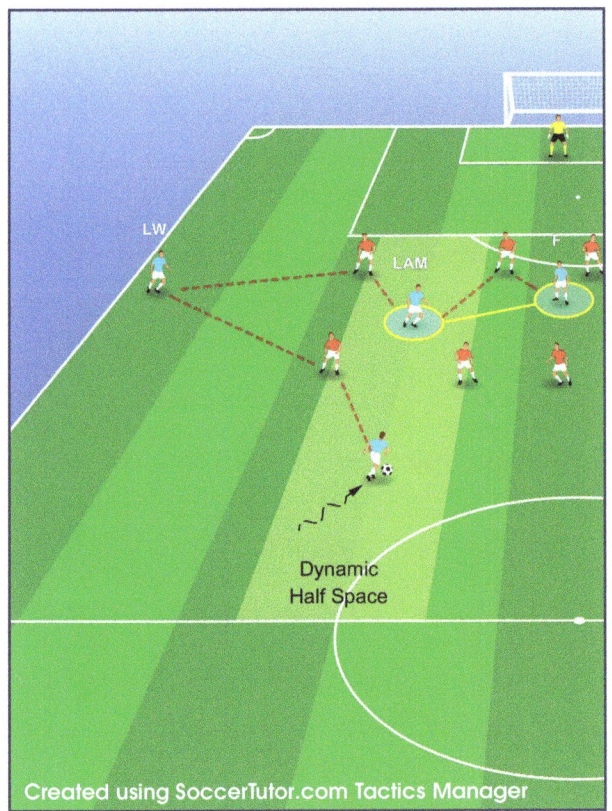

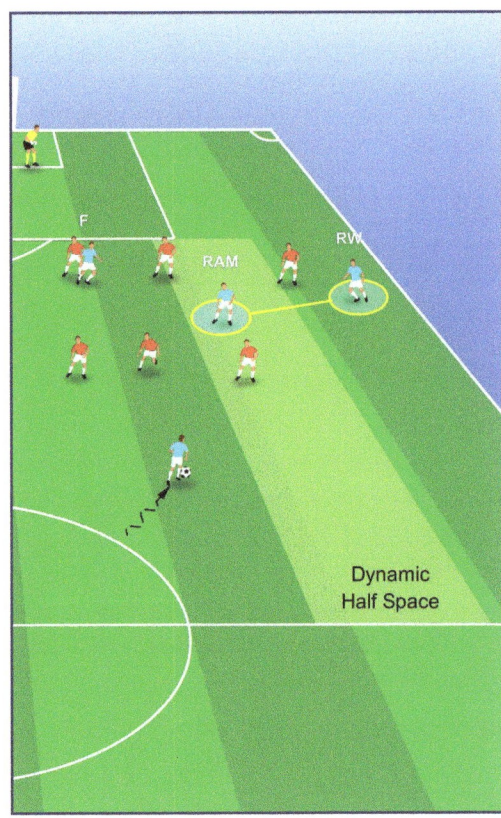

As explained on the previous page, a **"Dynamic Half Space"** is not a fixed zone but a fluid area that adjusts based on the position of the ball and the players.

For **attacks through the centre (see the left diagram above)**, **players in the half spaces (e.g. Attacking midfielder - LAM) are positioned quite narrow** to stay close to the forward (**F**).

For **attacks out wide (right diagram)**, the dynamic half spaces move to more open areas, enabling better coordination with teammates **e.g. Attacking midfielder (RAM) in a wider position**.

This space behind the opposition's midfield line (between full back and centre back) shifts with the ball position, team strategy, and opponents' decision making.

Key Point: Occupying the dynamic half space is crucial for Manchester City's attacking patterns, helping their fluid passing style and positional superiority.

Attacking midfielders like **De Bruyne, Bernardo, Gündoğan,** and **D. Silva** before them, **excel in these spaces**, using their quality and intelligence to create goals and assists, underlining their importance for Pep Guardiola's attacking strategy.

The Role and Decision Making of Dynamic Half Space Players

In the final (attacking) third, players stationed in the dynamic half spaces (see explanation on previous 2 pages) are key to unlocking the opposition's defensive line. Their role fluctuates between finishing and creating, depending on the space available and the defensive setup. The aim is to influence the attack decisively, either by scoring directly or by creating opportunities for others.

Finisher's Role

Dynamic half space players become direct threats when acting as finishers:

a. Receive a pass within the dynamic half space, set the first touch toward goal, and shoot.

b. Combine with a teammate to bypass defensive pressure and set up a scoring chance.

c. Make timed runs behind the defensive line to receive a pass and finish within the box.

Success in this role depends on the player's spatial awareness and adaptability, which enables them to exploit openings and convert chances.

Provider's Role

Focus on creating scoring chances for others:

a. Drawing defenders out of position by receiving and then playing a perfectly weighted through pass to a teammate.

b. Linking up with short and quick combination play, such as a one-two, to assist the forward.

The effectiveness of the provider role lies in quick decision making, precise passing, and smart positioning to consistently unbalance the defence.

By understanding and mastering these dual responsibilities, **dynamic half space players add a vital layer of unpredictability and effectiveness to their team's attack**.

In the pages to follow, we explore how Pep Guardiola's Manchester City team have used these players in coordinated patterns, and demonstrate how their movements, decisions, and technical execution are seamlessly integrated into the team's overall tactical approach.

Attacking Through Dynamic Half Spaces in the Centre

Quick Passing Combinations Through the Dynamic Half Spaces

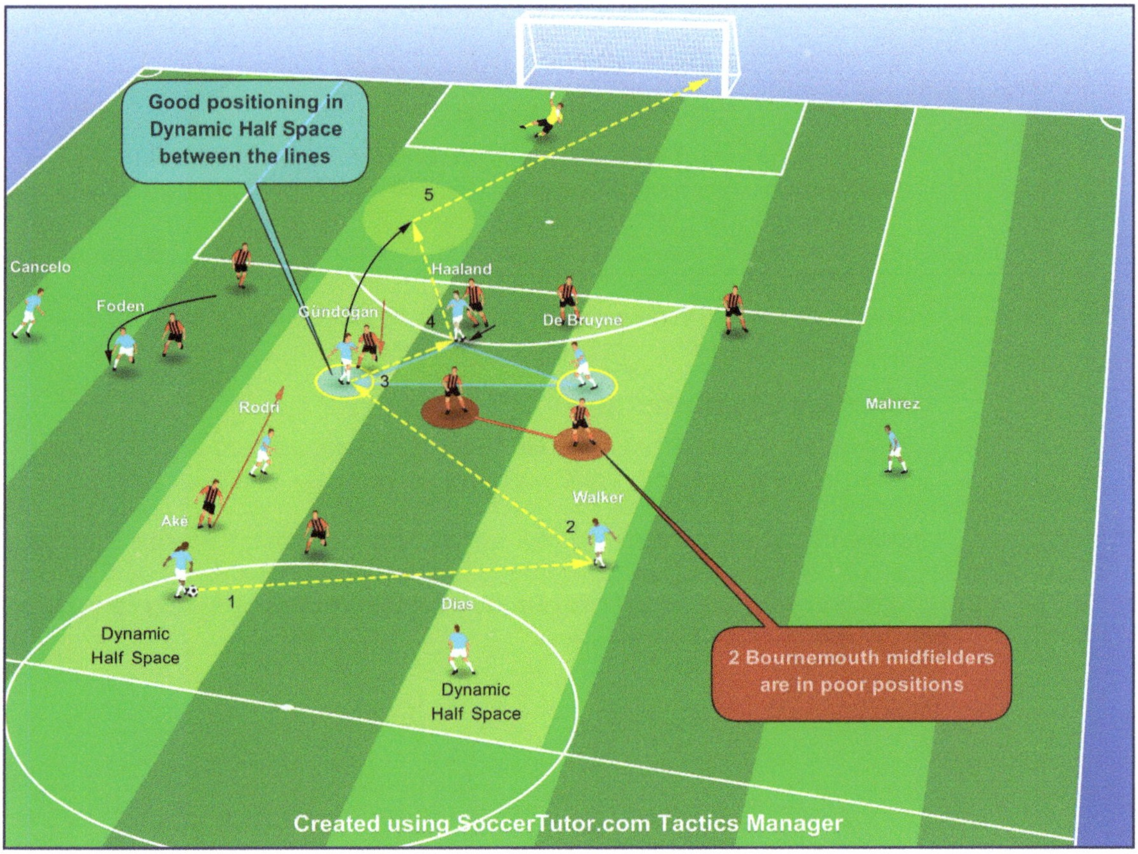

This example is taken from Manchester City's 4-0 Premier League win against Bournemouth (13th August 2022) and highlights their ability to exploit tight spaces with precise central combinations.

Facing a compact 5 player defensive line and a compact midfield, **Pep Guardiola's team patiently shifted play centrally** rather than forcing it down the left flank.

The left centre back (**Aké**) passed to right back (**Walker**), who was inverted in a midfield position. Attacking midfielders **De Bruyne** and **Gündoğan** occupied central spaces, forming a triangle with the forward (**Haaland**), while the left back (**Cancelo**) and right winger (**Mahrez**) provided width.

Walker spotted a diagonal passing lane and played a firm through pass to **Gündoğan** between the lines.

Under pressure, **Gündoğan** played a first time pass to **Haaland**, who pivoted and returned it in behind the defensive line. **Gündoğan** broke free, controlled the ball, and finished with a precise diagonal shot.

Attacking Through Dynamic Half Spaces in the Centre

Key Insights for "Quick Passing Combinations Through the Dynamic Half Spaces"

The sequence on the previous page highlights the **importance of utilising 2 or 3 player combinations to unlock compact defences in confined spaces**.

Key factors contributing to the success of this play are:

- **Positioning Between the Lines:**
  The attacking midfielder (**Gündoğan**) and the forward's (**Haaland**) intelligent positioning disrupted Bournemouth's defensive structure and created a good opportunity to combine.

- **Passing Precision:**
  The right back's (**Walker**) incisive pass and **Haaland's** deft lay-off showcased the technical quality required to navigate tight spaces.

- **Effective Combinations:**
  The quick interplay between **Gündoğan** and **Haaland** emphasised the value of synchronised movements and awareness in crowded areas.

By mastering these intricate combinations, Pep Guardiola's Manchester team City effectively bypassed Bournemouth's compact defensive block. This is a prime example of how their **coordinated movements and passing can create decisive moments in limited space**.

Attacking Through Dynamic Half Spaces in the Centre

Fluid Positional Rotations Through the Dynamic Half Spaces

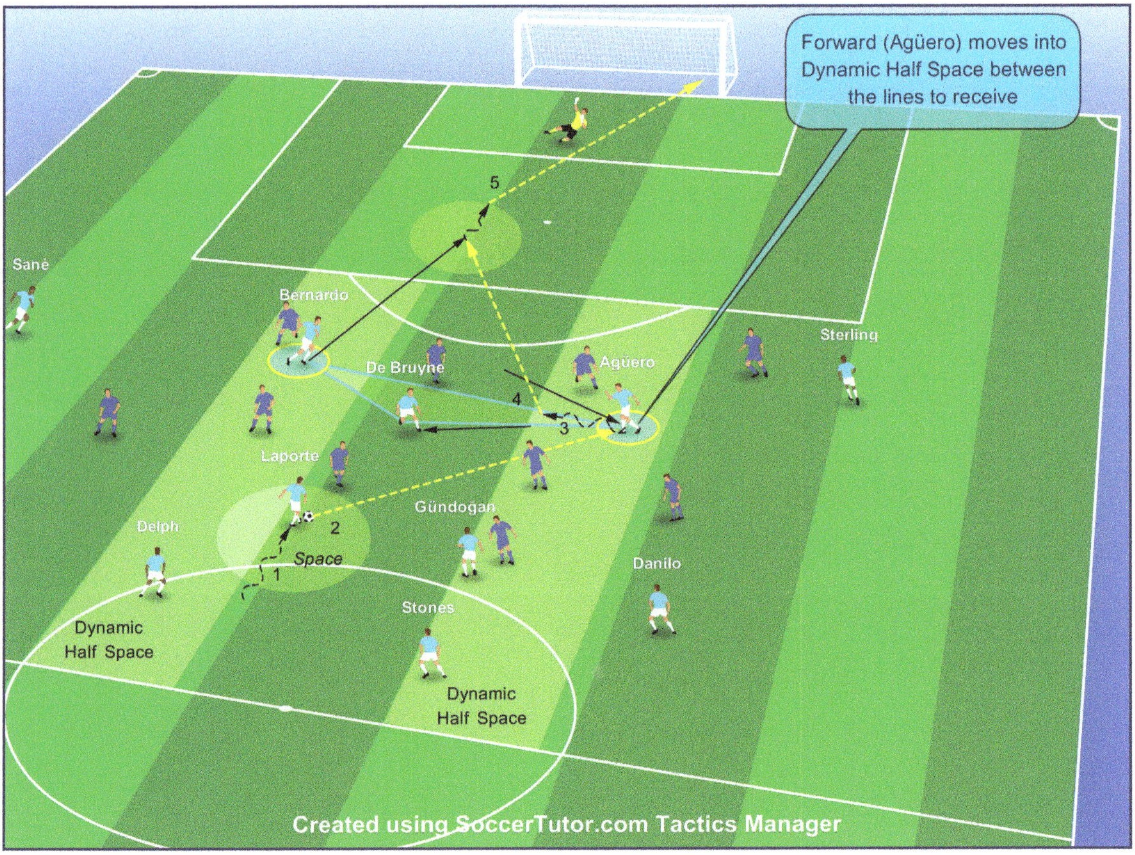

This example is taken from Manchester City's 2-1 Premier League win against Leicester (26th December 2018) and highlights the use of **internal positional rotation movements to exploit space**.

Facing Leicester's 4-5-1 defensive setup, City's 3-2-5 attacking phase shape pinned their opponents back, with 5 players positioned up against their defensive line.

The centre back (**Laporte**) advanced into open space, forcing a Leicester midfielder to press. The forward (**Agüero**) drifted right, the attacking midfielder (**De Bruyne**) moved central, and the other attacking midfielder (**Bernardo**) held the left dynamic half space. **Laporte's** diagonal pass found **Agüero**, who controlled inside, and drew a defender toward him. **Bernardo** capitalised, making a perfectly timed run in between the centre back and full back.

Receiving the ball in the box, **Bernardo** finished decisively. The sequence showcased **Agüero's** movement to link play, **De Bruyne's** positioning to create space, and **Bernardo's** precision in attacking in behind, demonstrating **Manchester City's tactical fluidity in breaking compact defences**.

Attacking Through Dynamic Half Spaces in the Centre

Crossing for Runs into the Box Against a Very Deep Defensive Line

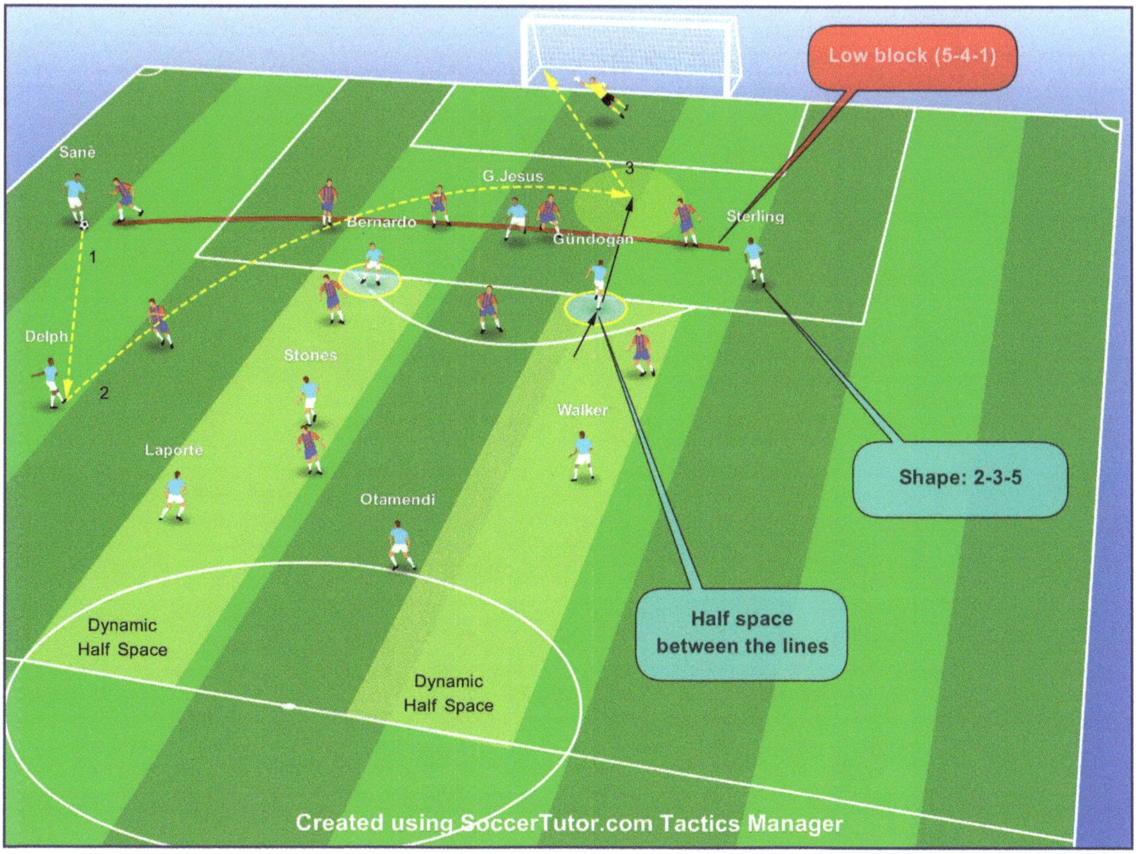

This example is taken from Manchester City's Premier League match against Crystal Palace (22nd December 2018) and highlights their ability to **exploit defensive repositioning**.

Crystal Palace defended deep (compact 4-5-1 formation) with their defensive line inside the box to block crosses. City used a 2-3-5 attacking phase shape, patiently circulating the ball to create an opening.

The action developed on the left, where left winger (**Sané**), who was pressed, passed back to the left back (**Delph**).

Delph delivered a cross into the gap between the centre back and full back.

Both attacking midfielders (**Gündoğan** and **Bernardo**) were positioned in the dynamic half spaces. Recognising the opportunity, **Gündoğan** made a decisive run into the space behind the defence, meeting **Delph's** precise cross with a header to score.

Key Point: This highlights Manchester City's ability to manipulate tight defences through intelligent positioning and synchronised movement, capitalising on small defensive lapses.

Attacking Through Dynamic Half Spaces in the Centre

Receiving in Dynamic Half Space to Finish Attacks Against Compact Block

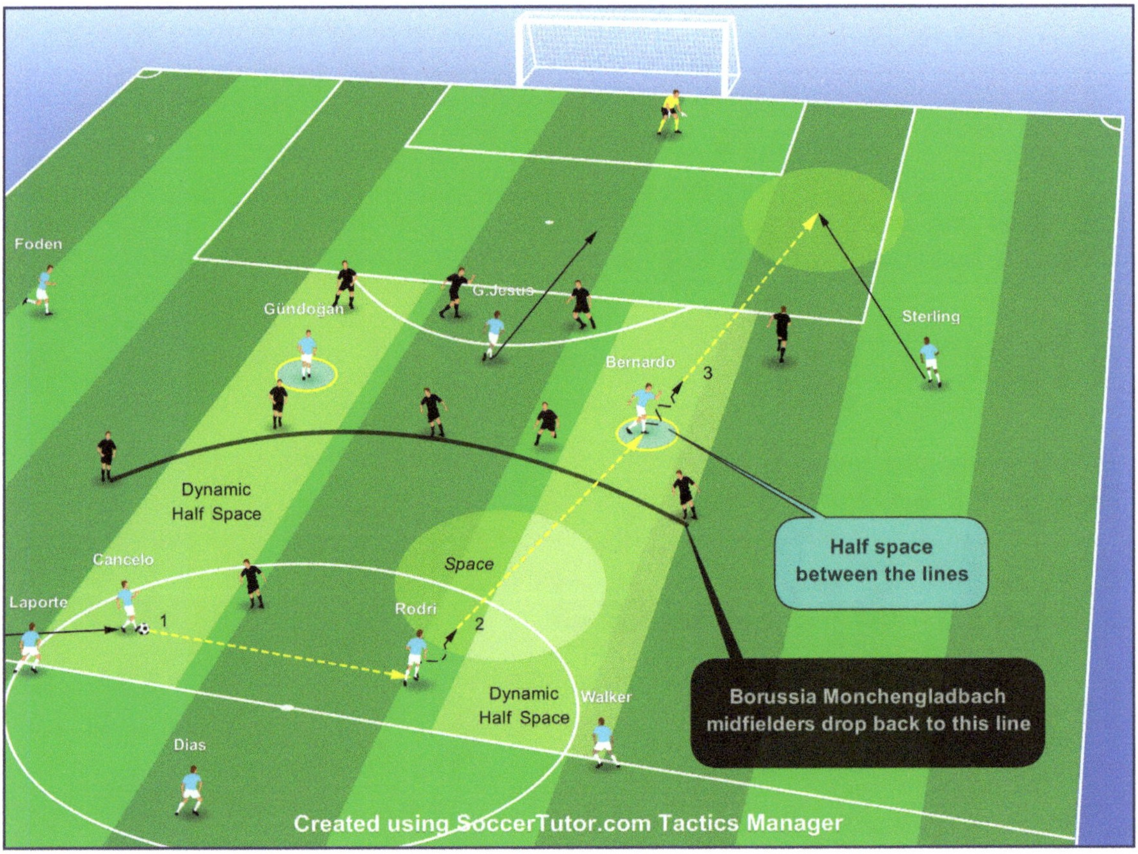

This example is taken from Manchester City's 2-0 Champions League win against Borussia Mönchengladbach (24th February 2021), where the role of the dynamic half space player was pivotal against a compact defensive block.

City shifted the ball from right to left. The left back (**Cancelo**) moved centrally inverting alongside the defensive midfielder (**Rodri**). **Rodri** carried the ball forward as Mönchengladbach's midfielders dropped deeper.

The attacking midfielder (**Bernardo**) was positioned in the dynamic half space and maintained his position behind the midfield line. The right winger (**Sterling**) helped stretch the width of the pitch.

Receiving from **Rodri**, **Bernardo** turned sharply and assessed 2 options:

1. Through pass to **Sterling** (inside run).
2. Through pass to **G. Jesus** in the centre.

Key Point: This highlights how half space players adapt based on available space and defensive setups, serving as providers or finishers depending on the situation.

SESSION BASED ON THE TACTICS OF **PEP GUARDIOLA**

Attacking Through Dynamic Half Spaces in the Centre

Session for PEP GUARDIOLA Tactics - **Attacking Through Dynamic Half Spaces in Centre**

SESSION FOR THIS TACTICAL SITUATION (3 PRACTICES)

1. Attacking Combinations Through Dynamic Half Spaces in the Centre + Finishing

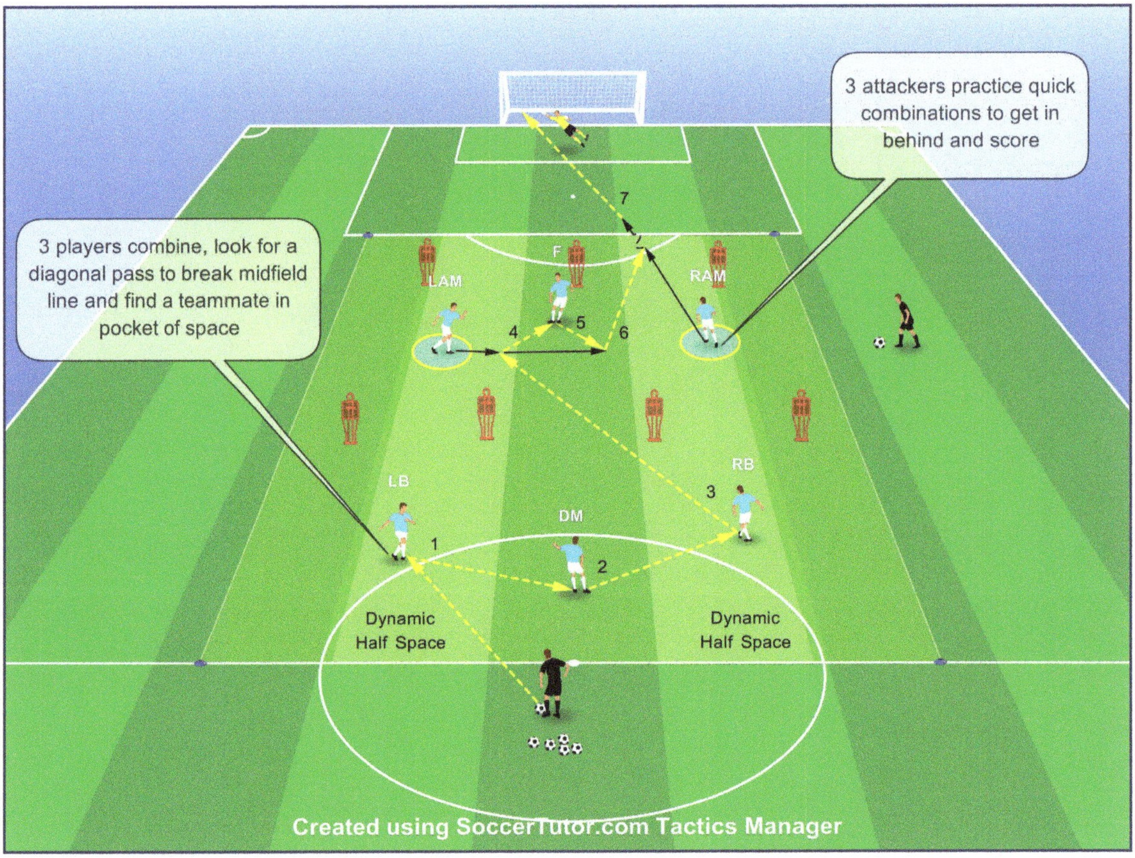

3 attackers practice quick combinations to get in behind and score

3 players combine, look for a diagonal pass to break midfield line and find a teammate in pocket of space

Practice Description

- The practice focus is **developing central attacking play through coordinated combinations (see analysis pages)**.

- 2 full backs (**LB** & **RB**) and the defensive midfielder (**DM**) start by exchanging passes before delivering a diagonal or forward pass to their teammates (3 attackers) positioned between the midfield and defensive line mannequins.

- The attacking midfielders (**LAM** & **RAM**) receive in the dynamic half spaces, forming triangles with the forward (**F**).

- In the example shown, **LAM** receives, combines with **F**, and plays a through pass for the third man run of **RAM** in behind the defensive line.

Coaching Points

1. Correct body shape and positioning in the dynamic half spaces for optimal receiving.
2. High technical quality in passing and combinations.
3. Timed runs to get in behind the defensive line effectively.

Session for **PEP GUARDIOLA Tactics** - **Attacking Through Dynamic Half Spaces in Centre**

PROGRESSION

2. Functional 6 v 5 (+GK) Attacking Through Dynamic Half Spaces in the Centre

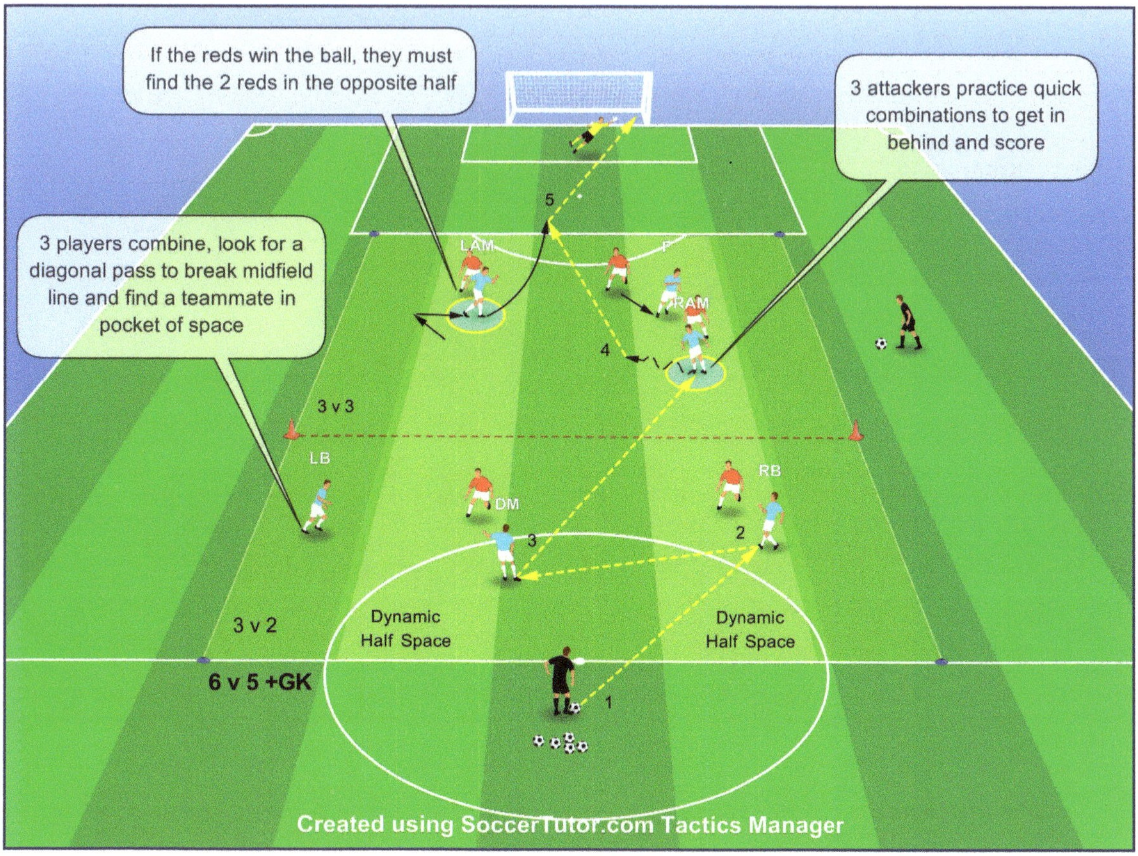

Practice Description

- The practice focus is **developing central attacking play through coordinated combinations (see analysis pages)**.
- The low zone has 3 blue players against 2 red midfielders (3v2) and the high zone has 3 blue attackers against 3 red defenders (3v3).
- **Blue Objective:** Pass to the 3 attackers, who are positioned in a triangle shape to force defensive decisions. They then combine to release a teammate into space behind the defensive line.
- In this example, the right attacking midfielder (**RAM**) receives from the defensive midfielder (**DM**), turns to evade his marker, and plays a through pass for the third man run of the left attacking midfielder (**LAM**) in behind.
- **Red Objective:** Win the ball in the high zone and pass the ball back to one of their 2 teammates in the low zone.
- **Key Point: If the attacking players struggle against 3 defenders (3v3), reduce the number of defenders in the high zone to 2.**

Session for PEP GUARDIOLA Tactics - **Attacking Through Dynamic Half Spaces in Centre**

PROGRESSION

3. Functional 8v5 (+GK) Attacking Through Dynamic Half Spaces in the Centre + Winger's Runs in Behind

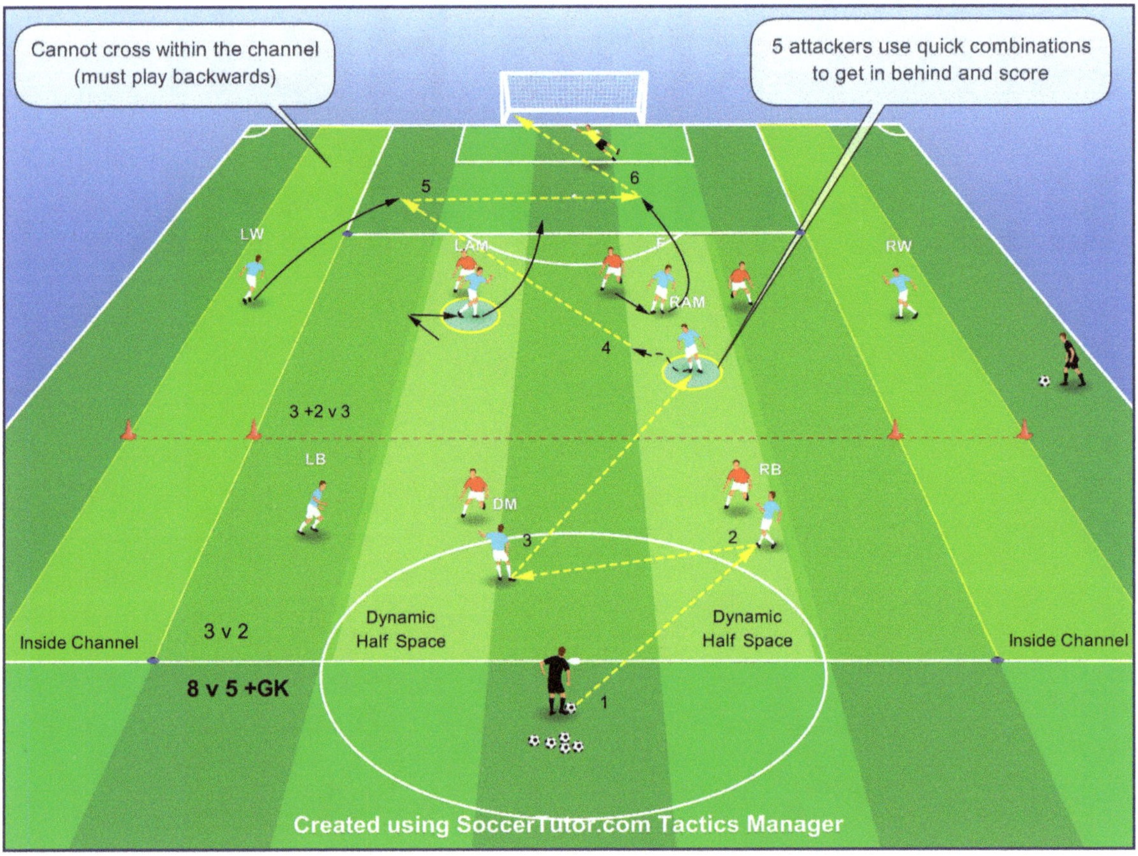

Practice Description

- This is a progression of the previous practice. We add 2 blue wingers who operate from the wide "Inside Channels."

- The low zone has 3 blue players against 2 red midfielders (3v2) and the high zone has 3 blue attackers against 3 red defenders (3v3).

- The **addition of the 2 wingers introduces more attacking options**, as these players can be activated with through passes from the 2 attacking midfielders positioned in the dynamic half spaces.

- The 2 wingers can make runs in behind the defensive line. In this example, the right attacking midfielder (**RAM**) plays a through pass for the run of the left winger (**LW**) into the box, who passes across for the forward (**F**) to score.

- **LW** and **RW** can receive to feet high up the inside channel zone, but they are not allowed to cross - they must pass back to a blue player in the low zone.

- **Red Objective:** Remains the same.

- **Variation:** Increase the difficulty by having 4 red defenders in the high zone.

Attacking High Up on the Flank

Attacking High Up on the Flank when the Winger Receives Near the Sideline

1. Winger Drives Inside + Attacking Midfielder's Underlap Run

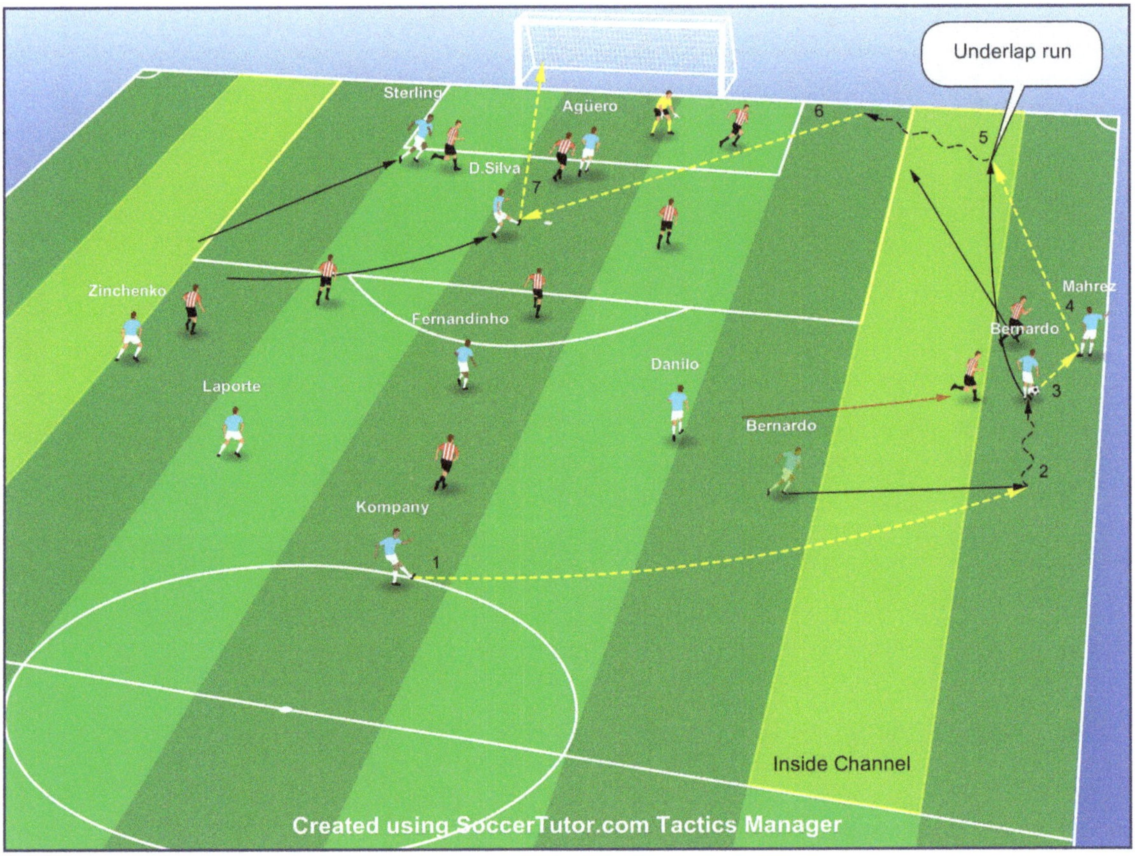

When Manchester City's perimeter players cannot find openings to attack through the centre of the pitch (previous section of the book), play is redirected to the flanks. Pep Guardiola's wingers are adept at receiving near the sideline and dribbling.

This example is taken from Manchester City's 3-1 Premier League win against Southampton (30th December 2018), where the **role of the attacking midfielder (Bernardo) was pivotal against a compact defensive block**.

After receiving from the centre back (**Kompany**), **Bernardo** advanced towards the opposing left back and combined with the right winger (**Mahrez**) via a quick give-and-go, before cutting the ball back for the other attacking midfielder **D. Silva** to score.

Key Point: This example highlights the importance of interplay and movement between players in wide and inside positions, which are crucial for exploiting defensive gaps near the box.

Attacking High Up on the Flank

2. Winger Drives Inside + Attacking Midfielder's Overlap Run

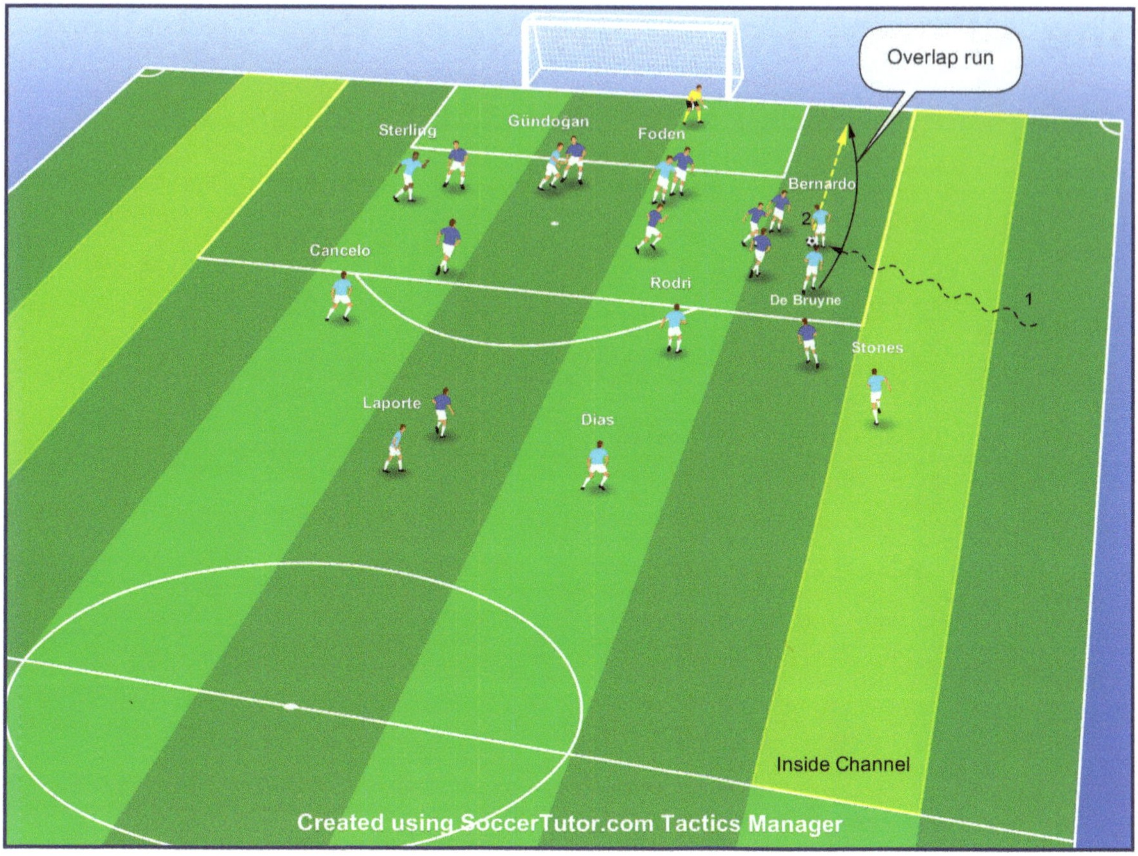

When the winger receives the ball to feet near the sideline, **Manchester City can use several different tactical options to attack the box from high up on the flank**. If they have space in front of them, they can drive forward inside with the ball and create space for an overlapping run.

Typically, the **overlapping run is made by an inside player** who times their movement to coincide with the player in possession's progression.

This example is taken from Manchester City's 1-0 Premier League win against Everton (26th February 2022), where the inside player's overlapping run created space for a decisive attack.

The right winger (**Bernardo**) receives near the sideline, drives inside with the ball into the box, and the attacking midfielder (**De Bruyne**) makes an overlapping run to receive in a dangerous position inside the box and close to the byline.

Attacking High Up on the Flank

3. Three Player Combination with Full Back's Overlap Run

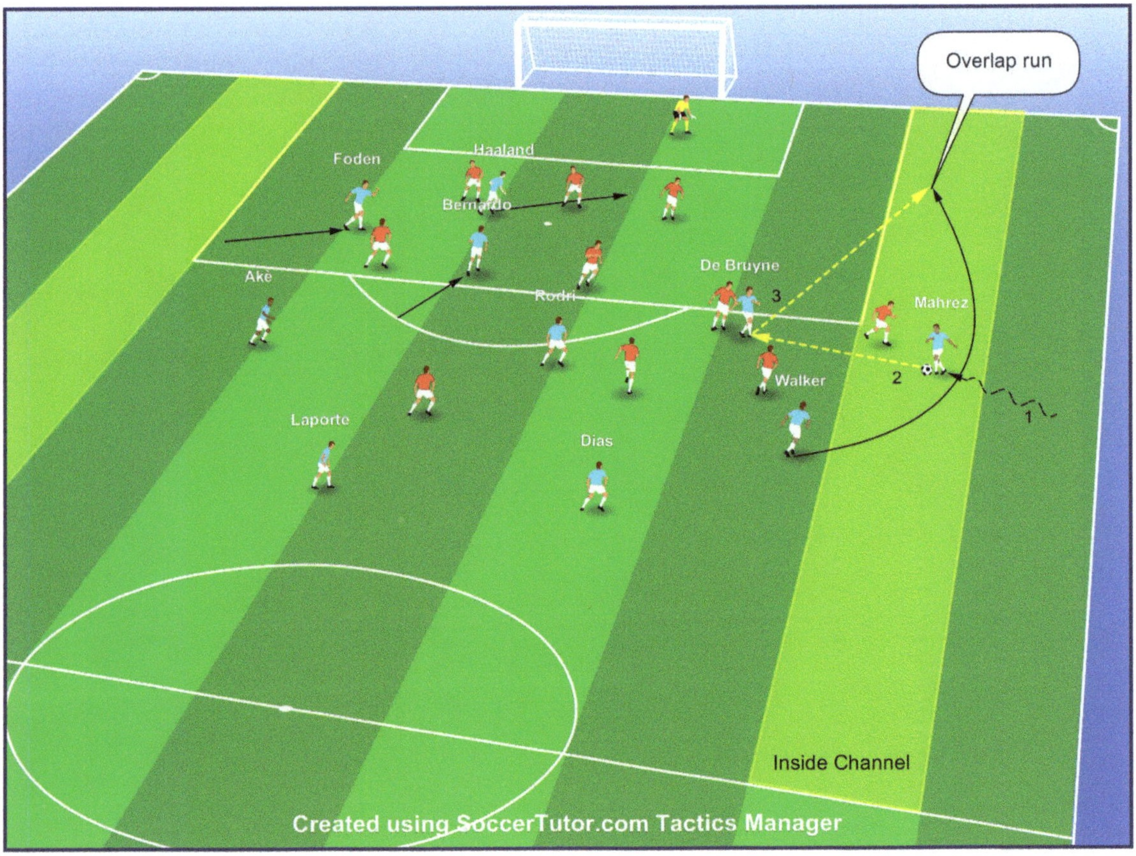

In situations when a Manchester City winger receives and dribbles inside (towards the centre), the overlapping run comes from a player positioned centrally, who shifts into the wide area to exploit the space vacated by the ball carrier.

This **coordinated movement stretches the opposition's defensive line and opens passing lanes** for a decisive finish or through pass in behind the defensive line.

Both options underline the importance of timing and spatial awareness, ensuring Pep Guardiola's Manchester City team can adapt their attacking patterns to exploit the opposition's defensive gaps.

In this example, the right winger (**Mahrez**) plays a short pass inside to the attacking midfielder (**De Bruyne**), who is marked. The right back (**Walker**) reads the situation well and makes an overlapping run to receive **De Bruyne's** first time pass in behind, and in a dangerous position.

Attacking High Up on the Flank

4. Three Player Combination with Att. Midfielder's Underlap Run

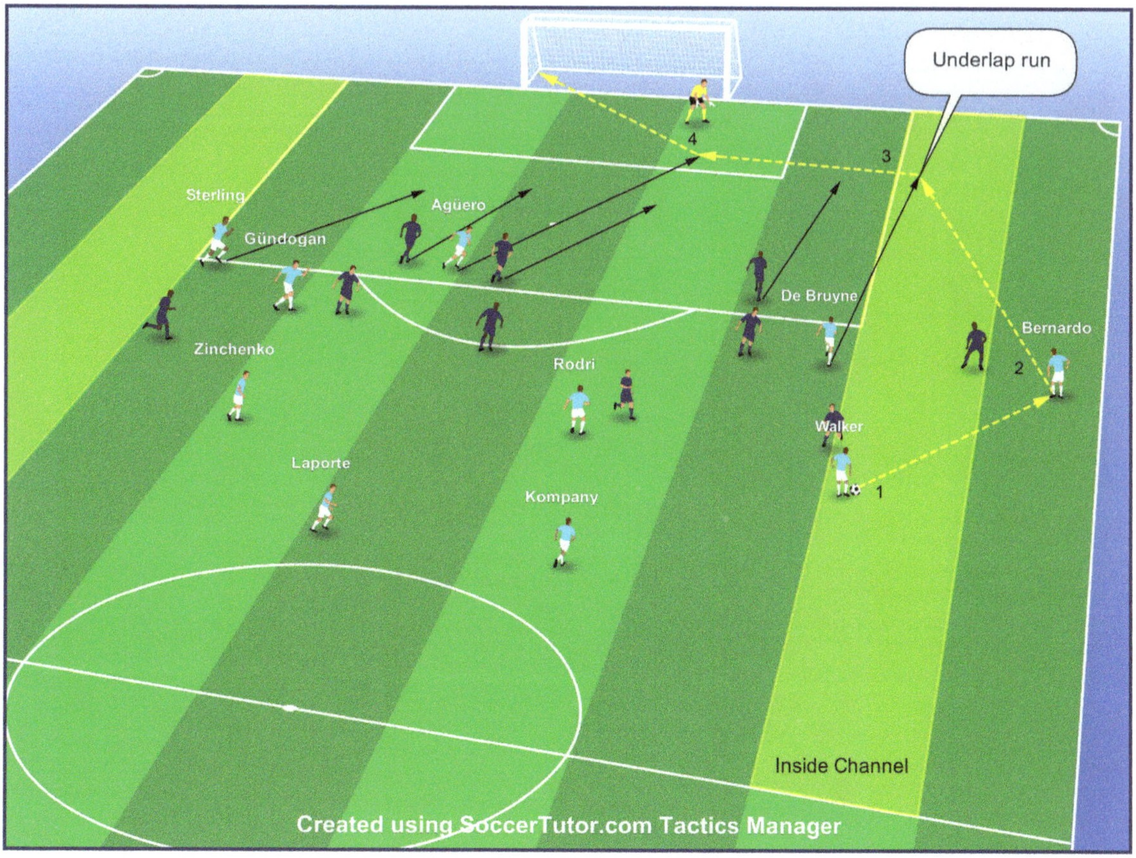

In situations when a Manchester City **winger receives and is unable to pick up speed due to close marking from the opposing full back**, the inside player can exploit the available space by making an underlapping run in behind the defender.

This provides an effective alternative to progress the play and create a goal scoring opportunity.

This example is taken from Manchester City's 1-0 Premier League win against Tottenham (17th August 2019). The right winger (**Bernardo**) received from the right back (**Walker**) and played a perfectly timed pass for the underlapping run of the attacking midfielder (**De Bruyne**).

De Bruyne then delivered a precise assist for the forward (**Agüero**) at the near post close to goal to score easily.

Key Point: This example highlights the effectiveness of coordinated movements and the ability to exploit defensive gaps through underlapping and overlapping runs.

Attacking High Up on the Flank

5. Full Back's Dummy Run to Create Space for Attacking Midfielder

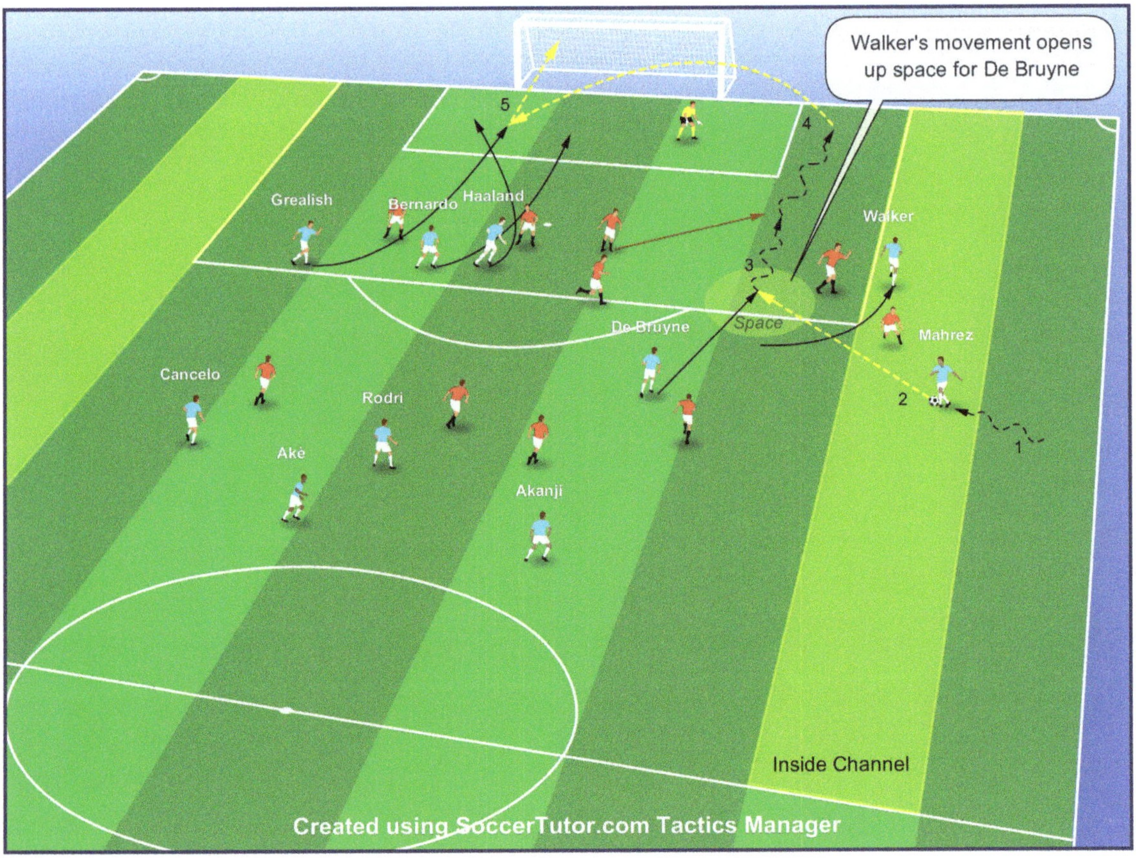

Here we show an interesting variation of Pep Guardiola and Manchester City's attacking play, where **dummy runs create space and confusion in the opposition's defence**.

This example is taken from Manchester City's Premier League match against Manchester United (14th January 2023).

As the right winger (**Mahrez**) drove inside with the ball, the right back (**Walker**) made a curved forward run in behind the defensive line. This movement forced the Manchester United defenders to adjust and created space inside. The attacking midfielder (**De Bruyne**) moved forward to receive from **Mahrez** within this space.

De Bruyne exploited the available space in front of him by dribbling to the byline. From there, he crossed towards the back post for the left winger (**Grealish**) to score.

Key Point: This example highlights how coordinated movements and positional flexibility can disrupt defensive structures and create high quality scoring opportunities.

Attacking High Up on the Flank

Alternative Option 1:
Deep Cross Towards the Far Post

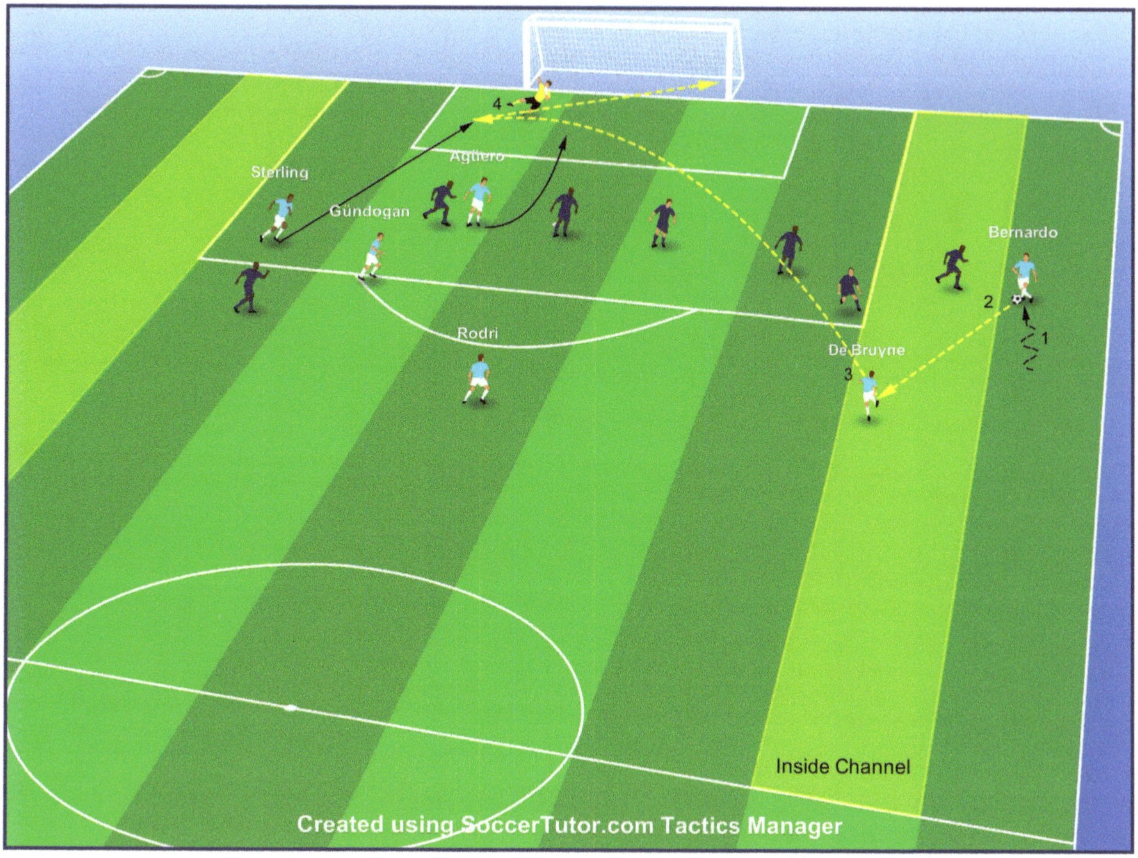

An alternative method to attacking high up on the flank involves **reversing the direction of play**. Rather than progressing towards the byline for a traditional cross, this change in direction creates opportunities by **destabilising the opposition's defensive block and opening new angles** to deliver the ball into the box.

This textbook example is taken from Manchester City's 1-0 Premier League win against Tottenham (17th August 2019).

After receiving a pass from the right winger (**Bernardo**), the attacking midfielder (**De Bruyne**) delivers a precise cross to the back post. The left winger (**Sterling**), having timed his run perfectly, escaped his marker and finished clinically to score past the goalkeeper.

Key Point: This approach showcases Pep Guardiola and Manchester City's ability to exploit defensive vulnerabilities through intelligent ball circulation and movement when they decide (or are forced) to reset the attack.

Attacking High Up on the Flank

Alternative Option 2:
Switch Play to the Weak Side

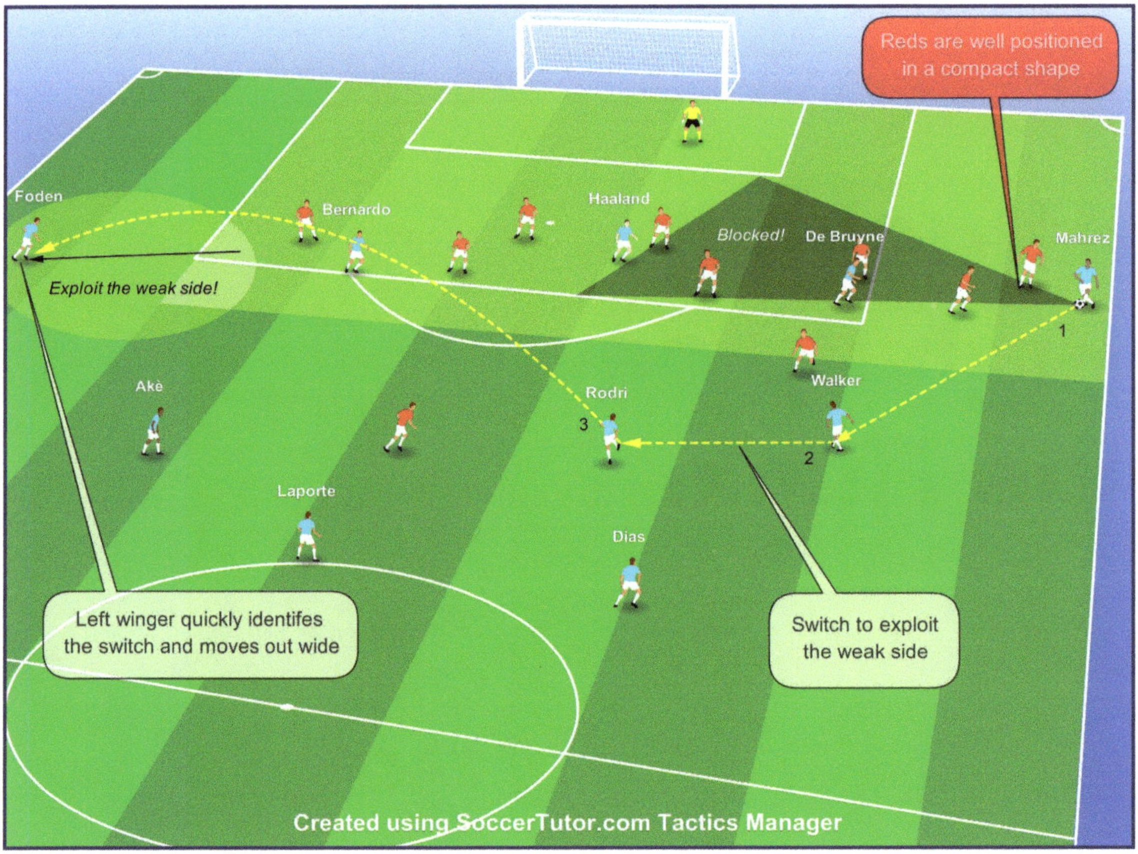

Pep Guardiola's Manchester City team typically attack through the centre or high up on the flanks (attacking the box). However, when the wingers and inside players in the perimeter structure cannot create or trigger opportunities, alternative approaches are needed.

Key Point: Against compact defences with most players positioned behind the ball, City focus on relentless ball circulation along the perimeter.

As highlighted earlier, blocking passes in behind leaves openings on the perimeter, and vice versa. The key is to move the ball to disrupt the defensive setup, using interchanges and chain rotations to create positional errors.

In this example, the **opposition are well positioned in a compact shape, so City need to switch the point of attack**.

The ball is first moved to the defensive midfielder (**Rodri**) in the centre. He plays a long switch of play to the left winger (**Foden**) on the weak side, who is free in space, and in a dangerous position to attack.

PRACTICES BASED ON THE TACTICS OF PEP GUARDIOLA

Attacking High Up on the Flank

Practices for PEP GUARDIOLA Tactics - **Attacking High Up on the Flank**

PRACTICES FOR THIS TACTICAL SITUATION (2 PRACTICES)

1. Attacking High Up on the Flank with Full Back's Overlap Run + 3v3 in Box for Cross

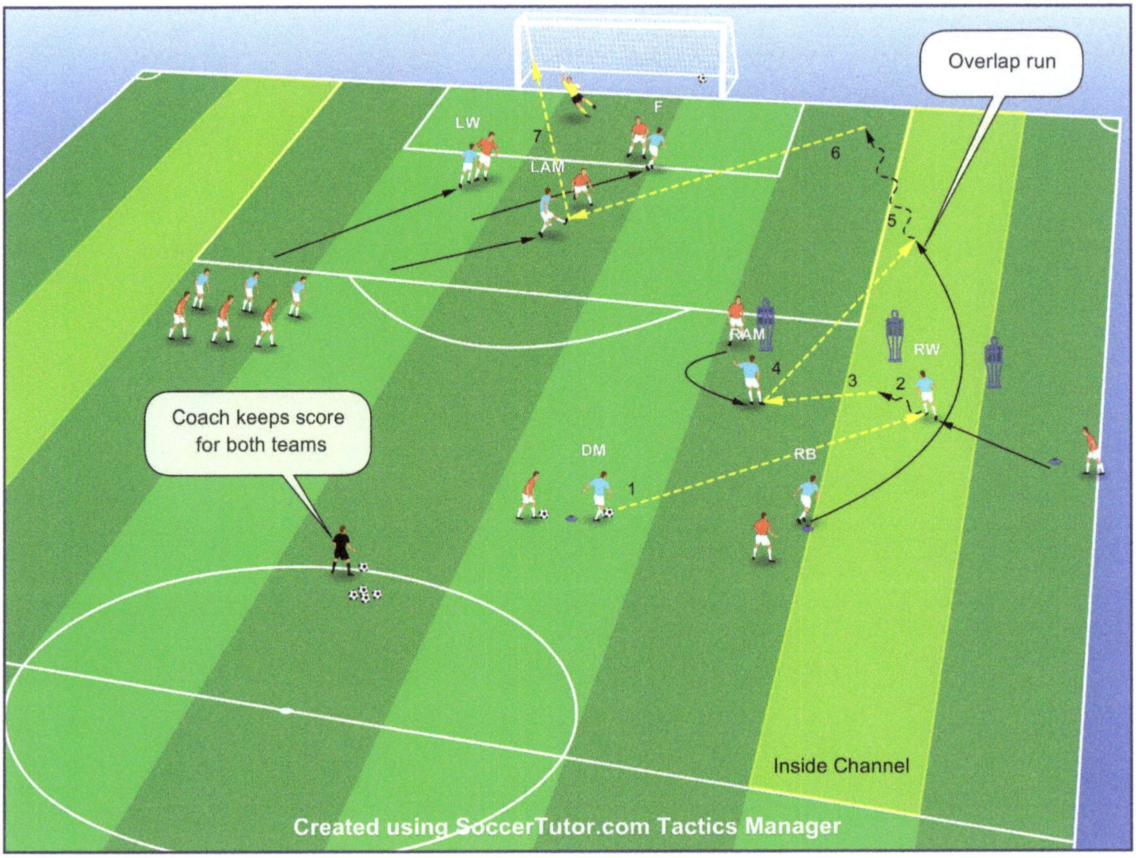

Practice Description

- Position 3 mannequins in the wide area as shown. We have 2 teams of 10 players alternate, focusing on one flank (right).
- The aim is to practice combinations on the flank with an overlap run. **See the analysis pages in this section for the different tactical solutions.**
- The sequence starts with the winger (**RW**) moving inside off the flank to receive from the defensive midfielder (**DM**), which creates space for the right back (**RB**) to overlap.
- **RW** passes inside to the attacking midfielder (**RAM**), who acts as the link player to play a well-timed pass for the overlap run of **RB** in between the 2 mannequins.
- **RB** receives, dribbles forward towards the byline, and crosses for the 3 blue attackers to try and score against 3 red defenders.
- **Rules:** Switch to practice on the other side (left) halfway through. **The team that scores the most goals is the winner**.

PEP GUARDIOLA - COACHING FLUID POSITIONAL ROTATIONS

Practices for PEP GUARDIOLA Tactics - Attacking High Up on the Flank

VARIATION

2. Attacking High Up on the Flank with Attacking Midfielder's Underlap Run + 3v3 in Box for Cross

Practice Description

- In this variation of the previous practice, we now practice combinations on the flank with an underlap run.
- The defensive midfielder (**DM**) passes to the right back (**RB**). The right winger (**RW**) receives from **RB** and dribbles inside off the flank.
- The attacking midfielder (**RAM**) makes an inside underlapping run, receives, dribbles towards the byline, and crosses for the 3 blue attackers to try and score against 3 red defenders.

- **Rules:** Switch to practice on the other side (left) halfway through. **The team that scores the most goals is the winner.**
- **Variation:** The players are free to decide whether to use an underlap or overlap combination/run.

Coaching Points

1. Precision timing for synchronised movements for the 3 player combination on the flank.
2. Competitive duels in the box.

Cutting Inside Off the Flank to Create Shooting Chances

Cutting Inside Off the Flank to Create Shooting Chances

When attacking high up on the flank was not possible (previous section), Pep Guardiola's Manchester City team adjust their strategy based on the spaces made available by their opponents.

An **effective solution involves playing through the centre to set up a shot at goal without needing to break through the defensive line**.

This approach provides an **alternative method to maintain attacking momentum while bypassing the opposition's compact structure**.

In this situation, the ball is controlled by the wide player, who moves inside (horizontally) instead of continuing attacking combinations on the flank. This movement allows them to connect with a teammate in the central area of the pitch (near the edge of the box), or switch play to the weak side.

The effectiveness of this tactic often stems from the actions of the attacking midfielder, who can **force the opposition's defensive line to drop back**, or **draw a midfielder out to follow their movement**, creating gaps that can be exploited.

As the opponents reacts, a horizontal corridor can open, giving the ball carrier several options:

1. **Combine with a teammate to progress closer to the goal.**
2. **Set up a teammate for a decisive shot.**
3. **Switch play to the weak side to exploit the free available space.**

This tactic not only relies on the initial positioning of the winger and attacking midfielder/s, but also their ability to destabilise the defensive block with precise timing and coordination.

To better understand these tactical dynamics, in the pages to follow we explore 2 examples taken from Manchester City's 1-0 Premier League win against Everton (26th February 2022), where these principles were executed perfectly.

Cutting Inside Off the Flank to Create Shooting Chances

Cutting Inside and Passing for a Shooting Chance on Edge of the Box

1/2. Cutting Inside when Attacking High Up on Flank is Not Effective

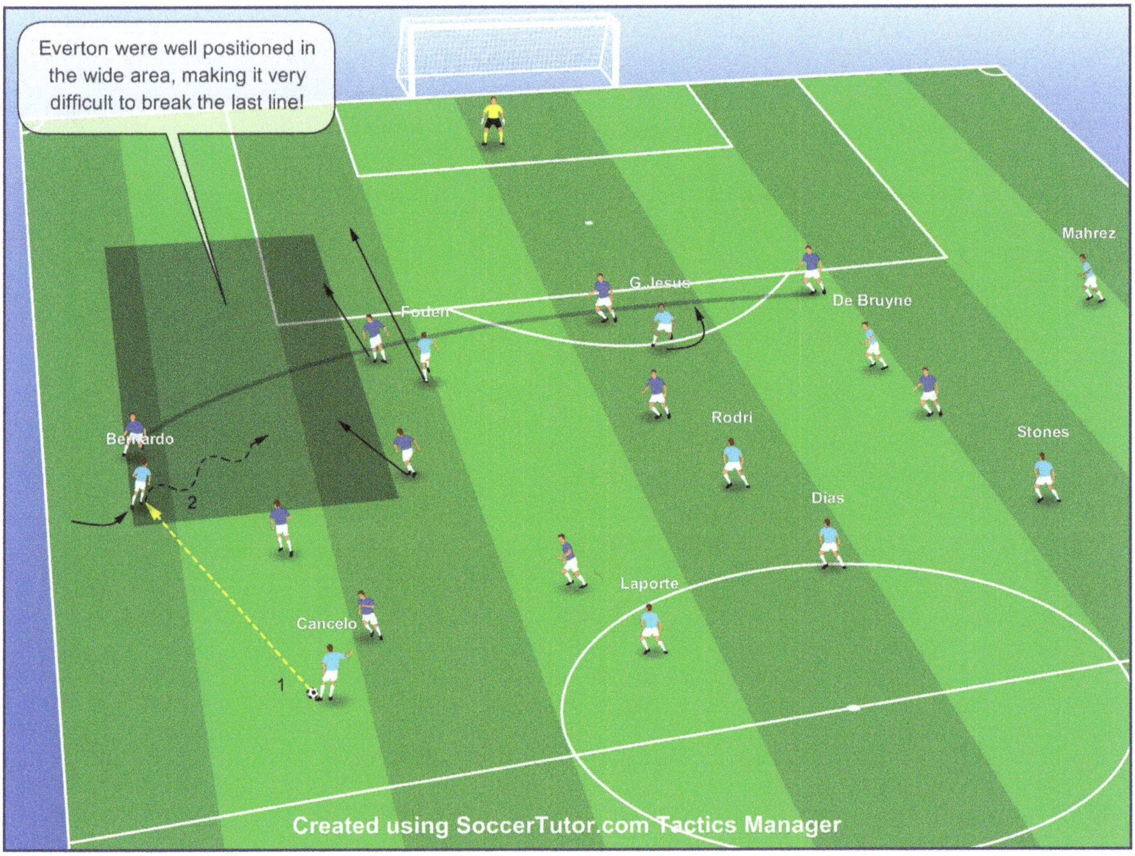

In this phase of play, the attacking midfielder (**Bernardo**) was positioned wide left and received a pass from the left back (**Cancelo**).

At the same time, the left winger (**Foden**) occupied an advanced inside position, ready to exploit any space available in behind.

Using his excellent ball control, **Bernardo** drives inside, effectively evading the opposing full back's challenge.

As **Bernardo** moves inside, **Foden** makes a well-timed run to attacking the space behind the opposing centre back.

This **forced the Everton defensive line to retreat and created opportunities for Manchester City to advance** their attack or finish this phase of play decisively.

The same phase of play continues on the next page.

Cutting Inside Off the Flank to Create Shooting Chances

2/2. Dribbling Past Opponents and Passing for Teammate to Shoot

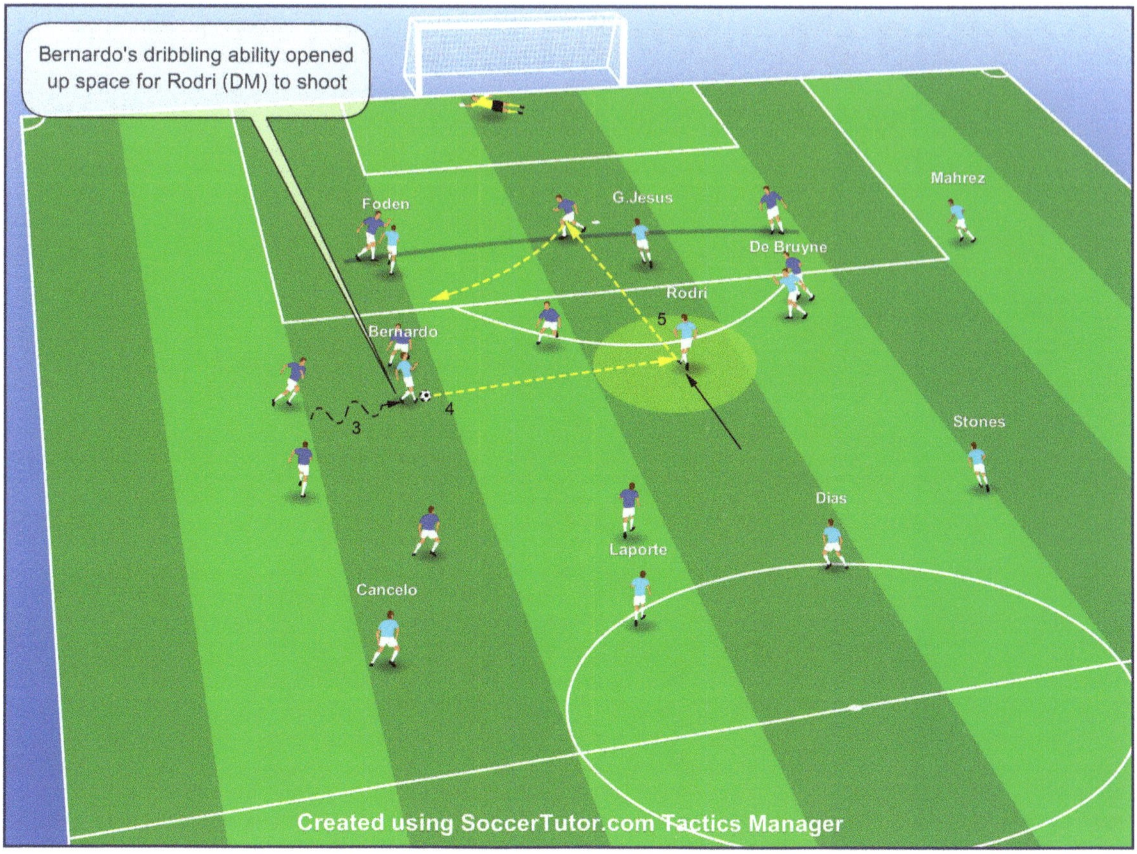

Bernardo dribbles past the opposing central midfielder, who attempts to recover and intervene.

With precise control, he advances further before delivering a pass to the defensive midfielder (**Rodri**), who is positioned at the edge of the box after moving forward.

Everton's defensive line, along with their midfielders, are drawn deep into the box, compressing the space.

Rodri receives the pass and unleashes a dangerous first-time shot. On this occasion, it was blocked by a defender.

As shown in the diagrams, Pep Guardiola's team opted against attacking in behind due to a numerical disadvantage on the flank, making it an ineffective choice.

Instead, **Bernardo** utilised his ability to draw defenders in and evade them. **Rodri** utilised his off-the-ball movement to get in position to shoot at goal.

Key Point: The runs of Foden and G. Jesus into the box created space for Rodri in this attacking move, which was developed strategically along the horizontal channel running parallel to the box.

Cutting Inside Off the Flank to Create Shooting Chances

Switching Point of Attack for the Opposite Winger to Shoot

1/2. Cutting Inside when Full Back Makes Advanced Run in Behind

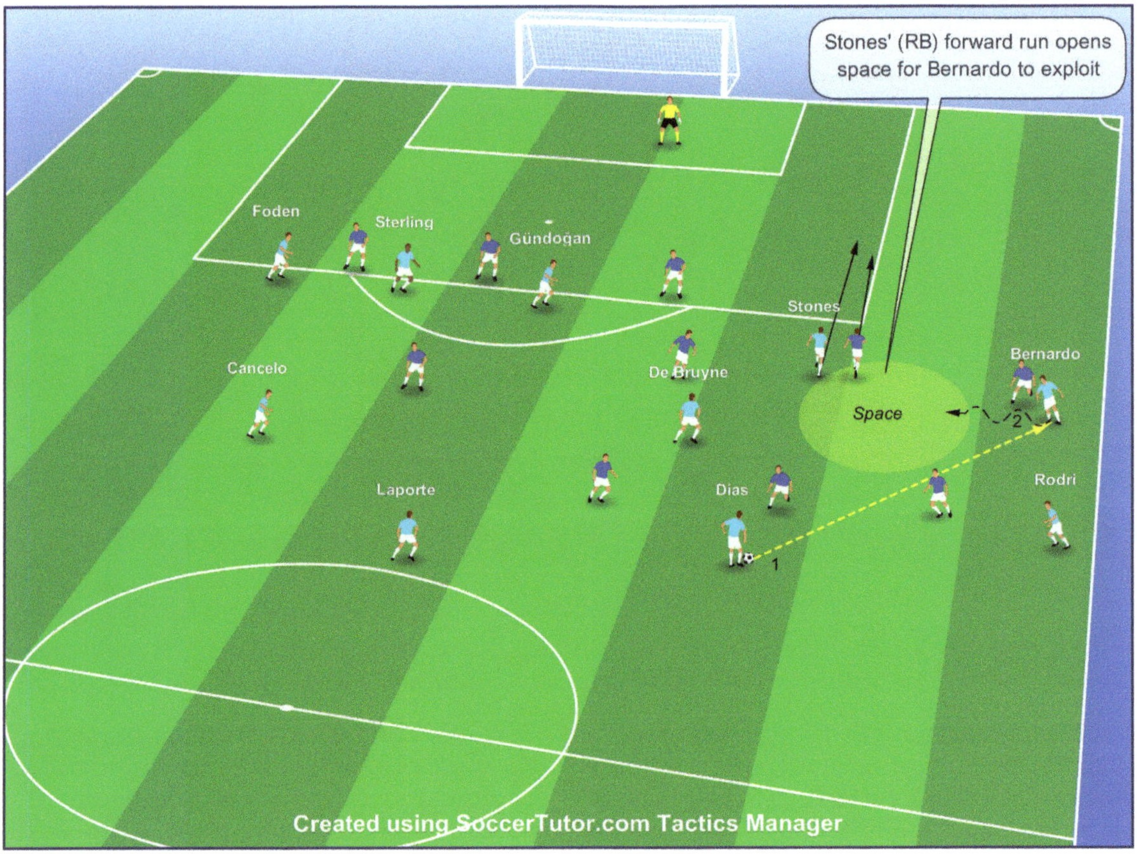

In this second example, **Bernardo** was positioned wide right and received a pass from the centre back (**Dias**). This followed an extended build up, during which Manchester City's players demonstrated quality movement, interchanging positions and occupying their usual corridors with fluidity.

The right back (**Stones**) and attacking midfielder (**De Bruyne**) are positioned in the central corridor and the defensive midfielder (**Rodri**) is out wide on the right.

Bernardo receives and starts to move centrally, dribbling inside. At the same time, **Stones** makes a run into the space between the Everton full back and centre back, forcing an opponent to follow his movement.

This coordinated movement clears the **"Horizontal Channel" (see next page)**, giving **Bernardo** the opportunity to exploit the space created by his teammates' off-the-ball movement.

Cutting Inside Off the Flank to Create Shooting Chances

2/2. Switch Play to Weak Side into Space for Teammate to Shoot

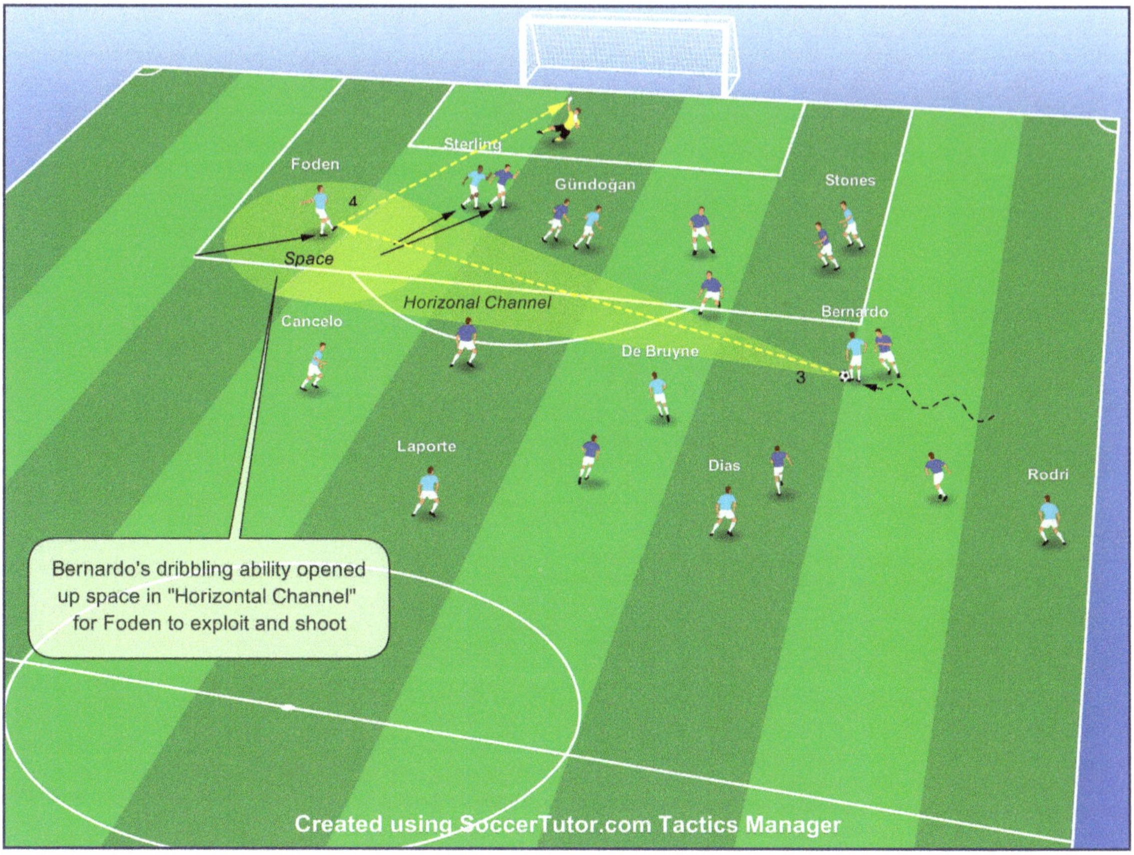

As **Bernardo** dribbled inside, **Gündoğan** and **Sterling** made synchronised runs into the box, **forcing Everton's defensive line to drop deeper**. Their movement **widened the "Horizontal Channel,"** creating more space for **Bernardo** to exploit.

Approaching the edge of the box, **Bernardo** delivered a precise diagonal pass to the opposite (weak) side of the pitch to **Foden**, who moves inside to attack the back post area.

Foden capitalised on the space left vacant as the opposing right back, who, preoccupied with **Sterling's** run, dropped back. **Foden** took a first time shot, which was well saved by the Everton goalkeeper.

Key Point: Pep Guardiola's Manchester City tactics highlight the importance of coordinated movement and decision making. Bernardo cutting inside triggers reactions from potential receivers like Gündoğan and Sterling, who attack spaces to force defensive adjustments. This movement creates the necessary width and depth in the Horizontal Channel, allowing Foden to exploit the space and shoot.

SESSION BASED ON THE TACTICS OF **PEP GUARDIOLA**

Cutting Inside Off the Flank to Create Shooting Chances

Session for PEP GUARDIOLA Tactics - Cutting Inside to Create Shooting Chances

SESSION FOR THIS TACTICAL SITUATION (3 PRACTICES)

1. Cutting Inside to Create Shooting Chances in the Horizontal Channel

As the LW moves inside, teammates make dynamic runs to receive and attack the goal

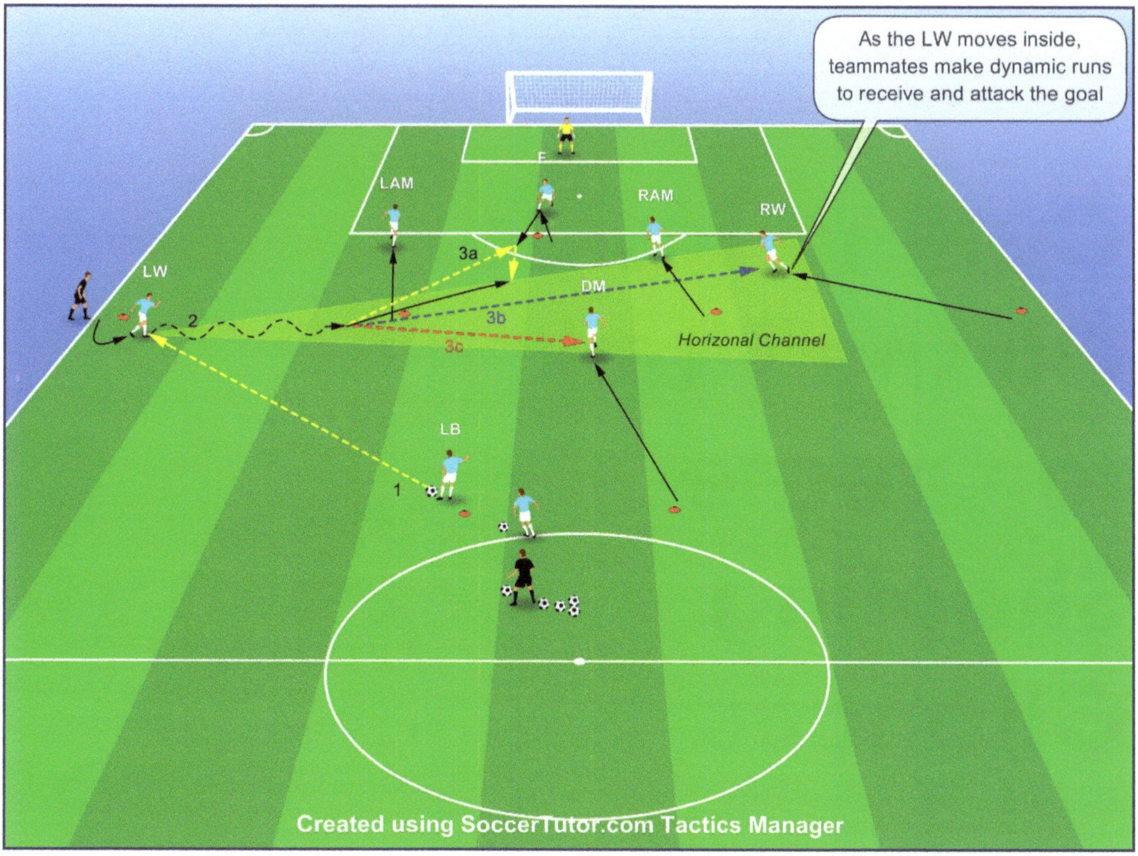

Practice Description

- The players start in specific positions on the red cones. The sequence starts with the inverted left back (**LB**) passing to the left winger (**LW**).
- **LW** receives and dribbles inside into the horizontal channel. At the same time, the attacking midfielder on that side (**LAM**) makes a run in behind and into the box, while other teammates adjust their movements to connect with **LW**. From this setup, various solutions can be developed:

3a. Pass to the forward (**F**), who sets it back for **LW** to shoot or play a final pass.

3b. Pass to the opposite winger (**RW**), who capitalises on the space created by his teammates' forward runs into the box to shoot.

3c. Pass to the defensive midfielder (**DM**), who moves forward to shoot.

- After each repetition, restart from **DM** position with a first pass to **RW**.
- See **pages 178-181** for analysis of the different tactical solutions.

Session for PEP GUARDIOLA Tactics - Cutting Inside to Create Shooting Chances

PROGRESSION

2. Cutting Inside to Create Shooting Chances
7 v 5 (+GK) Functional Attack

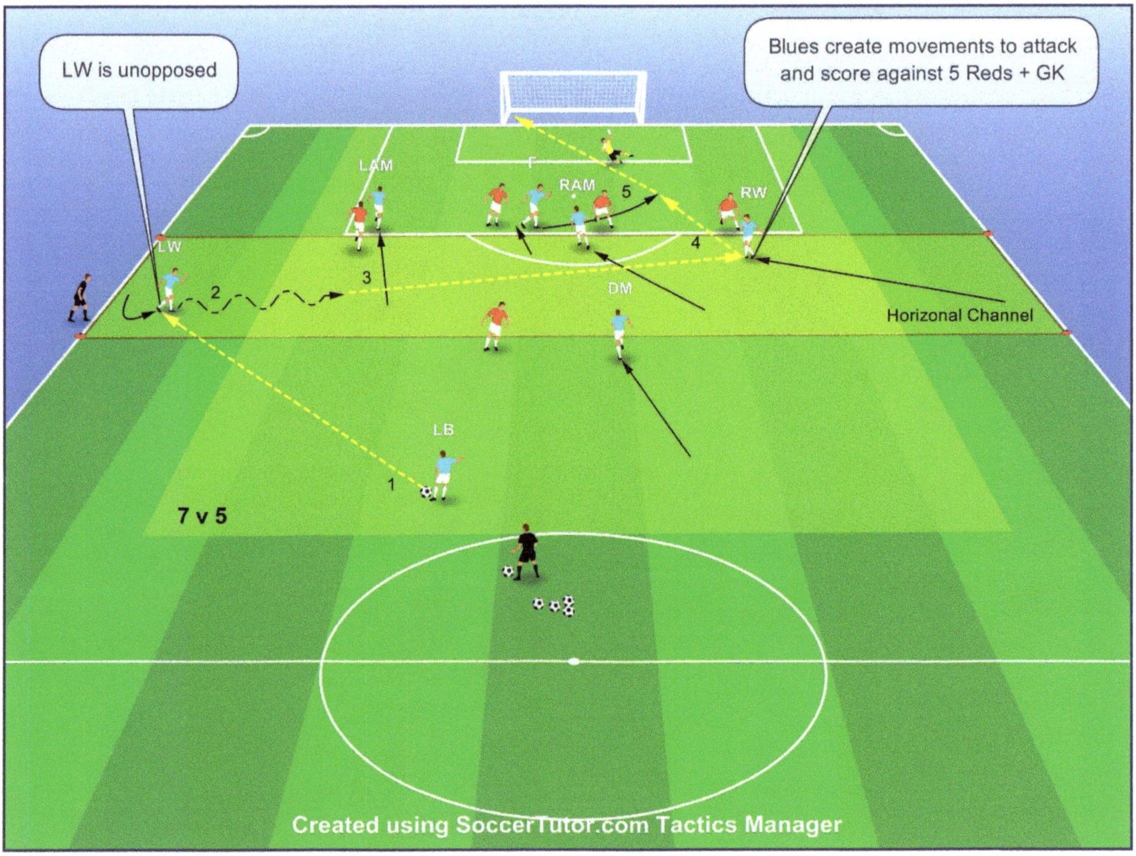

Practice Description

- In this progression of the previous practice, the horizontal channel is a marked out zone (yellow) and 5 red defenders are added.

- The practice starts with the left back (**LB**) or defensive midfielder (**DM**), who are a double pivot, passing to a winger (**LB** to **LW** in diagram).

- **LW** cuts inside and the opposite winger (**RW**) moves inside. There is a 7v5 attack against defence situation in the central space which is highlighted (white area).

- **Blue Objective:** Score using specific tactical solutions, adapting to defensive reactions **(see analysis pages 178-181)**.

- **Red Objective:** Win the ball and pass to the coach = 1 Point. The blues counter-press to try and regain possession.

Coaching Points

1. Effective decision making based on opponents' reactions.
2. Precision and creativity in combinations.
3. Timing of runs and quality finishing.

Session for **PEP GUARDIOLA Tactics** - Cutting Inside to Create Shooting Chances

PROGRESSION

3. Attacking in the Final Third 10v10 (+GK) with Transitions Game

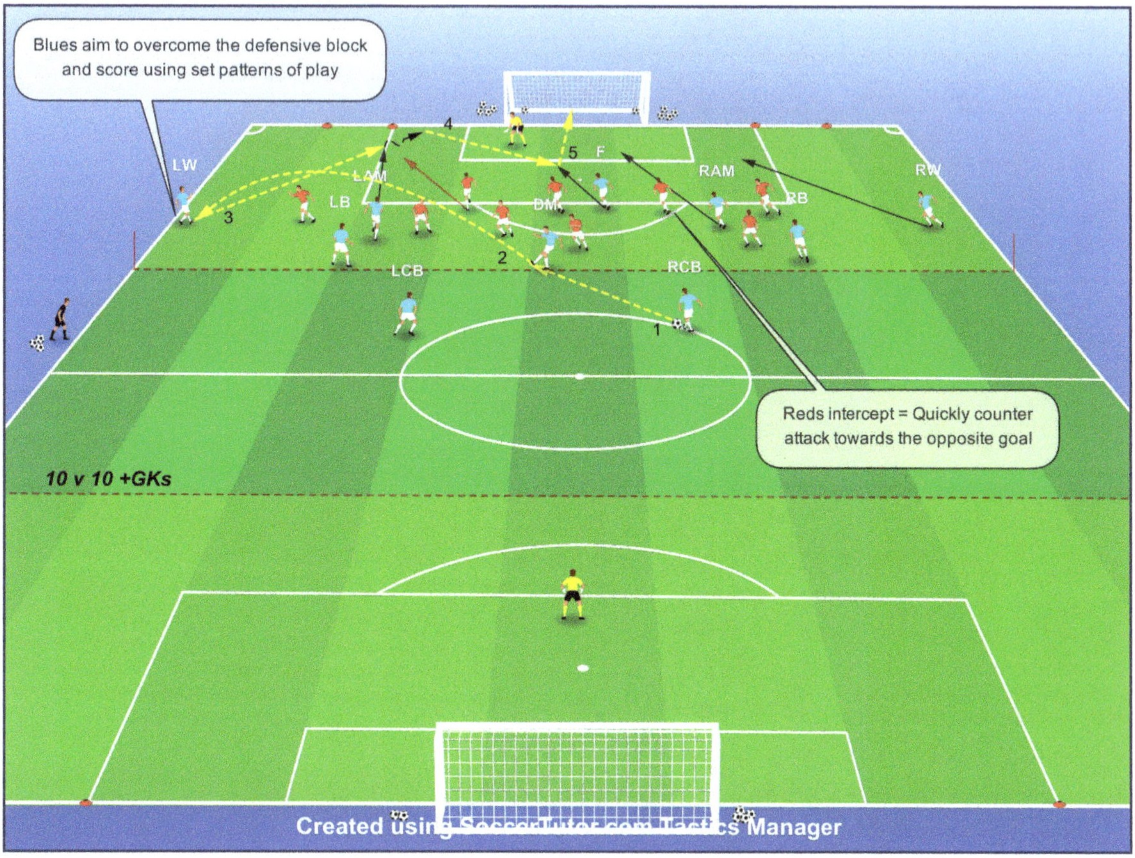

Blues aim to overcome the defensive block and score using set patterns of play

Reds intercept = Quickly counter attack towards the opposite goal

10 v 10 +GKs

Practice Description

- The end zone is marked out 35 yards from goal. All apart from the blue centre backs, who start, play in there.
- **Blue Objective:** Break through the defensive block (inside or outside) while maintaining effective ball circulation.
- **Red Objective:** Win the ball and launch a counter attack to score at the opposite end (with all the zone rules removed). Once the red counter attack ends, the teams reset and the blues restart for another attempt.
- Team roles and objectives switch after a set number of repetitions.

Coaching Points

1. Quality and speed of ball circulation during the build up phase.
2. Precision in timing and decision making based on opposing players' positioning.
3. Coordination of team movements to maintain structure and exploit spaces.
4. Execution in the final third to complete attacks decisively.

Bibliography

Combined Drills: Developing Tactical Relationships While Improving Individual Skills
A.S.T Coach.net (Coach.net Editions - September 2022).

Pep Guardiola - History, Anecdotes, Methodology, Tactical Evolution
Carlo Pizzigoni, Micaela Acevedo (ESI Editions - November 2021).

Guardiola Workshop
Matteo Cocco (Allenatore.net Editions - June 2022).

Free Trial

Football Coaching Specialists Since 2001

Tactics Manager
Create your own Practices, Tactics & Plan Sessions!

Tactics Manager App

SoccerTutor.com

Football Coaching Specialists Since 2001

PEP GUARDIOLA

Coaching High Pressing Tactics & Sessions Against Different Formations

Terzis Athanasios

SoccerTutor.com - Football Coaching Specialists Since 2001

Coaching Books Available in Full Colour Print and eBook
PC | Mac | iPhone | iPad | Android Phone / Tablet | Chromebook

FREE Coach Viewer APP

SoccerTutor.com

Football Coaching Specialists Since 2001

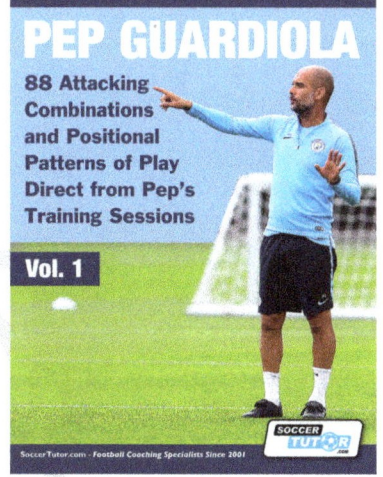

Pep Guardiola Books Available in Full Colour Print and eBook
PC | Mac | iPhone | iPad | Android Phone / Tablet | Chromebook

 **FREE** Coach Viewer **APP**

SoccerTutor.com

Football Coaching Specialists Since 2001

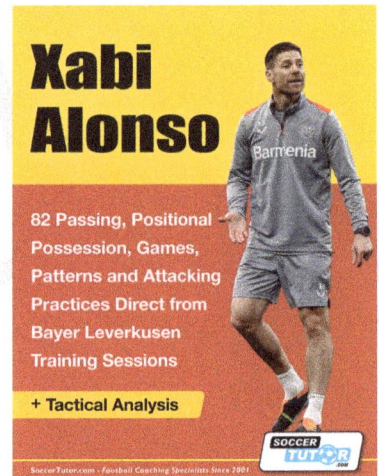
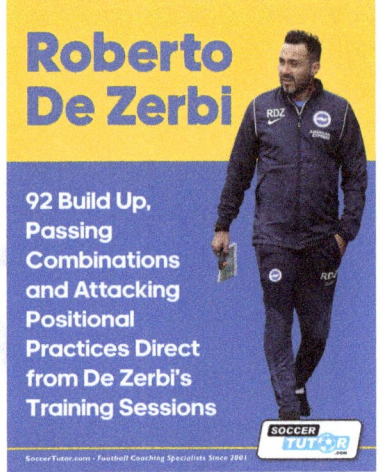

More Coaching Books Available in Full Colour Print and eBook
PC | Mac | iPhone | iPad | Android Phone / Tablet | Chromebook

 **FREE** Coach Viewer **APP**

SoccerTutor.com

www.ingramcontent.com/pod-product-compliance
Lightning Source LLC
Chambersburg PA
CBHW040932240426
43673CB00051B/1956